A CELEBRATION OF
WESTERN NEW YORK POETS

Edited by Patricia Tansey

A Celebration of Western New York Poets

Edited by Patricia Tansey

Editorial Consultants: Verneice Turner, Lewis Bowman and David Landrey

Printed in the United States of America

Book and cover design by Patricia Tansey, with technical help from Mary Kinney
Chief Copy Editors: Irene Sipos and Patricia Tansey
Assistant copy editing by Celeste Lawson, Nava Fader, Stephen Baraban and Gunilla Kester
Logo design by Michael Morgulis

First International Edition

ISBN: 978-1519699640

Buffalo Legacy Publications
Buffalo, NY

To my son, Joseph, my friend, Lewis Bowman and my "midwife," Verneice Turner, all of whose help and encouragement made this book possible.

Acknowledgments

Grateful Acknowledgments to all publications in which these poems have appeared and to the poets who have given permission to print these works:

Gay Baines "In the Rapturous Grass" (*Poem*), "Eugene Onegin at the Regal Cinema" (*REAL*), "Tape Watcher" (*Hiram Poetry Review*), "Walking After the Blizzard" (*ELF: Eclectic Literary Forum*). All four previous poems appear in *Don't Let Go* by Gay Baines (Xlibris, 2010). "Earthly Heaviness" ("Lighter Than Air" *Icarus* 12/19/98).

Ansie Baird "The Earth In Its Orbit," "Bonnard's Wife Speaks," "Take A Right Turn At Oneida," "And All Of Us Alive" and "Nothing Of You" were all first published in *In Advance of All Parting* by Ansie Baird, WHITE PINE PRESS POETRY PRIZE 14 (White Pine Press, 2009).

Stephen M. Baraban "From The Murk Of His Tiger Dome He Steps Into The Lucid Air" (*intent.*), "Lot's Wife Turns to the Lot of the City" (*intent.* and *Home Planet News*), "After Robert Creeley" (*BlazeVOX Online*). "Untitled" (God, it's delightful) and "To Get to the Post-Blizzard" (*House Organ*).

Michael Basinski "There Was Light that Was Alone," "I am that July Night that Returns like Zorro," "SOUND POEM 5," "Poem in 8 parts," "Buffalo Snow Poem" and "Once Upon a Time in East Buffalo: Mary, Faith and the Imagination" are published here for the first time with the generous permission of Michael Basinski.

E.R. Baxter III "Country" and "My Baby Loves Them Old-Time Movies" appear in *Niagara Lost and Found: New and Selected Poems* by E.R. Baxter III (Abyss Publications, Yarmouthport, MA, 2013).

Kathleen Betsko Yale "TWO PARTY SYSTEM: TAKING THE HOUSE" appears in *POEMS FROM THE CROOKED CIRCLE* (Crooked Circle Press, 2013). "UNDOCUMENTED IMMIGRANTS" and "RESURRECTION" are published here for the first time with the generous permission of Kathleen Betsko Yale.

Michael Boughn "I.3.iv - Economic reality" and "I.3.vi - No further *adieu*" appear in *City, Book One, Singular Assumptions* by Michael Boughn (BookThug, 2014).

Lewis Bowman "At Jekyll Island" appeared in *Jean's Journal of Poems*, Kanona NY, c. 1967 and *Leevz* (United Student Government of State University College at Buffalo, 1978). "Nineteen Fifty Five" is published here for the first time with the generous permission of Lewis Bowman.

Kastle Brill "The Flyer," "Harry" and "Bioluminescence" are published here for the first time with the generous permission of Kastle Brill.

Jennifer Campbell "The Way I Saw It" appears in *Supposed to Love* by Jennifer Campbell (Saddle Road Press, 2013). "First Born," "The One Where We Dance Around the Pain and Suffering of the World," "Nachtmusik" and "Late Frost" are published here for the first time with the generous permission of Jennifer Campbell.

Charles Case "Poetry Chores" and "Afternoon" are published here for the first time with the generous permission of Charles Case.

Elaine Chamberlain "Departure," "Mexico City" and "Huertas Delicias" are published here for the first time with the generous permission of Elaine Chamberlain.

Lynn Ciesielski "Pizza Again," "Sticky Decisions," "Chain Reaction," "Let the Whistle Blow" and "To the God of Song" appear in *I Speak In Tongues* by Lynn Ciesielski (Foot-Hills Publishing, 2012).

Marten Clibbens "Refugee" appears as "Immigrant" in *Sequence* by Marten Clibbens (Lost Pages Press, 2006).

Sandra Cookson "After" (*Common Ground Review, Vol.9, No.1,* Summer, 2007). "After," "Nocturne," "Venue," "*Four Songs of Desire*," "Late Quartets" and "Prospero's

Sacrifice" appear in *Two Loons Taken for Vultures* by Sandra Cookson (Finishing Line Press, 2011).

Martha Deed "Poppycock" appears in *The Lost Shoe* by Martha Deed (Naissance, 2010). "The Stubbornness of Chocolate" and "Duplicity of Sand" appear in *The Last Collaboration* by Martha Deed with Millie Niss (Furtherfield.org/friendsofspork, London, UK, 2012). "Morris Island Mockingbird" appears in *Truck*, 3/17/2013 and *Climate Change* by Martha Deed (FootHills Publishing, 2014). "Checkpoint on the I-10" is published here for the first time with the generous permission of Martha Deed.

Alexis De Veaux "A VIA CURCIS do CORPOS/THE STATIONS of the BODY" appears in *For the Crown of Your Heads; Poems for Haiti* (an independent publication printed in 2010 by Soho Reprographics). "HOUSEWORK," "MIGRATE" and "SNOW: December 2008" are published here for the first time with the generous permission of Alexis De Veaux.

Christina Woś Donnelly "Let There Be Silk" *(Venus Afflicted)*. "Something Like the Truth," "Apology for Mrs. R" and "Cassandra in Captivity" are published here for the first time with the generous permission of Christina Woś Donnelly.

Nava Fader "My hunger, Anne, Anne! Flee on your donkey. (From Rimbaud)," "And so it was that I entered the broken world (H. Crane)," "False translation of Hunger, Rimbaud, A Season in Hell" and "...fossil ribs and saws embedded there (Ciarán Carson)" all appear in *all the jawing jackdaw* by Nava Fader (BlazeVOX, 2009).

Irving Feldman "Apocalypse" appeared in *Works and Days, and Other Poems* by Irving Feldman (Atlantic-Little, Brown, 1961), and was reprinted in *New and Selected Poems* by Irving Feldman (Penguin, New York, 1979). "The Dream," "Immortality" and "Malke Toyb" were originally published in *The Life and Letters* by Irving Feldman (University of Chicago Press, 1994) and reprinted in *Collected Poems, 1954-2004* by Irving Feldman (Schocken Books, a division of Random House, New York, 2004).

Kenneth Feltges "if I told you," "Daddy-time" and "need" are published here for the first time with the generous permission of Kenneth Feltges.

Sally Fiedler "No Mercy" appears in *Earth's Daughters* and *Eleanor Mooseheart* (Weird Sisters Press, 1992). "No Mercy," "Griffith Court" and "Unfinished Business" appear in *A Trick of Seeing* by Sally Fiedler (Finial Press, 2007). "The Poet and the Painter," "All is Real Here and Clear" and "To Continue" *(The Buffalo News).*

Gail Fischer "The Mob of the 21st Century" appears in *Red Ball Jets, Poems by Gail Fischer* (Outriders Poetry Project, 2011).

Lisa A. Forrest "Field Song," "An April Mood," "White-breasted Nuthatch, Singing" and "Of the Hill" were published as a series in *Kadar Koli*, July, 2010.

Eric Gansworth "Dusk to Dusk" and "While Hendrix Played a Solo: 'Burning of the Midnight Lamp'" were published in *From the Western Door to the Lower West Side: Photography by Milton Rogovin, Poetry by Eric Gansworth* (White Pine Press, 2010).

Geoffrey Gatza "Fifteen Hundred Hours," "Eighteen Hundred Hours" and "Twenty Three Hundred Hours" were first published in the series of poems, "The Twelve–Hour Transformation of Clare" in *House of Forgetting* by Geoffrey Gatza (BlazeVOX, 2012) and also appear in *Apollo* by Geoffrey Gatza (BlazeVOX, 2013).

Jimmie Margaret Gilliam "What the Mountains Say" *(The Buffalo News*, 3/2009, *July Literary Press* and *Earth's Daughters # 80, Perennial Forte, Fortieth Anniversary Issue).* "burning flowers" *(Black Mountain II Review, Vol. 3, No 1*, Sub Board 1, Inc., SUNY/Buffalo). "Four Years Old at the A & P" appears in *Translation of Silence: Poems by Women of the Crooked Circle* (Just Buffalo Literary Center), and in Broadside, Poem by jimmie gilliam, Priscilla DeVantier Bowen, artist, Burchfield Penney Art Center Poetry Reading Series, jimmie gilliam, Buffalo, NY. "Graveside" appears in *Poets at Work: Contemporary Poets - Lives, Poems, Process*, Betty Cohen, ed. (Just Buffalo Literary Center, 1995); in *Pieces of Bread* by Jimmie Gilliam Canfield (Priscilla DeVantier

Bowen, artist) (White Pine Press, 1987); and in Our Family Project DVD, Jenny C. Chalk, *Exposing Digital Photography,* Harvard University Final Class Project (Graveside and other poems by jimmie gilliam, paintings by Aidan Chalk), Boston, MA. "Love Poem" is published here for the first time with the generous permission of Jimmie Margaret Gilliam.

Ann Goldsmith "Emy's Breath," "Alpine Honeymoon," "Leaves" and "Facts and Figures" appear in *No One Is the Same Again* by Ann Goldsmith, Quarterly Review of Literature Poetry Book Series, Volume XXXVII-XXXVIII, ed. T. & R. Weiss (Quarterly Review of Literature, Princeton NJ, 1999). "Maisie's First Blood" appears in *The Spaces Between Us, Poems by Ann Goldsmith* (Outriders Poetry Project, 2010). "Annunciation" is published here for the first time with the generous permission of Ann Goldsmith.

Gene Grabiner "Recess" appeared in *Rosebud Magazine* in 2013, and was a runner up in their William Stafford Award competition. "Spare a Dime?" appeared in an earlier form, "Journeys," in *Blue Collar Review.* "Fingered" *(J Journal).* "Uncontacted Tribes" is published here for the first time with the generous permission of Gene Grabiner.

George Grace "Narcissism Is the Answer," "Dresden" and "Mystified" are published here for the first time with the generous permission of George Grace.

Jorge Guitart A slightly different version of the poem, "Dear All," appeared in the April, 2011 issue of *The Potomac: A Journal of Poetry and Politics.* "Three Anecdotes on Types of Bones Missing From Bodies," "Fragments of Skewed Reports" and "A Page from a Chronicle" are published here for the first time with the generous permission of Jorge Guitart.

Mac S. Hammond "Charlottesville, Virginia" appears in *The Horse Opera and Other Poems* by Mac Hammond (Ohio State University Press, 1966). "Charlottesville, Virginia" and "Disappearing Acts" appear in *Mappamundi: New and Selected Poems* by Mac Hammond (Bellevue Press, 1989). "Catching a Crab on Wednesday" and "The Bride of Frankenstein I" are published here for the first time with the generous permission of Katka Hammond.

Barbara Holender "Facing the End" appears in *IS THIS THE WAY TO ATHENS?* by Barbara Holender (Quarterly Review of Literature Poetry Books, 1996). "Our Last Best Perfect Day," "Facing the End," "Standing In Front Of the Met Looking Up On a Night Unseasonably Cold" and "Eppur si muove" appear in *OUR LAST BEST PERFECT DAY* (Jewish Women's Resource Center, 2007).

Anne Huiner "Rousseau's Tiger," "Aliens," "Pieta" and "Carrying over" are published here for the first time with the generous permission of Anne Huiner.

S.M. Hutton "The Post-Modern Shaman" (*Artvoice,* June, 2006), "On a Photograph by Mimi" (*Artvoice,* v9n11). "Positions" and "Louisiana Suite: Crude" appear in *Brigid's Fire,* ed. Frederick E. Whitehead (No Frills Buffalo, 2011).

Olga Karman "Shadow On Stone" (*The New Republic,* c. 1990), "Crossing Harvard Yard" *(The Nation,* c. 1990). The two preceding poems and "Couscous" appear in *Border Crossing, Poems by Olga Karman Mendell* (Buffalo Press, 1990). "Come and Be Born" is published here for the first time with the generous permission of Olga Karman.

Norma Kassirer "The Moving Architecture of the Japanese Fan" (*Yellow Edenwald Field 1,* collator, Edric Mesmer, The Buffalo Ochre Papers, Winter, 2006-2007).

Michael Kelleher "But Do They Suffer?" and "The Librarian" are published here for the first time with the generous permission of Michael Kelleher.

Loren Keller "To Silence" *(The Buffalo News).* "When They Flew Away" appears in *As I Might Hold A Bird* by Loren Keller, 1983. "This Place She Returns To" *(The Buffalo News).* "When They Flew Away," "Charles Burchfield: Orion in Winter" and "Ageless" appear in *Evening Everything: The Collected Poems of Loren Keller* (Harborage Press,

2005). "Recurring Dream" is published here for the first time with the generous permission of Loren Keller.

Joyce Kessel "Intonations" appears under a different title in *Describing the Dark* by Joyce Kessel (Saddle Road Press, 2013). "At Abiquiu" and "Buffalo Icons" are published here with the generous permission of Joyce Kessel.

Gunilla T. Kester "This Time of Sand and Teeth" appears in *Poetic Voices Without Borders*, ed. Robert L. Giron (Gival Press, 2005) and in *Waging Words for Peace: Buffalo Poets Against War*, ed. Chuck Culhane (Niagara River Press, 2004). "Spires and Tunnels" appears in *Poetic Voices Without Borders 2*, ed. Robert L. Giron (Gival Press, 2009). "Shiri's Piano" won *Atlanta Review's* International Publisher's Prize and was published in its International Issue, Oct., 2008. All of the above poems appear in *Time of Sand and Teeth* by Gunilla T. Kester (New Women's Voices Series, Finishing Line Press, 2009). "How I Wish You'd Traveled by Boat" and "Write Me like Ashes" appear in *Mysteries I-XXIII* by Gunilla T. Kester (Finishing Line Press, 2011). "How I Wish You'd Travelled by Boat" appeared first in *The Buffalo News*, 2/14/2010 and, as "Boat on the Hudson," in *The Empty Chair, Love and Loss in the Wake of Flight 3407*, ed. Gunilla T. Kester and Gary Earl Ross (The Writer's Den, 2011).

Rosemary Kothe "I Would Like to be a Tree" appears in *Ashes of Remembrance* by Rosemary Kothe. "Dream Dancer" and "Boychild in the Sky With Monsters" were published by Richard K. Olson, Buffalo, NY.

Richard LaClair "Alfred" (*Beyond Bones II*). "Running Light" and "Stolen Stones" are published for the first time here with the generous permission of Richard LaClair.

David Lampe "After Cataract Surgery" appeared in *The Trees Walked* by David Lampe (Toronto: Exile Editions, 2006). "Prague Castle," "All-Hallows" and "The Rocky Mountaineer : Vancouver-Banff" are published here for the first time with the generous permission of David Lampe.

David Landrey "VII," "XIV," "XXIII," "XXXIII" and "XLII" appeared in *Consciousness Suite* (Spuyten Duyvil, New York, NY, 2007). The last two untitled poems are from his new collection, *Dancing in the Dark*, and are published here for the first time with the generous permission of David Landrey.

Celeste Lawson "Passing Through Her" *(Earth's Daughters)*, "Taylor Arrives" *(The Buffalo News)*, "Encounters with Nature (1)" (*Earth's Daughters # 83, Dancing on the Edge*). "Portrait of Love in Pieces," "On Parting," "Grocery Store Parking Lot" and "Seaside" are published here for the first time with the generous permission of Celeste Lawson.

Karen Lee Lewis "Roots (The Pedregal), 1943" (*The Buffalo News* and *The Society, Canada*), "The First Hands" *(The Buffalo News)*. "Frail Grace" appears in *What I Would Not Unravel* by Karen Lee Lewis (The Writer's Den, 2010). "Parting Gift" and "Shiver" are published here for the first time with the generous permission of Karen Lee Lewis.

David Lewitzky "SUN DANCE" *(Mochila Review)*, "WALTZ NOTES" *(Storm Cellar)*.

Alexis Machelor O'Donnell "Out of the Blue" and "Untitled" (Mountains I've Climbed—) are published here for the first time with the generous permission of Alexis Machelor O'Donnell.

Sam Magavern "Balinese Ritual" appears in *Noah's Ark* by Sam Magavern (BlazeVOX, 2014). "The Plough Horse's Morning," "The Discovery of Atlantis," "The Acropolis Diner," "The Eleusian Mysteries" and "Manhattan Sidewalk" are published here for the first time with the generous permission of Sam Magavern.

Dennis Maloney "Crossing the Yangtze," "Children's Drawings" and "Sometimes in Winter" are published here for the first time with the generous permission of Dennis Maloney.

Susan Marie "Shahada," "aerials," "such perfect death" and "Alive in a Time of Dying" are published for the first time here with the generous permission of Susan Marie.

John Marvin "What's So Spatial About Time?" (*William and Mary Review*, 2011), "Écriture from the Black Lagoon" (*Timber Creek Review*, 2006), "differ defer nature" (*The Same*). "We seem to be a seam" is published here for the first time with the generous permission of John Marvin.

Janet McNally Versions of these poems have been published in the following journals: "Lilith, Happily" in *Alaska Quarterly Review*; "O–" in *Mid-American Review*; and "Maggie As Sleeping Beauty" in *Southern Poetry Review*.

Kristianne Meal "Untitled" (voice of the mustcracker), "Untitled" (sphery sea words) and "Untitled" (when were we last tangible) appear in *TwentyTwo, first pallet* by Kristianne Meal (Little Scratch Pad Editions, 2007). "Untitled" (oooo mummy I go crazy) (*Boog City*, 2008). "Untitled" (here is/ the dark of day), "Untitled" (I cannot translate you), "Untitled" (we both had to go out n learn), "Untitled" (in raccoon circles) and "Untitled" (oooo mummy I go crazy) appear in *TwentyTwo, here, now now* by Kristianne Meal (purple loose strife productions, 2010).

Marge Merrill "Hand in Hand," "Walk the Floor Blues," "Back of the Classroom View," "Best Friends," "Untitled" (I am more), "In Response to a Bewildering Poem" and "Standing Before Unblinking Gods" are published here for the first time with the generous permission of Marge Merrill.

Edric Mesmer "A khimera" appears in *Aufgabe 6*, ed. E. Tracy Grinnell (Litmus Press, 2007). "Flagging legends" and "A khimera" appear in *of monodies and homophony* by Edric Mesmer (Outriders Poetry Project, 2015). "The Alstons surround their reflexions" is published here for the first time with the generous permission of Edric Mesmer.

Perry S. Nicholas "It's Been Years Since I Was Read *Goodnight Moon*" and "On the Porch With My Daughter, Now a Woman" appear in *What the World Sees* by Perry S. Nicholas (Saddle Road Press, 2011). "A Momentary Gift" appears in *Small Crafts* by Perry S. Nicholas (The Writer's Den, 2012). "On the Light Side of 2 AM" and "Hotel Filoxenia" appear in *Beginnings: Poems to Greece and Back* by Perry S. Nicholas (2012).

Joe Nickell "The Discovered Daughter" (*Secular Humanist Bulletin*). "The Gift, Among the Wildflowers," "The Fortune Teller" and "The Wait" are published here for the first time with the generous permission of Joe Nickell.

Millie Niss "Slightly Fictionalized Version Of Bush's Speech At the Site of the Minneapolis Bridge Disaster" (*New Verse News*), "The Carmelites" (*Magazine Sudden [Canada]*). The preceding poems, "A Cross-Cultural Linguistic Mistake" and "It's a Whitman Morning!" were published in *City Bird: Selected Poems (1991-2009)* by Millie Niss, ed. Martha Deed (BlazeVOX, 2010).

Marjorie Norris "Kitchen by the Sea," "Squaw Island," "Foretelling" and "Redwing" appear in *Woodland Heart, New and Selected Poems* by Marjorie Norris (The Writer's Den, 2011). "Soyez Sage," "History" and "How Grief Travels: Poems about 9/11, After: Airborne Pieces in NYC" appear in *resilience* (Aventine Press, 2007).

Susan Dworski Nusbaum "Shore, Mountain" (*Chautauqua Literary Journal*), "Departures" (*Chautauqua*). "Shore, Mountain," "Departures" and "Vanishing Point" appear in *What We Take With Us* by Susan Dworski Nusbaum (Coffeetown Press, 2014). "Star Music" is published here for the first time with the generous permission of Susan Dworski Nusbaum.

Marc Pietrzykowski "The Insult" appears in *...and the whole time I was quite happy, Poems* by Marc Pietrzykowski (Zeitgeist Press, 2008). "The Grinding Wears the Stone Down, Too" appears in *Mastodon Dentist* and in *Following Ghosts Upriver, Poems* by Marc Pietrzykowski, Main Street Rag's Editor's Select Poetry Series (Main Street Rag Publishing Company, 2011). "In the Train Station Watching Footage of a Plane Striking a Building" appears in *Napalm Health Spa* and in *The Logic of Clouds* by Marc Pietrzykowski (BlazeVOX, 2009).

Peter Ramos "Birthday" (*Indiana Review*, 28.1, 2006), "The Nineteenth Century" (*Fugue*, 30.1, 2005), "Watching Late-Night Hitchcock" (*Painted Bride Quarterly*, No. 76 [online version] and in Print, 4.76, 2008). "Birthday," "The Nineteenth Century" and "Watching Late-Night Hitchcock" also appear in *Please Do Not Feed the Ghost* by Peter Ramos (BlazeVOX, 2008). "Our Lady of Porn" (*Puerto del Sol*, 46. 1 & 2, 2011). "Still Life" and "Our Lady of Porn" appear in *TELEVISION SNOW* by Peter Ramos (Back Pages Books, 2014).

Sara Ries "Christmas is Three Days Away and it's Raining," "Prayer at Johnson's Corner" and "Becoming Waves" are published here for the first time with the generous permission of Sara Ries.

Sherry Robbins "Another Silent Night," "The Castaway," "The Quarter-Deck," "The Grand Armada" and "The Symphony" all appear in *or, The Whale* by Sherry Robbins (BlazeVOX, 2010).

Gary Earl Ross "Evil—An Abridged Autobiography" previously was heard on WBFO-FM and was printed in *The Buffalo News*.

Jane Sadowsky "Two Worlds" appeared in *Journey* (with photographs by Jane Sadowsky) by Jane Sadowsky, 2008. "Early April Woods" (*The Buffalo News*).

Amrutansh (Amol Salunkhe) "The Headmaster and the Planted Tree," "The painter next door" and "The Goodbye" are published here for the first time with the generous permission of Amol Salunkhe.

Peter Siedlecki "Two Field Mice," "Going With The Flow," "Bruce Defines Eternity" and "Pain" appear in *Going with the Flow* by Peter Siedlecki (BlazeVOX, 2014).

Irene Sipos "We Run We Run" (*The Jewish Journal of WNY*), "Poetry" (*The Buffalo News*). "Freelance" and "Everyone Says I Love You" are published here for the first time with the generous permission of Irene Sipos.

Judith Slater "Star Nursery," "Birth Mother," "Christmas Afternoon" and "Home with a Cold, Reading" all appear in *The Wind Turning Pages* by Judith Slater (Outriders Poetry Project, 2011).

Josh Smith "You Might Be A Poet," "Stalling" and "Tienes" are published here for the first time with the generous permission of Josh Smith.

Carole Southwood "Shuffling Off to Buffalo," "I Get a Kick Out of You.," "Portulacas" and "Meredith on the Verge of Her" are published here for the first time with the generous permission of Carole Southwood.

Trudy Stern "April Fool" (*Beyond Bones II*), "Summer Heat" (*Earth's Daughters*). "April Fool," "Pneumonia" and "Untitled" (High wire) were published in slightly different forms in the chapbook, *Taurus in Lake Erie* (Saddle Road Press, 2013).

William Sylvester "When We Are Small Again In Heart," "'Some animals love humanity'" and "Balustrade" appear in *Nightmares—They Are Zeros* by William Sylvester (The Buffalo Ochre Papers, 2009). "This is the Poem of Our Great Grief" was published in another form, as part of a longer poem called "Lost Poem," in *War and Lechery, The Poem* by William Sylvester (Ashland Poetry Press, 1995), after *War and Lechery* appeared in *House Organ* and *Exquisite Corpse*. "Quick Within Slow Change" was first published by Stacy Szymasztk. "Suppose a Dream Swept King" is published here for the first time with the generous permission of William Sylvester. Another poem by the name of "Suppose a Dream Swept King" was published in *Nightmares—They Are Zeros*.

Patricia Tansey "Honey" (*Beyond Bones III*). The excerpt from "At Kenneglenn" is published here for the first time by permission of Patricia Tansey.

Ruth Thompson "Bless You, Father Walt" (*Eclipse*), "Our Father's Deafness" (*Clackamas Literary Review*). The excerpts from "Spring Along Cazenovia Creek" appear in *Here Along Cazenovia Creek* by Ruth Thompson (Saddle Road Press, 2011).

"Bless You, Father Walt," "Our Father's Deafness," "Walking Akolea Road" and "Humus" appear in *Woman With Crows* by Ruth Thompson (Word Press, 2012).

David C. Tirrell "The Long Road and Perfect Visions" appears in *The Dublin Sonnets, Poems by David C. Tirrell*. "Vision of Christ, of the Holy Tree" (*Inc.,* c. 1981). "Five-twenty p.m." is published here for the first time with the generous permission of the Tirrell family.

Michael Tritto, Sr. "Locked in Ages" *(The Buffalo News)*, "Memory Fire" *(Artvoice)*, "Flights" *(PoetLore)*, "Live at the Philharmonic" *(The Buffalo News)*. "A Twice a Day Wonder" is published here for the first time with the generous permission of Michael Tritto, Sr.

Verneice Turner "me" and "crescendo (a woman's prayer)" appear in *Sweetness, a collection of poems by Verneice Turner* (D.H. May Fair Publishing, 2011). "River" and "poor man's dance" are published here for the first time with the generous permission of Verneice Turner.

Katharine Tussing "Tree of Life" appears in *Trees of Surprise*, a 2007 anthology of poems edited by Marjorie Norris about the 2006 October snowstorm. "Winter Night" appears in *Poetpourri* anthology, 1991. "Tree of Life," "Winter Night" and "Cosmic Neighborhoods" appear in *Colored Pebbles* by Katharine Tussing (2010).

Sinéad Tyrone "Memories Disturbed" and "Red Haired Boys" appear in *Fragility* by Sinéad Tyrone (No Frills Buffalo, 2014). "Jupiter and Venus" and "Altered View" are published here for the first time with the generous permission of Sinéad Tyrone.

Alfonso Volo "Constellation for Vincent," "Stepping From a Train," "Untitled" (For Victor Volo), "Balboa Park, San Diego," "Untitled" (For Sonny Rollins at 81), "Sun Ra," "Untitled" (Midst my microscopic self) and "Untitled" (Beneath the ice, fish) are published here for the first time with the generous permission of Alfonso Volo.

Anna Walsh "Resonance" and "Wildflower" appear in *The Poetry of Anna Walsh & Alex Mead: Invisible Fire* (AMProSoft Books, 2005). "Untitled" (how we speak/the green languages) is published here for the first time with the generous permission of Lazuli Campbell, Anna's daughter.

Celia White "The Poet Whose Youth Was Pursuit of Wind Waits for April" and "Spring in Beautiful River" both appear in *Letter, Poems by Celia White* (Ambient Books, 2007). "November, For Mom" is published here for the first time with the generous permission of Celia White.

Frederick E. Whitehead "sweet spaces," "residual heart effect" and "under scars" appear in *Water From A Toad* by Frederick E. Whitehead (No Frills Buffalo, 2012). "the river waits" was published on Frederick's blog, fewhitehead.wordpress.com.

Max Wickert From *"Departures—for Esther"* was first published in *Michigan Quarterly Review* X: 3, Summer, 1971. From *"Departures—for Esther"* and *"Serenade 3"* both appear in *All the Weight of the Still Midnight* by Max Wickert (Outriders Poetry Project, 1972). *"Pat Sonnet 31"* was first published in *Poetry*, CXL: 1, April, 1982, and *"Pat Sonnet 31"* and *"Pat Sonnet 25"* were both published in *Pat Sonnets* by Max Wickert (Street Press, 2000). *"The Figures Beneath"* appears in *Poems Inspired by Art in the Albright-Knox* (Orchard Press, 1982) and in *Pat Sonnets* (Street Press, 2000). *"Blows"* is a collage of sections from *No Cartoons: Fortune Cookie Version* (Outriders Poetry Project, 2011). *"The You Who Homages 32"* is published here for the first time with the generous permission of Max Wickert. Max Wickert's translation from the Italian of two excerpts from Torquato Tasso's *The Liberation of Jerusalem* (Canto XVI:14-15) appear in *The Liberation of Jerusalem* by Torquato Tasso, translated by Max Wickert (Oxford World's Classics, Oxford University Press, USA, 2009, by kind permission of the publisher).

Lisa Wiley "Alice," "Somewhere Between Locks 34 and 35" and "Under a Bipolar Sky" appear in *Chamber Music* by Lisa Wiley (Finishing Line Press, 2013). "Return to

Goldfish Point" is published here for the first time with the generous permission of Lisa Wiley.

Janna Willoughby-Lohr "Death is Not Pastel," "The Scornful Look" and "Soap" are published here for the first time with the generous permission of Janna Willoughby-Lohr.

Robin Kay Willoughby "The Field Behind the Row of Pine Trees III," the excerpt from "Electric Buffalo," "An Invitation to the Dance" and "Swimming" appear in *Earth's Daughters 65* (Earth's Daughters, 2004).

Blue Wojciechowski "Ode to That Guy" and "Mom's Table" are published here for the first time with the generous permission of Blue Wojciechowski.

Theresa Wyatt "Trostle Farm at Plum Run" (*CircleShow, Seven CirclePress Journal*, 2009 and *The Buffalo News*, July, 2010). "Niagara Falls" (*Earth's Daughters # 80, Perennial Forte, Fortieth Anniversary Issue*, 2011). "After the Flamenco Lecture, I Can Not Sleep" and "Restoration on Church Street" are published here for the first time with the generous permission of Theresa Wyatt.

Ryki Zuckerman "on the ponte milvio" (poetrysuperhighway.com). "on the ponte milvio," "the tower" and "gentleman caller" (in another version, called "the man in the moon") appear in *Looking for Bora Bora* by Ryki Zuckerman (Saddle Road Press, 2013*)*. "the absence of joy" and "patina: copper entry roof" are published here for the first time with the generous permission of Ryki Zuckerman.

Photo Credits

E.R. Baxter III
Marten Clibbens
Lisa A. Forrest
Jorge Guitart
Olga Karman
Gunilla T. Kester
Celeste Lawson
Janet McNally
Marc Pietrzykowski
Gary Earl Ross
Alfonso Volo

Suzanne Parry
Anne Reed
Ginny Rose Stewart
Bruce Jackson
Errol Daniels
Enid Bloch
Cheryl Gorski
Symon Mink
Ashley Pietrzykowski
Karen Lee Lewis
Michael Volo

Celia White, Susan Marie and
Marge Merrill

Richard Wicka

Nava Fader, Jimmie Margaret Gilliam,
Norma Kassirer and Edric Mesmer

Nancy J. Parisi

Stephen M. Baraban, Lewis Bowman, Elaine
Chamberlain, Ann Goldsmith, George
Grace, Loren Keller, John Marvin, Marjorie
Norris, Jane Sadowsky, David C. Tirrell,
Verneice Turner, Katharine Tussing, Blue
Wojciechowski and Frederick E. Whitehead

Patricia Tansey

Preface

Welcome to *A Celebration of Western New York Poets*! In it you will hear some of the unique and diverse voices of the rich Western New York poetry scene.

I will start by saying that for every poet included here, there are at least one or two others, including well known ones, that also deserved to be in this anthology, and were not included only because of the limitations in the time I had, and obtainability, and the size of the book I was able to produce. Hopefully, at some point, I will be able to do a second volume.

I have listed the poets in alphabetical order, so you, the reader, will be able to easily find the poets you want to explore and go back to. In the preface, I will adopt the practice of putting the names of the poets mentioned who are included in the anthology in bold font, so you know they can be found here. I did not list poets by age or literary affiliations, since the ages are often irrelevant and the affiliations are often so intertwined as to be confusing. I will try, however, to give a sense of the history of the literary scenes that these poets have emerged from and some insight into their unique poetic voices.

The roots of the Buffalo associations for many of these poets go deep. **Mac Hammond** was hired by Albert Cook to teach in the UB English department in 1963, the same year that Charles Olson came to teach there until he left in 1965. **Irving Feldman** started teaching there in 1964. **Bill Sylvester** was hired in 1965. **Max Wickert** arrived in 1966, about the same time as Robert Creeley joined the faculty. **David Tirrell** and **Lewis Bowman** were undergraduates in the English department during the Olson years, and took a summer course together with Basil Bunting, and remained friends until David died in February of 2012. David later studied under Leslie Fiedler and Jack Clarke as a graduate student. **Stephen Baraban** was at UB in the early 70's, and was affiliated with Robert Creeley and Jack Clarke, and also became a close friend of David's, as I did later. We were both with him when he died three years ago.

The 60's and 70's were a very exciting time in the Buffalo literary scene. Allen De Loach brought his Intrepid Press here in 1966, attracting major figures from the Beat movement. Leslie Fiedler was continuing to develop a new type of criticism. Robert Creeley, **Irving Feldman**, **Mac Hammond**, **Bill Sylvester** and other members of the stellar cast of professors hired by Al Cook, including Raymond Federman, John Logan, John (Jack) Clarke, Carl Dennis, Robert Hass and John Barth were writing significant works and teaching a young generation of writers new approaches to poetry and fiction. Robert Creeley's presence, along with that of John Clarke and John Wieners, and Charles Olson's lingering influence, caused UB to be referred to as "Black Mountain II," after the famous experimental college in the hills of North Carolina that they, and other luminaries of that whirlwind of cultural and intellectual innovation in all of the arts, dispersed from after it closed in 1957. Judith Kerman started *Earth's Daughters* in 1971, creating the first real outlet for feminist creative writing, and **Max Wickert** was running a reading series at local bars, Alliota's and The One Eyed Cat. Some of the illustrous writers that visited Buffalo and did readings in the 60's and 70's were e.e. cummings, W.D. Snodgrass, Randall Jarrell, John Berryman, Robert Graves, Galway Kinnell, Robert Bly, Anne Sexton, Denise Levertov, Allen Ginsberg, Adrienne Rich, Gregory Corso, Ishmael Reed, Diane Wakoski, Gary Snyder and Donald Barthelme.

Small presses flourished in the 60's and 70's. The Institute of Further Studies, directed by John Clarke (and founded with George Butterick, Albert Glover and Fred Wah), published its Curriculum of the Soul series and *Magazine of Further Studies*. Niagara Frontier Press published books by Ed Sanders, H.D. and William Carlos Williams. *Audit*, edited by **Mac Hammond** and Ralph Maud, produced special issues on Frank O'Hara and Robert Duncan. *Choice: A Magazine of Poetry and Photography*, edited by John Logan and Milton Kessler, combined new writers with more established ones. *Paunch* gave a voice to radical Romantic criticism, and *Farthar*, in the early 70's, published work by John Clarke, Charles Olson, Ed Sanders, John Wieners, Michael McClure and **David Tirrell.**

If we look back in the pages of the old Niagara-Erie Writers newsletters, to the late 70's, we will encounter a still amazingly vibrant time in Buffalo's literary history, and the names of many of the poets included here can be found there. NEW was started by local writers in the late spring of 1978 and was headed initially by Dan Zimmerman. The newsletter was edited by Allen and Joan De Loach, and later, in the 80's, by Nancy Barnes, and then by **Robin Kay Willoughby** (who also did layout and graphics). It is a wonderful source of information about the goings-on in Buffalo from 1978 to 1989, when it folded for financial reasons. I happen to have a set of them, which I inherited as a board member of NEW, and I will use them to take you back in time to get a glimpse of Buffalo's writing scene in the late 70's and the 80's. If you would like to look into them further, you can find a set of them at UB's Poetry Collection.

In the February '79 issue, we find **Dennis Maloney's** personal history of White Pine Press, which he named after a tree that grew in part of the original virgin forest of the United States. He had gone to Japan in 1973 to study garden designing and met the expatriate poets, Edith Shiffert and Cid Corman. He had the idea of starting a magazine to publish them and other expatriate poets. Beginning with a series of postcard folios, they went on to publish small books by many local and expatriate writers, including Judith Kerman's *The Jacoba Poems, Pictures from the Beehouse* by **Elaine Rollwagon Chamberlain,** *Zodiac Poems* by **Robin Kay Willoughby,** *I am the Sun* by Maurice Kenny, *Rimrock* by **Dennis Maloney,** as well as works by Gary Lawless, Steve Lewandowski (who became coeditor of White Pine), Bill Pruit, and the Chinese poet, Lu Yu.

As well as already being a prolific publisher, Dennis took the reins of NEW in November, 1978, when Dan Zimmerman stepped down. In the newsletter pages, you can also find him giving a workshop at the wonderful 1978 summer poetry festival organized by **Max Wickert**, attending the NYC Book Fair with Max and Joy Walsh, and participating in a White Pine benefit reading with Max, **Elaine Chamberlain, Robin Kay Willoughby** and **Sherry Robbins.**

Late in 1978 White Pine published a biogeographic anthology of New York State poetry, *On Turtle's Back*, which included **Sherry Robbins, Robin Kay Willoughby, Elaine Chamberlain, Max Wickert, Dennis Maloney,** and many others, and went on, to this day, publishing many renowned writers, such as Pablo Neruda, John Briandi, William Golding, John Gardner, James Wright and Robert Bly, as well as many fine emerging writers, and well-known local writers, including **Ansie Baird**, Paul Hogan, **David Lampe** and **Eric Gansworth**.

Max Wickert started the Outriders Reading Series when a group of UB faculty members, himself, John Logan, Robert Hass, and two graduate students, poets Daniel Murray and Shreela Ray, were invited to read at Syracuse University in November, 1969. This series continued until the summer of 1979, featuring well-known writers such as Allen Ginsberg, Robert Creeley, James Wright, William Stafford, Marvin Bell, Anselm Hollo, David Ignatow, and many local writers, some of whom are included here, such as **Ansie Baird, Mac Hammond, Elaine Chamberlain, Sherry Robbins, Dennis Maloney, Jimmie Margaret Gilliam, Irving Feldman, Ann Goldsmith, Gail Fischer, Judith Slater** and **Bill Sylvester.** To get a fuller experience of this, you can look to his superb collection, *An Outriders Anthology: Poetry in Buffalo 1969-1979* *and After,* which has an informative and insightful introduction by Max Wickert, and a brief chronology of Buffalo's significant cultural scene.

In the NEW newsletter pages of the late 70's, Max can be found organizing, in coordination with UB, the impressive 1978 Artpark Poetry Festival (which he gives a wildly colorful account of with pictures in NEW newsletter Vol. 1, No 2, July-August, '78). It featured David Ignatow, Marvin Bell, James Wright, Anselm Hollo and Louis Simpson, as well as many well-known local writers, such as Raymond Federman, Allen De Loach, Judith Kerman, Dennis Maloney, **Sherry Robbins**, Carl Dennis, Dan Zimmerman, **Mac Hammond**, Steve Lewandowski and Dan Murray. In 1979, he organized and participated in the 1979 Summer Festival at UB, with William Stafford, David Ignatow, **Irving Feldman**, John Frederic Nims, Anselm Hollo and Mark Rudman.

Outriders Reading Series was revived as Outriders Poetry Project, and has published books by **Ann Goldsmith**, **Gail Fischer**, Jerry McGuire, Martin Pops, **Judith Slater**, Jeremiah Rush Bowen, **Edric Mesmer** and **Max Wickert**.

In those same NEW newsletter pages, we can find **Robin Kay Willoughby**, who had, along with **Kastle Brill** and **Ryki Zuckerman**, emerged as a leader in the Earth's Daughters' Collective after Judith Kerman had left for Michigan. We can find her displaying a new logo she had designed for NEW, designing layout for *Terra Poetica*, a bilingual magazine started by Boria Sax and **Jorge Guitart**, participating in a benefit reading for Los Ninos, a charity for the poor in Mexico, and organizing the NEW summer poetry festival in 1979, which was held at Griffis Park, Delaware Park and other locations thoughout the city, and included workshops and readings by Edith Shiffert, Grace Amigone, Joel Lippman, Manny Fried, **Dennis Maloney**, Joy Walsh, Judith Kerman, Michael Hopkins, Ed Sanders, Joel Oppenheimer, and collaborations of poetry and jazz. Later, from 1982 to 1988, Robin edited *Swift Kick*, which published work by Joel Oppenheimer, Lawrence Ferlinghetti, Maurice Kenny, **Bill Sylvester**, **Dennis Maloney**, **Jorge Guitart**, **Ryki Zuckerman** and Stephen Lewandowski.

Other poets included here who are frequently seen in the NEW newsletter doing readings and workshops in the late 70's are **Sherry Robbins**, who ran Orchard Press and Weird Sisters Press from 1979 to 1985, **Gail Fischer**, **Bill Sylvester**, **Jorge Guitart**, **Mac Hammond**, **Elaine Chamberlain**, who was a member of Earth's Daughters in the 70's, **Sally Fiedler**, **Ann Goldsmith**, **Ansie Baird**, **Jimmie Margaret Gilliam**, who with Nancy Barnes, ran a small press called Serendipity Arts Unlimited, and **Michael Basinski**, who with Joy Walsh, cofounded *Moody Street Irregulars*, a Jack Kerouac newsletter, in 1978.

Many illustrious writers passed through Buffalo during this time, attracted by the presence of Allen De Loach's Intrepid Press (which had moved to Buffalo from NYC in 1966), the Outriders series, Just Buffalo, the Hallwalls Fiction Diction Series, the Oscar Silverman Memorial Poetry Series and the UB summer residencies and festivals. They included Allen Ginsberg, Victor Hernandez Cruz, Peter Orlovsky, Robert Duncan, Ed Dorn, Irving Layton, Alice Notley, Ted Berrigan, Amiri Baraka, Ed Sanders, Joel Oppenheimer, Denise Levertov, Lawrence Ferlinghetti, Diane Wakoski, Richard Wilbur, Stanley Kunitz, Robert Pinsky and Galway Kinnell. It was a time of great interchanges among poets of many cities. The poets that were active during that period, and earlier, in the 60's and 70's, had been for years in the process of developing their own unique poetic voices; **Max Wickert**, a style of intricate imagery, romanticism and bittersweet irony that plumbs the hidden corners of the human heart and psyche; **Dennis Maloney**, a Japanese influenced contemplative style, dealing with nature and social issues. **Robin Kay Willoughby**, who passed away too soon in 2002, after studying to be in the ministry, evolved a totally original style combining deep poetics and unpredictable, quirky humor, influenced by her teacher and mentor, **Bill Sylvester**. **Sherry Robbins**, in *or, The Whale*, originally published in its first version by **Mike**

Boughn's shuffleoff books, and later published in an expanded version by **Geoffrey Gatza's** BlazeVOX in 2010, has created an astounding tapestry of the mythical tale of Melville's *Moby Dick* embodying the physical and psychological perils of being, woven into the particulars of the life of an everywoman in Buffalo, NY. **Gail Fischer** uses amazing verbal pyrotechnics, reminiscent of Hart Crane's, to depict hyper-real, yet dream-like worlds of raw, unfiltered perception, which have a familiar, and at the same time, alien quality. In "Mob of the 21st Century," she depicts the corporate world as a savage ecosystem, whose inductees are seduced into the will to dominate by being ground down at the bottom of the pecking order. **Elaine Chamberlain** uses searingly vivid collages of powerful memories, emotions and images.

Irving Feldman, who had already become a major poet before he came to teach at UB, emerged as a great painter of contemporary civilization, a visionary writer of unsurpassed depth, moral acuity and almost superhuman perception. The poems included here are from his monumental collection, *Collected Poems 1954-2004*. **Bill Sylvester**, who taught at UB until 1988, became a poet of expansive cosmology, dealing with modern consciousness, war and the mechanistic age, and both human and animal conditions, illustrated by Greek lore, and employing a gloriously rich, compact style which creates gorgeous spaces for the imagination. "This is the Poem of Our Great Grief" appeared in another form in his astounding multilingual book length poem, "War and Lechery." **Ann Goldsmith** also taught at UB for a number of years, and her book, *No One Is the Same Again*, was chosen for the Quarterly Review of Literature Poetry Book Series. Her poems open a magical, enchanted realm where everything comes alive with metaphorical transformation and wonder. **Ansie Baird**, who did her master's thesis on W.H. Auden, which is reflected in the bittersweet cadences of her poetry, deals with memory and loss with immaculate elegance, courage and sheer power. Her book, *In Advance of All Parting*, won the White Pine Press Poetry Prize in 2009. **Jimmie Margaret Gilliam's** strong woman's voice was a force of nature in itself, which inspired many generations of her students at Erie Community College and her fellow poets. Her new book, *TORN FROM THE EAR OF NIGHT*, is forthcoming from White Pine Press. Tragically, she died of cancer in 2015. **Sally Fiedler's** poetry is eloquent and personal, combining delightful whimsy, profound empathy and spiritual awareness in her own voice, and in the persona of her delightful alter ego, Eleanor Mooseheart. **Mac Hammond**, who, sadly, passed away in 1997, offers a museum of beautifully drawn bygone worlds, haunted by regrets and doubts. His last collection of poems, *Mappamundi: New and Selected Poems*, came out in 1989. **Jorge Guitart** has adopted a linguistically playful style with a touch of tongue-in-cheek surrealism, and a sly dislocation of the reader's cognition, and has also done highly experimental linguistic poetry in *Film Blanc* and some of his recent work. **Michael Basinski**, who now runs the Poetry Collection at UB, is also an experimental poet of broad innovation and endless imagination, exuberance and a delightful, sometimes rambunctious sense of humor. He is also an amazing performer, often "winging it" with brilliant improvisations, accompanied at times by his friend, musician, composer and Burchfield Penney administrator, Don Metz, and his ensemble.

The three friends of mine and each other, **David Tirrell**, **Lewis Bowman** and **Stephen Baraban**, went in very different directions in their poetic styles. After starting as a traditional writer of sonnets, followed by an avant-garde period of stylistic experimentation, in which he maintains the spiritual emphasis shown in his sonnets, David became a poet of simple language, which conveys and condenses his immense knowledge and feeling for literature, from the medieval, to the early English, to the romantics and moderns, to the beats and the Olsonites he studied with. His work crosses space-time and spiritual dimensions, which he accomplishes by the use of seamless and lyrical montage. In **Stephen Baraban's** poems, there is an almost startling element of surprise, which is wonderful, and at the same time, a sense of resignation and inevitability, which, along with his highly original imagery, give his poems a strangely satisfying aesthetic. **Lewis Bowman** is steeped in the literary traditions of both England and America, as well as other cultures, from the ancient Greek and Chinese to contemporary world poetry. His early poems have a vivid dream-like quality, full of metaphors and images. His later poems are elegiac, reflective, and reminiscent of other eras and specific events of the past.

In the early 1980's, **Ryki Zuckerman** and **Kastle Brill** were featured often in many reading series. They have continued at *Earth's Daughters* to this day, accompanied by **Joyce Kessel**, a professor at Villa Maria College, **Jennifer Campbell**, a professor at Erie Community College and **Janna Willoughby-Lohr**, a performance poet, musician, graphic artist, and the daughter of **Robin Kay Willoughby**.

Earth's Daughters continues to publish its unique, consistently high quality journals, most of them theme oriented, the latest ones being *Shift, small things, Light, Dancing on the Edge, one if by land* and *Both Sides Now*. The issues feature talented writers from all over the US and beyond, including local writers, such as **Jimmie Margaret Gilliam, Elaine Chamberlain, Bill Sylvester, Ann Goldsmith, Celeste Lawson, Janna Willoughby-Lohr, David Landrey, Irene Sipos, Barbara Holender, Joyce Kessel, Trudy Stern**, Emmanuel Fried, **Sally Fiedler**, Joy Walsh and **Peter Siedlecki**, and expatriate Buffalonians, Nita Penfold and Bonnie Johnson. Their invitational 40th anniversary issue #80, *Perennial Forte*, with cover art by Catherine Parker, includes Ralph Black, Diane di Prima, **Irving Feldman, Sherry Robbins**, Lynn Lifshin, Marge Piercy, Jerome Rothenberg, **Bill Sylvester** and **Michael Basinski**. Most of the covers contain artwork by **Ryki Zuckerman** and **Kastle Brill**, and more recently, by other artists, such as **Karen Lee Lewis** (photography) and **George Grace**, Catherine Parker, Priscilla Bowen and Michael Morgulis (art and graphics).

Ryki also runs the Earth's Daughters Gray Hair Reading Series, which features established local and formerly local writers over 50, and Wordflight, which combines accomplished featured readers and an open mike. **Jennifer Campbell** co-hosts the Center for Inquiry Literary Café, and was one of the editors of *Beyond Bones*, a poetry anthology series, which has published many of the writers included here.

Ryki Zuckerman's poetry is eloquent, personal and fanciful, combining erudition, boundless imagination and a playful, sometimes bittersweet humor. **Jennifer Campbell's** have exquisite, yet unflinching perception and depth of emotion. **Joyce Kessel's** poems have tenderness, deep perception and bemused wit. **Kastle Brill's** often have a transcendent dreamlike quality, and always have acute, beautifully chosen detail. **Janna Willoughby-Lohr** brings memories and dialogues to life with amazing fidelity and power, and soaring imagination.

Many of the poets here have been associated with perhaps the most important and pervasive literary organization in Western New York, Just Buffalo. It was started in 1975 with a reading by Diane di Prima, organized by Debra Ott. Its success inspired her to initiate a series of readings at the Allentown Community Center. In the late 70's many nationally known writers were included in the series, including Allen Ginsberg, Robert Creeley, Victor Hernandez Cruz, Laurence Ferlinghetti, Ishmael Reed, Diane Wakoski, Ted Berrigan, Nikki Giovanni and Ed Dorn, in addition to well-known local writers, Leslie Fiedler, **Max Wickert, Elaine Chamberlain, Bill Sylvester** and **Dennis Maloney**. In the early 80's, many of these writers returned to the series, as well as poets Alice Notley (the wife of Ted Berrigan), Jim Carroll, Fielding Dawson, Robert Duncan, Anne Waldman, Gary Snyder, Grace Paley and W.S. Merwin, and local writers, **Sherry Robbins, Ansie Baird, Ann Goldsmth, Robin Kay Willoughby**, Allen De Loach, John Daley, Nancy Barnes, **Ryki Zuckerman, Carole Southwood, Norma**

Kassirer, **Olga Karman** and **Jorge Guitart**. A local radio show Just Buffalo sponsored on FM 88 featured many of them, too.

Just Buffalo also put out a small magazine and published the chapbooks, *Snapshots of Paradise* by **Sherry Robbins** and *One Night Stands & Other Pieces of Time* by **Kastle Brill**. Just Buffalo sponsored workshops by many writers in the 80's, too. John Clarke gave a workshop, "Blake and the Modern Poetics," and a fiction workshop was given by Robert Pohl, who has maintained a poetry column in *The Buffalo News* since early 1987, and more recently, also, a blog, and has worked tirelessly to raise awareness of poetry in Western New York.

Just Buffalo also sponsored wonderful multimedia programs, including collaborations with visual artists and jazz musicians, readings featuring Latin American and Native American writers, and a collaboration with St. Mary's School of the Deaf to explore the possibilities of using American Sign Language in poetry. They also sponsored a production of *Gilgamesh* by the National Theater for the Deaf.

On April 6, 1983, Just Buffalo sponsored a multimedia celebration honoring the publication of *The Collected Poems of Robert Creeley, 1945-1975* by the University of California Press. Robert Creeley, who was, of course, one of the greatest poets of the past and present centuries, was unfailingly generous to the literary community of Western NY. He remained in Buffalo as a David Gray Professor of Poetry and Letters, and later as a Samuel P. Capen Professor of Poetry and the Humanities, until he left for a position at Brown University in 2003, which he had until he died in 2005.

Olga Karman, who was featured in Just Buffalo readings in the 80's, and is now on their board of directors, is a superb poet and writer of fiction and memoirs about her experiences as an expatriate Cuban. Her first collection of poetry, *Adios*, was published by Just Buffalo in 1984, and another collection, *Border Crossing*, was published by Buffalo Press in 1990. Her poetry captures the most profound human longings in rich, powerful and majestic language.

Norma Kassirer, who died in February, 2013, was a longtime Buffalo poet, artist, teacher and fiction writer, and an author of classic children's books. She was much loved by the poetry community, especially by her close friends among the poets who have the longest roots in Buffalo. She had worked as a social worker at Buffalo Family Services and began writing after her two daughters were born. She studied fiction writing under John Barth and Donald Barthelme. She was published by **Edric Mesmer's** *Yellow Edenwald Field,* and had books published by **Mike Boughn's** shuffaloff books, **Edric Mesmer's** Buffalo Ochre Papers and **Geoffrey Gatza's** BlazeVOX (see bio). Her writing was versatile, and ranged from the avant-garde experimental, to poetry of amusing and witty anecdotes, to the marvelously entrancing dream-like tales, like the one included here, which release a childlike sense of mystery and wonder.

Carole Southwood, who read in the early 80's in the Hallwalls Fiction Diction readings and the radio program sponsored by Just Buffalo, now teaches at Empire State College, and runs a poetry reading series at the campus there which has featured many of the poets included here. She studied with several major poets, including **Irving Feldman**, **Mac Hammond** and Carl Dennis. Her existentially startling poems convey the feeling of how much of what we know is generated from the inside, and how difficult it is to really know reality, ourselves or others.

Marjorie Norris can also be found in the pages of the 1980's NEW newsletters, sitting in a circle at the Essex Street Art Gallery with **Robin Kay Willoughby**, Lee Franke, **Dennis Maloney** and Joan De Loach, reading Japanese NO plays, which are a short dramatic form related to opera, ballet and religious ritual, and involve total immersion in their sound, physical action and meaning. It's not surprising, as to read a **Marjorie Norris** poem is to be totally engulfed in its sensory and imaginative possibilities, incredible intensity, striking metaphors and compelling musicality. She is a poet who has been celebrated in many venues and organizations, including Just Buf falo (as a Writer in Residence), Chautauqua, Center for Inquiry Literary Café, the Gray Hair Reading Series, the Wordflight reading series and the 4th Friday Poetry Series at Dog Ears bookstore, run in South Buffalo by **Frederick Whitehead**. Her books have been published by Aventine Press, **Gary Earl Ross'** press, The Writer's Den, No Frills Buffalo and **Ruth Thompson's** Saddle Road Press.

Some of the poets included here, myself as well, were involved with Niagara-Erie Writers during the mid-eighties, when we used to have meetings in a little office on W. Northrup Street and open mike readings at the Central Park Grill on Main Street, and readings, organized by poet, Cheryl Bell, that featured well-known out-of-town and local writers, including **Irving Feldman**, Robert Creeley, Charles Baxter, Tomas Tranströmer, Joe Bruchac, **Olga Karman, Ann Goldsmith, Ansie Baird, Bill Sylvester, Jorge Guitart** and **Sally Fiedler**. The small presses that were active at that time, and which published many poets here, were *Pure Light*, coedited and cofounded by the poet, Tom Piccillo; *Slipstream*, which still operates in Niagara Falls under Dan Sicoli, Livio Farallo and Robert Borgatti (also fine poets); Textile Bridge Press, which was run by Joy Walsh, and published *Moody Street Irregulars*, a Jack Kerouac newsletter, and other titles; Buffalo Arts Review, edited by George Sax; and, of course, Earth's Daughters.

Many who were involved with NEW then, like Jack Shifflett, John Lawton, Nancy Rybczynski and Francine Witte, have since left the area, and greats, Manny Fried and Joy Walsh have passed away. But some are still here, among them, Cheryl Bell, Tom Piccillo, **Gary Earl Ross, Kenneth Feltges, Alfonso Volo, Katharine Tussing** and **George Grace**, who, with Dee Script, in the late 80's, ran a series called Circleformance, which was revived, co-hosted by **Lynn Ciesielski,** at George's Meridian Gallery, a beautiful venue which unfortunately closed last year. It's now held at different locations in Buffalo.

Gary Earl Ross is a successful playwright, novelist and publisher, as well as a poet, whose riveting work often deals with the dark side of human nature. His press, The Writer's Den, has published work by himself, **Karen Lee Lewis, Perry Nicholas, Marjorie Norris** and **Lisa Wiley. Kenneth Feltges**, a retired teacher and award winning photographer, has a hard hitting and very absorbing cinematic style, which paints in-depth portraits of its subjects, and often explores the irony of human self-delusion, but always with great sensitivity and compassion. **George Grace**, a superb visual artist, as well as an excellent and prolific writer, combines unflinching realism with penetrating humor and a great ear for dialogue. **Alfonso Volo**, an artist who has had major exhibits throughout Western New York and other areas, and who studied philosophy in college, uses the same combination of thought and vision in his condensed and vivid poetry. My close friend, **Katharine Tussing**, also a widely exhibited painter, is distinctive for her ability to transform strong emotions into powerful metaphors and images. In my own poetry I draw on my background in science and my personal experiences, and am inspired by my love for the lyrical poetry of the past, the vision of the moderns and the endless possibilities of contemporary poetry.

Michael Boughn was studying under John Clarke and Robert Creeley in the 80's, and in 1988 founded shuffleoff books, which published, as I mentioned before, the first version of Sherry Robbins' *or, The Whale*, **David Tirrell's** *Half-House Poems, Places* by Robert Creeley, *In the Analogy 1* by John Clarke, as well as books by Lisa Jarnot, Bruce Holsapple, Randy Prus and Elizabeth Willis. In the late 1980's, Michael also helped John Clarke to run *intent. Letter of Talk, Thinking & Document*, which published work by John Clarke and himself, Charles Olson, Robert Duncan, Ed Sanders, Ben Friedlander, Diane di Prima, Daniel Zimmerman, **Stephen Baraban** and **David Tirrell**. He now teaches at the University of Toronto, and has written many books of poetry, and books for young adults, as well as numerous critical articles. He also coedited Robert Duncan's *The H.D. Book* with Victor Coleman. In these selections from his latest work, *City*, with subtle and illuminating language, he deals with the constraints and conditioning society imposes on consciousness; in "I.3.iv - Economic reality," with the "bill of goods" and misuse of religion proffered by exploitative financial hierarchies, and in "I.3.vi - *No* further *adieu,*" with perceptual and cognitive ones, though he celebrates the beauty of perception in spite of all the barriers.

Loren Keller has been a poet since the 60's and a playwright throughout the last three decades, publishing over a dozen plays, five of which were performed at Buffalo Ensemble Theatre, where he had been Playwright-in-Residence for many years. He is also an actor, and has appeared in *The Elephant Man, Of Mice and Men, The Night of the Iguana* and *On Golden Pond*, for which he won a Best Actor Award. He is the author of many chapbooks and a major volume of poetry, *Evening Everything*, which was published in 2005. He uses shifts in perspective and light that originate from his deep knowledge and understanding of visual art, and striking imagery and sound from his deep knowledge and understanding of the poetic art, both spoken and on the page. His poetry has a folksy plainspoken feel to it, but its elegance, subtlety, sophistication and elevated vision give it a power that is regal and sublime.

Gay Baines is another very fine poet, who has been published in innumerable journals from the mid-eighties to the present. She is the cofounder of July Literary Press, which publishes collections of poetry and fiction. Her poetry is beautiful, mysterious and romantic, and yet tough minded and witty. She makes the past seem so vivid, it seems to be happening as we read, and she can scope out and capture the whole cosmos in an instant. Her poems are classic, yet have a fresh, contemporary feel.

Alexis De Veaux is a widely published, much awarded and internationally celebrated writer of poetry, plays, fiction and biography. She is also an artist, and a lecturer who has given talks all over the world. Her poems, which are extraordinary, have a sense of flowing and connectedness. Each word multiplies the meaning of the other, so each poem is an infinite expansion of its parts.

Celeste Lawson, who started as a dancer, is rooted in the dance traditions of ancient North Africa and the Middle East. Her performing arts background shows in the dramatic tension of her poems, which lend themselves so well to spoken performance with their powerful imagery, metaphors and musicality. She, like **Marjorie Norris** and **Kathleen Betsko Yale,** has been part of the venerable women's writing group, Women of the Crooked Circle, as was the late **Jimmie Margaret Gilliam**.

Kathleen Betsko Yale, who came to Buffalo from the UK, is another poet whose work is influenced by drama. She is a successful playwright, an acclaimed actress, and a scholar who is a leading authority on the subject of women's contemporary theater. Her poetic work is dazzling, dramatically effective in its social and emotional impact, and often hilarious. She says she is influenced by Mother Goose, Bob Dylan, Sojourner Truth, Leonard Cohen, Charles Dickens and Mae West, who was, unbeknownst to many, an influential and controversial director and screenwriter. No wonder Kathleen's work is so colorful and original!

Judith Slater, who was mentored by Carl Dennis and **Irving Feldman**, abandoned teaching literature to study and practice clinical psychology. Her book, *The Wind Turning Pages*, was published by **Max Wickert's** Outriders Poetry Project in 2011. In her poems, memories are recalled with a dream-like quality and powerful emotional resonance.

Trudy Stern, who calls herself the shortest lived member of Earth's Daughters, was involved in creating broadsides for Just Buffalo in its earliest days back in 1978. She's a mother, a teacher and a nurse, and is married to the prominent artist and printmaker, Michael Morgulis. In the 2000's, she ran a wonderful tea house called

Tru-Teas, which hosted a poetry reading series, which many of the poets here participated in. She and Michael now run the popular Cherry Blossom Festival, which is held each spring at The Buffalo History Museum and in the gorgeous Japanese Garden behind it. Her poetry is steeped in traditional and contemporary forms of poetry, and is brimming with infectious humor.

Anna Walsh, who I was privileged to get to know in the latter part of the last decade, was born in Buffalo, but moved to Washington, DC after marrying in 1957, then to San Francisco, where she wrote and performed poetry, and associated with well-known Beat poets. In 1985, she came back to Buffalo to care for her mother, and continued to write her "sacred human text," which is an amazing tribal poetry for the human race, in which the personal becomes historical, mythical and sublime.

Ruth Thompson has been a professor, a librarian and a yoga teacher. Formerly a resident of Colden, NY, she makes her home in Hilo, Hawai'i, where she runs a small press called Saddle Road Press, which has recently published books by **Jennifer Campbell, Perry Nicholas, Ryki Zuckerman, Trudy Stern, Joyce Kessel** and **Frederick Whitehead**, as well as her own. Ruth's poetry is fresh, celebratory, and blazingly original. It penetrates to the roots of things, and to the heart of experience, unfolding its joy with deep resonance and exuberance.

Michael Tritto, Sr. was a teacher, who won the Just Buffalo Writer in Residence award in 1988. He read at the Rooftop Series (run by **Lisa Forrest** at Buffalo State College), at the Burchfield Penney Art Center and at the Screening Room. He was widely published, in the US and abroad, and had a narrative poem about the Holocaust performed as a ballet at The Pfeiffer Theatre. His poems are full of light and fire, and he had the gift of the poetic magician, the illusive sleight of hand knack to express the inexpressible, and to capture those rare moments when everything is illuminated by something beyond the ordinary. Tragically, he died of cancer in January, 2015.

Irene Sipos, who studied with Robert Creeley and Leslie Fiedler, taught writing for over 20 years at Buffalo State College, and also taught poetry workshops through the Rooftop Poetry Club. She has read in the Earth's Daughters Gray Hair Reading Series, the Burchfield Penney reading series, and many others. Her poetic voice is direct and warm, and full of wisdom and spontaneity, and her train of thought is highly original and associative, with a contemporary edginess.

Peter Ramos is a professor of American Literature at Buffalo State College, and has been widely published in prestigious journals. His latest book is *TELEVISION SNOW* (Back Pages Books, 2014). His poetry paints pictures, in detail that becomes metaphorically heartbreaking, of modern life, and its shaky emotional and ethical foundations. It strikes chords that wake us up to the fact that something is terribly wrong at the core, something that is almost indefinable, though its consequences may be obviously negative.

Lisa Forrest was a librarian at Buffalo State College until she recently took a position at Hamilton College. While at Buffalo State, she founded the Rooftop Poetry Club, which sponsors a reading series that has featured many local poets, including **Ryki Zuckerman, Michael Tritto, Sr.** and Barbara Cole, who is now artistic director at Just Buffalo. Lisa's poems are condensed and multifaceted, allowing us to experience their subjects from a prismatic array of perspectives.

Sandra Cookson teaches writing and literature at Canisius College. Her book, *Two Loons Taken for Vultures*, was published by Finishing Line Press in 2011. She writes with a pristine clarity, and a vocabulary of pure aesthetics, which penetrate to the heart of consciousness, dreams, love and fear.

Eric Gansworth, also a professor at Canisius College, is a successful novelist and visual artist, as well as a poet. In his book, *From the Western Door to the Lower West Side: Photography by Milton Rogovin, Poetry by Eric Gansworth*, he writes about the

Native American culture, experience and spirituality with a stunning combination of classic elegance, beautifully detailed realism and breathtaking understatement.

Janet McNally teaches creative writing at Canisius and was included in Best New Poets 2012, an anthology of emerging poets published by University of Virginia Press, and won the White Pine Press Poetry Prize in 2014. Her poems show how myth and memory haunt reality. They pose many questions they don't answer, creating chasms she invites the reader to bridge for themselves.

E.R. Baxter III is a professor emeritus of English at Niagara Community College, an environmental activist, and a mentor of **Eric Gansworth**. He is a versatile writer who can write in any mode from intensely personal and romantic, to biting political and social commentary, to hilarious self-spoof, with vivid fidelity. The poems included here are beautifully evocative memories of young love.

Gene Grabiner taught sociology and American history at Erie Community College and is a SUNY Distinguished Service Professor Emeritus. His poems have a wide range of subjects, from family and personal memories to victims of social injustice. They slice into reality with a laser sharp edge and cut with deft precision.

Barbara Holender is the author of several books of poetry, including Quarterly Review of Literature Award winner, *IS THIS THE WAY TO ATHENS?* She has also written children's books in Hebrew, and has had many essays and poems published. She is a colorful, funny, dramatic and gripping writer, even in the face of the heartbreaking loss of her young grandson, which she writes about in *OUR LAST BEST PERFECT DAY*, the book that the poems included here are chosen from.

S.M. Hutton's background in video and film media gives her poetry a cinematic feel of changing perspectives and intense imagery, to which she adds the dimension of beautiful, mysterious and surprising language. She won the Arthur Axelrod Memorial Award for poetry in 2006.

Marten Clibbens moved to Buffalo from the UK to study with Robert Creeley in the 1980's. His work often uses a skillful weaving of abstract and concrete images, of inner and outer landscapes to express alienation of the self from the encroachment of its surroundings. In "Refugee," he sets the self apart from the incidental circumstances of its being and asserts its freedom as a "refugee" from all superficial aspects that could define it.

Anne Huiner has worked and volunteered at several community organizations, and is a member of a women's writing group that includes **Ann Goldsmith**. She is also an actress who has been reading and performing poetry for decades. Hers is a superbly crafted poetry of intense vision, beauty and power.

David Lewitsky is writing a book length series of poems with the theme of dance as a metaphor. In his poems, the words dance through space and time in a sophisticated mixture of imagination and erudition.

From the fall of 1990, and into the 2000's, the UB English department ran a program called Wednesdays at 4 Plus, sponsored by the David Gray Chair of Poetry, (Charles Bernstein), the Samuel P. Capen Chair (Robert Creeley) and the Poetry/Rare Books Collection. It featured legendary writers such as John Ashbery, Adrienne Rich, Robert Kelly, Ron Silliman, Robert Pinsky, David Foster Wallace and J.M. Coetzee, as well as UB professors Raymond Federman, **Irving Feldman**, Carl Dennis, Robert Creeley, Steve McCaffery and Charles Bernstein, local writers, **Michael Basinski** and **Peter Ramos**, and many poetic innovators from all over the world.

Many small presses sprung up in the 90's, such as shuffaloff books, which I mentioned before, Leave Books (1991-1995), a cooperative edited by Juliana Spahr and Kristen Prevallet, which published 58 chapbooks by authors including Will Alexander and **Michael Basinski**; Meow Press, which published books by Charles Bernstein, Benjamin Friedlander, Loss Pequeño Glazier, **Jorge Guitart** and **Michael Basinski**; O-blek, No. 12 (1993) which sprung out of a conference for young writers organized by Juliana Spahr; and Tailspin Press, which published books by **Michael Basinski** and other experimental writers.

Some of the poets here who were connected with the Olson influenced group of the 60's and 70's, like **Stephen Baraban**, **David Tirrell** and Stephen Ellis, were published more recently in *House Organ*, founded by editor Kenneth Warren, a highly original poet and critic, who was retired from being the director of Lakewood Public Library near Cleveland and was living north of Niagara Falls, when, sadly, he passed away in 2105. *House Organ*, though associated with a lot of Olson influenced writers, is a publication independent of any academic trends, and publishes a very diverse group of writers dedicated to expressing themselves through the poetic art.

Since the early 2000's there have been readings at a small bookstore in Allentown called Rust Belt Books, in which some of the poets here were featured. **Kristianne Meal** was managing the bookstore formerly owned by Brian Lampkin, and she has since taken it over. An open reading series was run by Livio Farallo, and featured anthology poets **Celia White, Kristianne Meal** and **Lewis Bowman**, among others. Rust Belt has also hosted the Just Buffalo Small Press Reading Series and the Tangential Readings, organized by George Georgakis and Andrea Zysk, which featured many poets in this anthology, including **Lynn Ciesielski** and **Blue Wojciechowski**. Rust Belt has recently acquired a trendy new space on Grant Street.

Kristianne Meal is an amazingly original poet. Steeped in science, especially physics, she gives emotive language to the phenomenon of consciousness in our time of discovery of the vastness, ancientness and minuteness of our existence. Some of her recent performance pieces have been "Trust-body in Digital World" (Trimania 2013, Buffalo Arts Studio) and "In-La'kech: I Am Another Yourself" (Universal Technology Porn Application, Rust Belt, Buffalo).

Celia White often read at Nietzsche's and Rust Belt, did readings and workshops for Just Buffalo, and until recently, ran Urban Epiphany, a marathon reading each spring which included almost every poet in Buffalo. She is an extraordinary poet, who writes with astounding imagery, exhilarating passion and absolute honesty.

Also in the early 2000's, a boutique theater in Amherst, NY, called The Screening Room, became the venue for once a month Wednesday night and Sunday afternoon poetry readings. **Rosemary Kothe** and her husband, Bill Kothe, were the prime movers in starting the series, and **Verneice Turner** was involved in the early days of it, too. Most of the poets in this anthology have given readings there, and it's still going now, with Marek Parker and **Lynn Ciesielski** as its hosts.

Rosemary Kothe, who died in 2005, was a school teacher, a poet, and mother figure to all the poets that read at The Screening Room. She and her husband, Bill, gave legendary parties for which she cooked an amazing array of food. She wrote wonderful poetry, with exuberant innocence and consummate empathy for all living things.

Verneice Turner is an actress, director, a marvelous poet, a mechanical designer and the founder and coeditor of the *Beyond Bones* series of anthologies, in which many of the poets in this anthology have been included. She hosted The Screening Room for many years, looking everywhere to find talented writers to schedule for its events, and fostered a warm, supportive atmosphere, where poets could grow and improve. She has also been one of my best friends and a great supporter of this anthology. Her poems are powerful invocations of the Divine Light and hope that manifest themselves through all human struggle and suffering.

Many of the poets who have read at The Screening Room are also involved in a reading series at the Center for Inquiry, which is a publishing house for secular books in Amherst near UB. The series is called the Center for Inquiry Literary Café, which is cosponsored by Just Buffalo. It was first hosted by Livio Farallo, then David Musella, and then, until recently, by **Perry Nicholas** and **Jennifer Campbell**, and is being hosted this year by Jennifer and **Lisa Wiley**.

Some of the poets who have read at the CFI Café, besides Jennifer and Perry, are **Verneice Turner**, **John Marvin**, **Martha Deed**, **David Landrey**, **David Lampe**, **Amol Salunkhe**, **Gunilla T. Kester**, **Marge Merrill**, **Jane Sadowsky**, **Lynn Ciesielski**, **Peter Siedlecki**, **Joe Nickell**, **Josh Smith**, **Theresa Wyatt**, **Lisa Wiley**, **Richard LaClair**, **Susan Dworski Nusbaum**, **Charles Case**, **Sinéad Tyrone**, **Christina Woś Donnelly**, **Sam Magavern**, **Alexis Machelor O'Donnell**, **Susan Marie** and **Blue Wojciechowski**.

Jennifer Campbell, as I've mentioned before, is an Erie Community College professor, a member of Earth's Daughters, coeditor of *Beyond Bones* and co-host of CFI Literary Café. She has published two books of poetry, *Driving Straight Through* (Foot-Hills Publishing, run by poet, Michael Czarnecki) and *Supposed to Love* (Saddle Road Press). She is a complex and eloquent poet, whose intense perceptions create an alchemy of emotional depth and feeling.

Perry Nicholas is also an Erie Community College professor, who was an editor of *Beyond Bones* and a co-host of CFI, and has co-hosted the Lewiston Arts Café with his wife, Maria. The author of many books of poetry, he has a very distinctive poetic voice that is a balance of opposites; stark honesty and imaginative whimsy, earthiness and refined ethereality, a sense of tradition and striking originality. It is a voice that reaches for the sky, but at the same time embraces the imperfections of life below.

John Marvin is a retired teacher who went back to school to take a PhD in poetics at UB. He is an incredibly prolific poet of consistently high quality, and is widely published. His poetry is a poetry of the future, sometimes scientifically and philosophically erudite and discursive, sometimes dream-like fugue comparing alternate dimensions of human destiny, often whimsical, profound and impishly funny conjectures about the human predicament.

Martha Deed is a retired psychologist, and the mother of **Millie Niss**, also a poet in this anthology, who died tragically at the age of 36 from a hospital related infection after being admitted for complications of Behcet's disease. Martha's heart wrenching poems about the loss of Millie show the incredible power of her writing. In her undergraduate years, she did an independent study under Reed Whittemore, who served two terms as "Consultant to the Library of Congress," which is equivalent to the Poet Laureate title today. She stopped writing poems for many years and returned to it in 2000, and has since completed several collections, including editing a full length volume of Millie's work, published by BlazeVOX. Her latest work, *Climate Change*, gives a panoramic look at American life, echoing many of the best American writers, offering biting social commentary, satirical humor, emotional power and delightful observations of nature.

David Landrey is a retired Buffalo State College literature professor, who studied briefly under Charles Olson at UB, and is a great admirer of Robert Duncan. He explores the mysteries of selfhood and otherness, connectedness and disconnectedness, and the ephemerality of love and life, in his beautifully transcendent, evocative and enlightening poems, which capture the music of consciousness.

David Lampe, a colleague and friend of **David Landrey**, also taught English at Buffalo State College, specializing in the literature of the Middle Ages and the Renaissance. He is the editor of *Mortals & Immortals*, a marvelous 2014 anthology of participants in the 35 year old Burchfield Penney Art Center Writers and Poets Series. His deeply reflective poems are endowed with a vivid sense of the sacred and the miraculous in life.

Amol Salunkhe is a software engineer by trade, and by vocation, a writer of vivid and enthralling poems, brimming with stories and colorful descriptions, set to the backbeat of the bustling streets of India.

Gunilla T. Kester, a native of Sweden, makes her home in two languages and on two continents, as well as at Heritage Academy in Ghana, her latest adopted favorite place. A gifted musician, she often performs and teaches classical guitar through the Amherst School of Music, and has performed at Roswell Park Cancer Institute's Music-in-the-Lobby program for the past seven years. Her deeply felt, intuitive poems peel away layers of personal and collective history, showing us the living, breathing core of who she is, and who we are as humans, as we experience loss, conflict, belonging and abiding love.

Marge Merrill's work involves taking care of the elderly, and she has been a long-time host of The Screening Room. Her poems are delicious slices of life, both earthy and dream-like, which bring full blown characters to life in their short verses.

Jane Sadowsky is a poet whose vision is so pristine and sparkling, that it makes the world seem reborn. To read her poetry, with its unexpected revelations, metaphors and dazzling imagery is to see a whole new world through her eyes. In "Two Worlds," a reflection on a wood burned painting of a Native American scene by a Mohawk artist, she enters the unspoiled world of the Native Americans before the white man came, and accounts, in their voices, the destruction and renewal of their culture and the endurance of their spirits, their ancient ways and their wisdom, which has distilled into America's. In "Early April Woods," a walk in her favorite hiking ground becomes a revelation of the rebirth of nature and of the human spirit.

Lynn Ciesielski is a retired teacher who has toured and read poetry throughout the United States and in England. Her poetry has the emotive power and vividness of a life fully experienced, rich with fascinating characters, humor, feeling and beauty.

Peter Siedlecki teaches literature and creative writing at Daemen College, and runs a reading series at the student center there, called the RIC, which has featured many of the poets in this anthology. His poetry is contemplative and powerfully written, sometimes humorous, and often deals with questions of existence and suffering.

Joe Nickell has had many occupations, the current one as a scientific investigator for the Center for Inquiry. He has written books on many aspects of paranormal investigation. His poems here, which are written in a haunting, musical style he calls "improvisational rhyming," involve a series of personal, yet archetypal, quests, which tell a true story of loss and reunification with his true love and his newly discovered daughter.

Josh Smith is a versatile, widely known poet in Buffalo, and in Toronto, where he has co-hosted the ArtBar Series. His work combines keen observation, unflinching realism, humor and subtlety.

Theresa Wyatt, who is an accomplished visual artist, as well as a poet, studied art history in Italy and is retired from teaching art and English, both in Iran and the NYS Department of Corrections. Her knowledge of the arts, history and literature informs her poetry, and her personal insight and experiences are eloquently ornamented with vivid metaphors and imagery, in a direct and forceful, yet intricate poetic style.

Lisa Wiley, like **Jennifer Campbell** and **Perry Nicholas**, teaches English at Erie Community College. In her first book, *Chamber Music* (Finishing Line Press), she writes of love, motherhood and friendship, in lyrical villanelles, which resonate with haunting emotions. Her second book, *My Daughter Wears Her Evil Eye to School* (The Writer's Den, 2015), paints a rich and reflective portrait of her home and family life.

Richard LaClair is a professor Emeritus at Erie Community College. His poems have a way of turning and examining transformative moments of reality, in all their intensity, intricate detail and complexity.

Susan Dworski Nusbaum is a retired criminal prosecutor whose poems have been published in many prestigious journals and have won many awards. Her poetry, with breathtaking imagery, captures serene oases of harmony in a universe that seems to be whispering its secrets to those who can really listen.

Charles Case is also an attorney, whose poems open wondrous unexpected worlds that are inevitably impinged on by a narrower reality. He presents life with all its quirks, and finds in it surprising metaphors, such as the depiction here of the afternoon as a naked dancing woman, which calls up remembrances of the unspoiled and unfiltered perceptions we learn to suppress.

Sinéad Tyrone works as an administrative assistant, and is a novelist as well as a poet. Her deeply moving, eloquent and powerfully written poems speak of the rootedness of love in memory, and beautifully echo the poetic traditions of Ireland. Her poetic voice, like those of her colleagues, **Loren Keller** and **Perry Nicholas,** is one of the wonderful things that seems to spring right out of the earth and sky.

Christina Woś Donnelly has been a freelance writer and an editor. Her poetry exposes the female condition with a scathing power. She writes with a savage beauty in which metaphor, story and image transform into the starkest of truths. The beauty of her writing can be gentle, too, when she writes of the more pleasant aspects of womanhood, as she does in "Let There Be Silk."

Sam Magavern is a Harvard graduate who teaches law at SUNY/Buffalo, and co-directs an organization that helps develop poorer neighborhoods and provides opportunity for their inhabitants. He has been published in the most prestigious journals in the country. His poetic voice is totally fresh, original and imaginative, painting emotions with captivating and charming imagery, and using his pervasive erudition with a lighthearted touch.

Alexis Machelor O'Donnell works as a counselor, and has loved literature since she was a kid. She is a member of a *Finnegan's Wake* study group, and is also an actress who has appeared in Bloomsday enactments of James Joyce's *Ulysses.* In addition, she plays in a band, and she and her husband, David O'Donnell, raise Monarch butterflies. She has a wonderfully fresh, totally in-the-moment style with spontaneous jazz and hip-hop rhythms.

Susan Marie is a publicist and broadcast journalist who works with many artistic and charitable organizations. She has a deeply original style of writing that is archetypal, elegant and transcendent, telling of the struggles and triumphs of the spirit.

Blue Wojciechowski is a humorist who writes side-splittingly funny rants about the ridiculousness of contemporary life. They are too long to be included here, but you can have a taste of her hilarious humor in "Ode to That Guy" and her warm recollections of her mom's dinner table in "Mom's Table."

Michael Kelleher worked from 1998-2012 as artistic director of Just Buffalo, where he initiated the enormously popular program, Big Night, which is held at the Western New York Book Arts Center, and has featured many poets in this anthology, including **Michael Basinski**, **Nava Fader** and **Geoffrey Gatza**. They also had a celebration of Earth's Daughters; **Jimmie Margaret Gilliam** and **Alexis De Veaux** in a reading honoring Adrienne Rich; and **Martha Deed, David Landrey**, the expatriate poet Kazim Ali and many others in a reading honoring the late **Millie Niss**. Big Night has featured many well-known out-of-town poets, too, such as Will Alexander, Lisa Jarnot, Kent Johnson and Dodie Bellamy.

Michael also founded the immensely successful program, Babel, which fills the auditorium at Kleinhans Music Hall for fascinating lectures by best-selling and critically acclaimed authors such as Amy Tan, Russell Banks, Naruddin Farah, Julia Alvarez, Amos Oz, V.S. Naipaul, and recently, Colum McCann, David Henry Hwang,

Chimamanda Ngozi Adichie and Patti Smith. It is currently being administered by a new artistic director, Barbara Cole, also a wonderful writer, who inherited the mantle after Michael left for a position as the Program Director of the Windham Campbell Literature Prizes at Yale University.

Michael studied poetics for his masters at UB, and has had two books published by BlazeVOX, *To Be Sung* (2005) and *Human Scale* (2007). He also coedits a blog with Ammiel Alcalay called *OlsonNow*, which is dedicated to the poetry and poetics of Charles Olson. In his own poetry, Michael has the gift of expressing complex and almost inexplicable feelings, using an entertaining and aesthetically pleasing anecdotal style, in which, in "But Do They Suffer," he explores questions of the true nature of what is real.

Edric Mesmer works at the Poetry Collection at SUNY/Buffalo, and publishes an international journal of poetry and commentary called *Yellow Field* (formerly called *Yellow Edenwald Field*). In it, he has published many of the poets featured here, including **Norma Kassirer, Lisa Forrest, Geoffrey Gatza, Marten Clibbens, Kristianne Meal, Michael Boughn, Michael Basinski** and **Ann Goldsmith**. He also published *Nightmares–They Are Zeroes*, a chapbook by **Bill Sylvester**, and recently coedited the collected works of **Norma Kassirer** with **Ann Goldsmith**. He has had several collections of his own work published as well. (See bios.) Edric's poetry fascinates with nuances of aesthetic and philosophical discourse found in ordinary things, like a night view at the window in "Flagging Legends," the fate of rotting plums in "The Alstons surround their reflexions," or the transmutations of a dream in "A khimera."

Sara Ries is often inspired to write by her experiences growing up around her parents' diner in Woodlawn, NY, south of Buffalo. She runs a reading series there called Poetry and Dinner Night at the Woodlawn Diner, which has featured many local poets, including **Lynn Ciesielski, Ken Feltges, Ryki Zuckerman, Jennifer Campbell, Karen Lee Lewis, George Grace, Elaine Chamberlain, Janna Willoughby-Lohr, Irene Sipos, Frederick Whitehead** and **Kathleen Betsko Yale**. Sara herself has a poetic voice so vibrant in its emotions, and so vivid in its descriptions, that life literally seems to jump off the pages of her poems, in all its nuances and idiosyncrasies.

Karen Lee Lewis has taught many workshops on art and poetry in the Buffalo area, including one on creative writing at the C.G. Jung Center. She's read poetry at Wordflight, Circleformance, and at the Woodlawn Diner series, and has a full length collection of poems, *What I Would Not Unravel*, published by The Writer's Den in 2010. Her poems are full of fierce, spontaneous and brilliant imagery and metaphors. She captures the vivid terror, pain and will to survive of the living organism in its organic and existential circumstances.

Frederick Whitehead is the host of the Dog Ears Bookstore 4th Friday Poetry Series, which has included as features or open readers many poets here, including **Marjorie Norris, Perry Nicholas, Sara Ries, Janna Willoughby-Lohr, George Grace, Ryki Zuckerman, Elaine Chamberlain, Martha Deed, Josh Smith, Theresa Wyatt, Karen Lee Lewis, S.M. Hutton, David Landrey, Stephen Baraban** and **Gene Grabiner**. In Fred's earthy, subtle and profound poems, there is a deftly suggested sense of the awareness of time, and often, of the mysteries and alternate possibilities of existence, that lingers just below the surface of conscious thought.

Geoffrey Gatza is the editor and publisher of BlazeVOX, a press which has published books by many authors here including **Michael Basinski, Michael Kelleher, Nava Fader, Marc Pietrzykowski, Peter Ramos, Michael Boughn, Jorge Guitart, Sam Magavern, Peter Siedlecki** and **Millie Niss**. BlazeVOX has released over 300 titles of poetry, prose and criticism by innovative and respected authors from all over the world, and also publishes, several times a year, an online journal of print and audio performances of poetry and fiction. Geoffrey does all this, in Wizard of Oz fashion, from a little desk in the living room of an apartment in Kenmore that he shares with his girlfriend, Donna White (who runs Brighton Place Library, where many BlazeVOX events are held). Geoffrey is also a Gulf war veteran and a haute cuisine chef, who for years cooked gourmet feasts which were included in the $5 admission price of Just Buffalo's Big Night.

The ppem excerpted here, "The Twelve Hour Transformation of Clare," is included in Geoffrey's extraordinary book length conceptual piece, *Apollo*, in which Marcel Duchamp plays Apollo and his female alter ego, Rrose Sélavy, represents the blind prophet, Tiresias, who, in his 900 years of life granted by the gods, has been transformed from male to female numerous times. Apollo's muses of rhetoric, dance and poetry are represented by well-known female artists connected to the surrealist movement in the 1930's, Gertrude Abercrombe, Leona Carrington and Dorothea Tanning. As Calliope, the muse of poetry, Dorothea Tanning becomes Clare, who over a period of twelve hours, becomes transformed entirely into symbols, starting with stories of literature, to random assortments of words in many languages, to scientific concepts and equations. The degradation of the human essence to impersonal knowledge speaks to the predicament of human consciousness in the digital age of limitless information, and also to the limitless possibilities of art in any age. The ballet goes on to a chess game where pieces and squares are assigned random common words, generating a strangely familiar poetry, and then to an enactment of a famous chess match between Duchamp and Frank Marshall, performed by Duchamp and Rrose Sélavy, while engaging in sophisticated banter about Duchamp's triumphs and limitations as a chess player, and the nature of life, gender, knowledge, war, death, love, and art in its infinite varieties, in a weaving of themes far too complex to do justice to here. It is a work of universal vision and deep insight.

Marc Pietrzykowski teaches English at Niagara Community College, and runs a small publishing company called pski's porch. He has had several books of poetry published, including *and the whole time I was quite happy* (Zeitgeist Press), *Following Ghosts Upriver* (Main Street Rag's Editor's Select Poetry Series), *The Logic of Clouds* (BlazeVOX) and *No Tribe, No Tribute* (pski's porch). Marc is a writer, who with broad leaps of imagination and fantasy, captures the true psychological landscape of America. He is one of the writers I like to think of as "high fidelity writers." Like many of the other wonderful writers of Western New York, like his friends, **Eric Gansworth** and **E. R. Baxter III**, and **Bill Sylvester, Ansie Baird, Ann Goldsmith, Jimmie Margaret Gilliam, Max Wickert, Peter Ramos, Gene Grabiner, Perry Nicholas, Gunilla T. Kester, Jennifer Campbell, Janna Willoughby-Lohr, Martha Deed, Millie Niss, Sara Ries, Charles Case, Ryki Zuckerman, Celia White, Josh Smith, Ken Feltges, Christina Wos Donnelly, George Grace, Lynn Ciesielski, Gay Baines, Olga Karman, Barbara Holender**, and the greatest high fidelity writer of all, **Irving Feldman**, and many others, he has an extraordinary trueness to life and its unpleasant realities, and yet, also like many of these others, a sense of the dreams, visions, hope, love and beauty that can rescue us from despair.

Millie Niss was the daughter of **Martha Deed** and a mathematician, who studied at Columbia and Brown until Behcet's disease ended her formal studies. She was also an accomplished software designer and web artist, whose poetry and graphics appeared in many print and online publications. Millie's poetry is always a complete delight, whether it's outrageously accurate satire, whimsical tall tales, wicked sociological spoof, serious aesthetic poetry or exuberant description, Millie always nailed it brilliantly. In an unspeakable tragedy, she died of a hospital infection in 2009. Her book, *City Bird*, edited by her mother, was published in 2010 by BlazeVOX.

Nava Fader is a school librarian who received her masters in poetry from UB. Her book, *all the jawing jackdaw*, was published by BlazeVOX in 2009. Most of her poetry starts with lines or whole poems by other poets, such as Sylvia Plath (*The Plath Poems by Nava Fader*, dancing girl press, 2009), Adrienne Rich, Arthur Rimbaud, Basil Bunting and Élise Turcotte. She reinterprets and fleshes out these lines and poems opulently from the roots of life and language, and from her own experience, in a wonderfully rich exploration of their implications and imaginative extensions.

So these are the poets of Western New York. They are all not only wonderful poets, but also wonderful people, too. They are people you would love to know, and people that I am proud to know. Every one of them has generously shared some of their best work for me to bring to you in this book, and have, to a person, helped me with the editing, sequencing, layout and proofing of their segments. The many of them who are publishers themselves have shared their expertise with me without reservation.

They are beautiful people, inside and out, and I wanted to set their images, their lives and their words, like priceless gems, in a setting worthy of them. They all speak with their own true voices, with heart, soul and imagination. They are poets of high fidelity to life, of wit and eloquence, of metaphorical transformation and unforgettable imagery, of affirmation and illumination, of drama and of comedy, of cinematic camera tricks and montage, of deeply realized and individualized literary influences, and of warm and enthusiastic affiliations with each other and the world of poetry outside the region. Their poetry is seasoned with life's experiences, imperfections and vulnerabilities, and addresses concerns common to all human beings. I want this to be a book that you, the reader, will treasure and return to because you hear the poets truly speaking to you.

Patricia Tansey, December 5, 2015

References:

"A Selected Bibliography of Buffalo Publications in Poetry & Poetics" compiled by Kristen Prevallet with a huge amount of help from Michael Basinski, from *chloroform: an aesthetics of critical writing*, eds. Nick Lawrence & Alisa Messer (1997).

NEWSletter (Niagara-Erie Writers) Vol.I, No 1-Vol. XI, No 7 (June, 1978- November, 1989) edited by Allen and Joan De Loach, Nancy Barnes, Robin Kay Willoughby, and later Tom Piccillo, Ed Kuzan.

An Outriders Anthology: Poetry in Buffalo 1969-1979 and After, Selected with an Introduction by Max Wickert (Outriders Poetry Project, 2013).

The Buffalo News archives at www.buffalonews.com

The *Artvoice* archives at http://artvoice.com/

Postscript: I just want to say that as much as I love the poems printed here as art, some of the points of view they express may not be in agreement with my own, as a person of the Christian faith. P.T.

Table of Contents

Gay Baines is a poet, publisher and fiction writer, who did graduate studies in poetry under Carl Dennis and John Brandi, and in fiction under J.M. Coetzee. She is the cofounder and poetry editor of July Literary Press, which publishes poetry, fiction and theme oriented collections. Her poetry collection, *Don't Let Go*, was published in 2010. In 2002 she published her first novel, *Dear M.K.*, and she is working on a second one. Her poetry has been published in *Nimrod, Rattapallax, RE:AL, Cimarron Review, Slipstream, Poet Lore, Icarus, Atlanta Review, Room of Our Own, South Carolina Review, Lullwater Review, Wisconsin Review, Louisiana Literature, The Texas Review, Poem* (#95), *The Art of Poetry: A Treasury of Contemporary Verse, The Buffalo News,* and too many more to mention. She received 1st prize in the 1991 National Writers Union Poetry Contest, judged by Donald Hall. Her poem, "Earthly Heaviness," received honorable mention in the International Icarus 5th annual poetry competition. She has been an active member of the Roycroft Wordsmiths for many years. She has always been a country person, and lives in the beautiful village of East Aurora, New York.

In the Rapturous Grass

sliding after summer rain,
we ran until aspens hid us,
fell to the rusty floor
of a spruce grove,
not a good place to be. All
those needles.
Their scent was too much
for us, we became part of it, or it—
and the needles—became part
of us. Somewhere
surf purred and sucked, but whether
the sea lay yards or miles away
we could not tell, nor care.

We laughed about it later,
mostly at the others, who sat
straitly on verandahs with
tumblers of gin disguised
as lemonade. We laughed
at ourselves too, remembering

our journey, the flight,
the limousine, the air-conditioned
room, our polished shoes,
and the two of us running away
to a distant, leafier, darker time.

Eugene Onegin at the Regal Cinema

After such distance from her own life
driving the mad road called Transit
away from the flats of the north suburbs
away from the ugly grotesque eating
and tax prep and engine shops   driving
with the darkening sun of a bitter day in
her eyes   driving toward the soft blue
rim of the hills where she lives she
thought I should not be here in jeans
sweater and old down coat
but in a long burgundy velvet
dress sitting in a soft leather booth
somewhere in a city   a northern city
Toronto perhaps   sitting and drinking
a Dubonnet while talking and talking
about Tchaikovsky about Fleming and
Hvorostovsky of the dark music the
passion the foolishness of arrogance
young love older love the
possible and impossible   To talk
and talk and talk until the afternoon
has become glittery night which she
does get to watch out in the country
from her window that looks over the
creek where she gazes at the
clarion sky   looks at it and realizes that
the sky is where we live.

Tape Watcher

Somewhere in New York City
he watches videos every day,
images of the bodies plunging
from the Twin Towers. He mutes
the sound, has heard the sirens' moan
quite enough, it is in his head, will
stay in his ear forever. He watches
each figure fall, a curious reversal
from hell to the mangle of death.
One figure interests him,
a slender person, possibly a woman,
wearing blue slacks, a classic white
shirt, a blue-and-green scarf that
floats about her shoulders and face
at first, then points skyward, as if in
horror, as its wearer passes the 20th floor.
He knows every pixel of this
record, has memorized the azure
sky, the drifting clutter of
shattered paper and dust. The
figure, he is sure, is his wife.
She often wore those slacks,
owned a scarf like that. The mix
of blues, the green, the slow tumble
of those delicate limbs he loved
is graceful, measured, as if she
had waited her whole life to
perform this final, sinuous dance
in midair for him, though untrained
in movement, yet beautiful,
a figure from myth, Pallas Athena
changing before his eyes.

Walking After the Blizzard
(February 1977; for Pearl)

Stars blaze. No one else walks the street,
sounds are smothered. They say crime goes down
after such storms. But look at the sky:
Cassiopeia, an uppity lady locked up
by her abusive husband to sit forever,
ferriswheeling round Polaris. The Archer
draws his poaching arrow, frozen in the flash
before some creature dies. Orion lifts his fist,
angry (as aren't we all) at life's vicissitudes.
The dogs run loose. The Gemini—are they
holding hands? Two crimes in one (if you know
what I mean). Who violated Leda's rights
to hatch them? And what of Daphne? Of Agamemnon?
If gods commit rape and murder, what hope have we?

In a city of five hundred thousand you are alone;
yet every eye that gazes on this hulk
of civilization, brought down by wind,
by piled-up snow on the lake, by rigidity
of office schedules, by worn-out buses,
gazes with you, as the ancient eyes
of those who painted the skies for us
gazed then. They knew in those clear days
our frailty, our beauty and our ugliness.
We can add little to that,
we can't even keep our world going.
Alone, in snow and stars
you don't despair. Hot tea
will warm you later, by and by
the snow will melt, and all the time
the pictures white-stitched across
the sky remain, reminders
of our mistakes, our hope and glory.

Earthly Heaviness
(a triple poem)

Drop to earth in wind
      Scratch the air to find
  Swept away with breath
        Starpricks, pinholes, black
        In a cushion of white
Silkweed gathered in forty-two
To send for flotation.
        Sky a tiara for space
Body a silvery pod
        Pavé seen from the swamp
Crinkly lips whispering
Spreads apart, flies apart
  I'm landing! I'm landing!
        Miles apart, light-years apart
Each sprout of silk bursts away
Floating to catch on loosestrife
        Flickering dust in the nighttime
        Coalstars caught on threads of aurora
Pips sunk in mud
White fingers gravid
        Glints set in the teeth of planets.
Mulch brings up branches
That fight with the wind.
        Light shoots straight down
        Through the coreholes of your eyes
        To the planted soles of your feet.

Ansie Baird holds degrees from Vassar College and the State University of New York at Buffalo, where she received her MA in English, and won first prize in the University's Academy of American Poets contest. She is Poet-in-Residence and a part-time English teacher at The Buffalo Seminary, a non-sectarian secondary school in Buffalo, where she has taught for more than 37 years. She has also taught for Just Buffalo Literary Center in their Writers in Education program. She was one of the editors of *Earth's Daughters* magazine, which is one of the oldest feminist arts magazines in the country. In 2010 she was poet-in-residence and a workshop coordinator at the Chautauqua Institute. She was also an original member of the Albright-Knox docent program entitled, "A Picture's Worth A Thousand Words."

Her work has been published in *The Paris Review, The Quarterly, The Southern Review, Western Humanities Review, Poetry Northwest, South Dakota Review, Denver Quarterly, The Recorder, Earth's Daughters*, and a number of other journals. She has read her poetry at the Burchfield Penney Art Center, the Earth's Daughters Gray Hair Reading Series, and at many other regional and non-regional events. Her book of poetry, *In Advance of All Parting*, was published in 2009 as the winner of the White Pine Press Poetry Prize. She is a lifelong resident of Buffalo, New York.

The Earth In Its Orbit

Aren't you glad we're third from the sun?
my daughter, age five, inquired of my mother.
The child had just mastered the planets, desired
to share her delight in their order with her grandmother,
who, frail and ancient, as I then conceived,
smiled and continued on her way to die.
Nine planets shuddered in their rigid route,
the moons receded, seven oceans gasped,
all oxygen burned out of the blue sky
when flames enveloped my mother's frame,
sending her hurtling through the universe.
And I, already older now than she had ever been,
observe the world's tilt, that which can be seen.
Look, here we are on Earth and the fields are green.

Bonnard's Wife Speaks

It isn't that easy being your wife.
You think I like lying around in
interminable bathtubs while the water
turns tepid, the drain clogs, I try dozing
as the scruffy little dog yaps
throughout the afternoon? And you
sketch on and on and on, oblivious.

Meanwhile those other women lurk always
at the edge of doorways or window frames,
gazing away from me, don't get me started.
You introduce us over café au lait
but they turn their ample backs in silence,
assuming I'm invisible, a sort of
intruder they refuse to recognize.

I'm going to confess something else.
Lavender skin? I mean, you know
perfectly well which tubes of paint
contain flesh tones, the ochers and umbers,
pale beiges and translucent peach. But no,
you go ahead and make my skin glow
violet or puce as inspiration strikes you.

I do the best I can with lotions but god knows
I'm not getting any younger. My sallow body
begins to sag in certain curious places, my
skin to shrivel and hang loose on my frame.
It must be all this time I've spent immersed
in tubs, indulging your view of me as some
sort of water sprite who revels in the damp.

The truth is, I've been longing for dry land,
an invitation to slake my thirsty days within
your vivid arms. There I'd be spritely indeed!
We'd paint the bedclothes every lurid
color in the spectrum: bolts of scarlet,
tangerine and gold. I keep suggesting this
but you insist I have to hold my pose

While you depict me floating in a trance
within the rigid confines of the tub,
a trapped beast wallowing amid the steam
on tiny speckled feet. You think

7

I don't know everything about your
golden girl? You think I do not churn
and shiver in this hot flush of pink?

My skin glows mottled in its quilt of hues,
Its vivid blues and greens.
The patchwork floor slopes forward
over space, transformed into tapestries
of light. And I lie bathed in purple
like a corpse, my coffined limbs
encased and glazed in shade.

I see your face reflected in the glass
above the porcelain sink, observing me
in all my amplitude. Duplicity, indeed,
to paint your naked wife while craving
someone else. Go ahead, embellish
my flesh with segments of absurd pastels
to keep me from escaping. Wretched love,

I clamber from the bath, a phantom wife
all absence in your view. You may
as well have hung me on the wall,
abandoned effigy within a frame.
Light from my undraped limbs spills
like water on the floor, a pool of blue,
an aureate, a scattering of gold.

Take A Right Turn At Oneida

For Hayden Carruth

Any day now I'll be heading out North
To visit the old man of Munnsville,
Carting along supper and two or three bottles
Of booze which we'll imbibe while I soak up
All his lunacy and wisdom,
Wrestled from eighty-six fretful years upon this planet.

The guy resembles a sort of Old Testament prophet,
Disheveled hair, scruffy beard resting on his chest.
Only the translucent plastic tubing jutting from his nose
And a tank trailing along from bed to desk to ancient kitchen chair
Betray his up-to-date condition, or, as he'd say, over-the-hill,
About-to-croak.

Meanwhile he sends me up-to-date indignant letters berating me
For sticking with the same old subjects:
For crissakes, forget about that bastard.
You're wasting time yearning for the past.
There's plenty to write about just outside your window:
Glint of ice on the downed power line;
Your spotted dog circling the swings.
You know as well as I do how the Earth exhales in beauty.

I write him back: You're right, of course,
Old pal, old microphone,
Ranting at the world's injustices
And all the dreck we find in poetry.
You never stray from telling me the truth.
Keep holding on. I cherish you for that.
When your forsythia blooms, I'm coming back.

And All Of Us Alive

So there we were and all of us alive,
Embracing on the Atlantic beach
Near midnight, Nantucket time in breezy May,
While the moon went through its paces
Of flash and dazzle and farewell
And the stars skimmed by on their
Oblivious errands through outer space,
Disinclined to stay in place so we five
Could trace their outlines into ancient
Constellations as the Greeks could.

Sure, we'd had plenty of fine wine,
Or anyway ample to the occasion.
One of us said, Let's go down to the shore
And we did and stood there amazed,
Gazing as though we'd never seen it all before,
This panorama, this flamboyant sky,
And one of us about to die
Although we couldn't say for sure which one or why.

So off we laughed and stumbled on the path,
Dipped and danced and strutted on the sand,
Grabbed hands and held each other in our arms
While the sea clamored and the winds churned
And we sang our mortal hearts out to the moon.

Nothing Of You

I

Sometimes I pretend you have tumbled
off the edge of the Persian Gulf,
dropped like a pearl
to the bottom of the sea.

You glimmer but the indifferent fish
swim on.

You are my exotic, my precious
non-possession.

I would have you hammered
into sheets of gold,
molded into a brooch
I could pin on my lapel.

See, I'd say. There he is.
Doesn't he shine?

II

Who's to say?
It may be all
for the best
this fall-
ing off
this dis-
sonance.

Still, when I
stumble
in the pitch
and tremble
of night's pit
      clamor
      clamor
      clamor
shakes me
awake

your name
engraved
in water
on my palm.

Stephen M. Baraban was born in Brooklyn in 1955. He moved with his family at the age of five to Nassau County, Long Island, where he was supremely bored, until he had the chance to escape to the University of Buffalo.

At the university, where he received both a BA and an MA, Baraban was inspired by such poet/professors as Robert Creeley, Blake/ Olson scholar John (Jack) Clarke and Albert S. Cook, the visionary who had reorganized and reimagined the UB English Department at the time that the university became public.

When Stephen reluctantly returned to the New York City area, continued correspondence with Creeley, Clarke and Cook helped sustain him as he occupied research and clerical positions. Participating in a Saint Mark's Poetry Project workshop with the incomparable Bernadette Mayer was a rejuvenating experience. In August 2009, he took the opportunity to return to Buffalo.

Stephen has published poetry in various journals, including Geoffrey Gatza's *BlazeVOX Online* and Ken Warren's *House Organ*. He is working on a series of ten explications of poems by Charles Olson, which was originally commissioned by the late Ken Warren. He has spoken at various gatherings of poet/scholars, including the Black Mountain North conference at the Rochester Institute of Technology and the First Annual Cloudburst Council in Naples, NY.

From The Murk Of His Tiger Dome He Steps Into The Lucid Air

for David Tirrell, keeper of the ancient stones

He fixes his eyes on the
sweating angels beneath us,
    pouring their jars of black magma,
and the pain-warped foreheads
of the massive masters, the human
    saints of orogeny—
wailing, he strums the tale
of the labors of the star-drunk craftsmen—
gaunt-framed, pacing, he wanders, his bones swinging as
    wind chimes

drinking in, and sprinkling
cadence of dharma through
each breeze
and greater thrust.

Lot's Wife Turns to the Lot of the City

Murderous fire and sulfur from the skies

not deflected by the force of enough

satisfactory citizens forming a *minyan*

as minimum constellation to

serve as shield of wonderful light for

the city's living flesh against

the knuckles of judging flame

the lucky woman couldn't take in her

stride, so halted,

turned to witness, with body and heart

bleeding as instantly she

solidified to

bitter intellectual tears standing

firm as eternal

saving saline

mercy of all

health and preservation.

After Robert Creeley

To be in love is also like sneaking
A thermometer into the mouth
Of the honeyed object of
One's attention.

Ah! freaked, she might fume and sniff
Regarding unsent bouquets,
Or you, pard, pace and flail
Regarding well-deserved Favors

While the fierce core is
What *fevers*
Also within her may
Stream.

* * *

God, it's delightful!
oh yes—treat and shining!
when you're in the presence of
the unhindered enthusiasm of
any soul that's truly child-like, jeez
but me, call me –ish—
rued and gnashed
the carefully avoiding all
eyes again
prodigiously wrecked and regretful
full-grown person.

To Get to the Post-Blizzard

To get to the post-blizzard
city-government snow-shoveling site
I walked listlessly to the bus-stop
beneath the black-blue sky,
and then managed
to bestir my feet to
a livelier pace, and later
strained beyond that
to a desperate, clumsy speed-walking,
not falling back
for a long time until
this gasping pace
could no longer be sustained.
And I still have to wonder
whether I seemed
more grotesque or more energetic
to anyone peering
through one of the
noble windows
of the ample, colorful houses of West Ferry
I strove and advanced beside
when before my bleary eyes
these houses changed
into stamped, addressed envelopes—
the houses I
love are messages
poised upright
fronting the air
had acquired by this time
a misty gleam.

Michael Basinski

is the Curator of the Poetry Collection of the University Libraries, University at Buffalo. He performs his work as a solo poet and in ensemble with BuffFluxus. Among his many books of poetry are *Trailers* (BlazeVOX); *Poems Popeye Papyrus* (Slack Buddha Press); *Of Venus 93* (Little Scratch Pad); *All My Eggs Are Broken* (BlazeVOX); *Strange Things Begin to Happen When a Meteor Crashes in the Arizona Desert* (Burning Press); *Heka* (Factory School); *Mool, Mool3Ghosts* and *Shards of Shampoo* (Bob Cobbing's Writers Forum); *Cnyttan* and *Heebie-Jeebies* (Meow Press); *By* and *The Doors* (House Press); *Un-Nome, Red Rain Two, Abzu* and *Flight to the Moon* (Run Away Spoon Press); *Poemeserss* (Structum Press); and many more. His poems and other works have appeared in many magazines, including *Dandelion, BoxKite, Antennae, Unbearables Magazine, Open Letter, Torque, Leopold Bloom, Wooden Head Review, Explosive Magazine, Deluxe Rubber Chicken, First Offense, Terrible Work, Juxta, Kenning, Witz, Lungfull, Lving, Generator, Tinfish, Curicule Patterns, Score, Unarmed, Rampike, First Intensity, House Organ, Ferrum Wheel, End Note, Ur Vox, Damn the Caesars, Pilot, 1913, Filling Station, fhole, Public Illumination, Western Humanities Review, Vanitas, Talisman, Yellow Edenwald Field* and *Poetry*.

There Was Light that Was Alone

not much left
or right of winter
night is when I is what
will become of us
keys unchained
jarlids unjarred
think of all the common
white moths
left to March
night need to fend toward
sewing off
of water buttons

I am that July Night that Returns like Zorro

there in is the thee I pangolions!
Julips delight of if off foreestoes
if O. e. night A.
personification ouF toasted
on the moon's hot-plate
or the thee characteristictocs
          of birds
     drinkin bourbon
or it of toasters
toasters toasters
      cocking of bread
we have mouths of sunflower seeds
      feed to each other
      our bees our moths released
where are yore fingers are before
persuasion's lips
released released
the tiny fish so the they may
be me about
your bathtub
butter

SOUND POEM 5

Calming

SHHH
Shhhhhhh
shhhhhhhhhh
shhhhhhhhhh

Poem in 8 parts

babble, bang, bark, blare, blow, boom, burst, buzz

Buffalo Snow Poem

it snows
in Buffalo
it's not that
in Buffalo
it snows
but it snows

and snows.
one hard winter
it snowed on Halloween
-not orange and black
it snowed on Easter
-not purple or resurrected

some say
it once snowed
in May
on the blue and yellow
croci it snowed

on Mother's Day
I don't remember
mother much
but it snows.

Once Upon a Time in East Buffalo: Mary, Faith and the Imagination

After workin away for a several hours on my kitchen sink, with snake, pipe wrenches, and plunger, frustrated, I informed my landlady, Florence, an elderly woman pushing 70 who lived with her mother, Mary, approaching 90, that my sink was hopelessly clogged. They had, by the way, a black velvet 2 by 6 and half-foot Last Supper in the dining room. I hoped that she would call a plumber. She told me with complete faith-filled conviction that she would say a prayer to the Virgin for me so that my drain would open. Needless-to-say, I had not expected her response. I was stunned. I was perplexed. I returned somewhat despondent to my flat, which is a Buffalonian term for an apartment, and began to work and instantly or almost instantly with my first twisting and banging, miraculously, the drain lost its clog. Oh foolish poet, I naively placed all my Bingo chips on the snake.

E.R. Baxter III, Niagara County Community College Professor Emeritus of English, has been a fellow of a New York State Public Service Award for fiction and a recipient of a Just Buffalo Award for Fiction. Previous publications include *Niagara Digressions* (innovative nonfiction); *Looking for Niagara* (poetry); and the chapbooks, *And Other Poems, A Good War, Hunger* and *What I Want. Niagara Lost and Found: New and Selected Poems* was released in March of 2013.

The Buffalo Audubon Society, Inc. presented him with the Henry Jay Kord Recognition Award in 2002 for "outstanding contributions to the cause of education and conservation in Western NY." In 2004 he was presented with the Friends of the Buffalo Niagara Rivers Award for his efforts to restore the Niagara River Gorge and the Niagara Reservation. Founding the Niagara Frontier Wildlife Habitat Council (www.nfwhc.org) was a part of those efforts. He is also a founding member of Niagara Heritage Partnership (www.niagaraheritage.org). His web site is www.erbaxteriii.com.

Country

It was not love
at first, among tender
rows of new corn. Or even
last, it was not, watching
burnished apples drop
into the hard frost.
Yet more than sexual
attraction held
at arm's length
for a summer.

It persisted until fall,
until the loft grew deep
with sweet hay, with dusk--
the young farm girl armed
with trust, following
down evening lanes,
small even milk teeth
smiling, wanting

to know what
love is.

And I, eager
to be away, ahead
of winter crashing
downward like an age,
gave no answer. And having
given none, packed what was
mine into the car, and drove off.

It was unsaid, undone,
what came away with me. It was
like a swath of wheat left uncut
at one end of the field suddenly
remembered after the first snow.
The country remains as it was,
suspended, a land of summer
between cities.

My Baby Loves Them Old-Time Movies

1.   where
       was it, the Bellevue,
       Strand, the Cataract?
       when you first
       took my hand
       his face
       filling the screen
       hair brilliantined
       mustache pencil
       thin, and
       her face
       soft, out
       of focus
       closeup kiss

spare
me, spare me
let us not hold
hands in the balcony
and where
is it this
time? the Amendola,
the Rainbo?
the movie
is a love
story, your
palm is moist
it is too much

the usher looking
on, leer behind
the stab of his
flashlight beam.

2.   your hand is
curled in mine
dim in the late TV
the sound
turned down
Niagara falling
silently over
the screen

I'm remembering
elephants screaming,
Johnny Weissmuller
come down
a vine
to Jungle
Jim huffing
and puffing
through undergrowth
fighting clogged
arteries, thoughts

of Jane
keeping company
with a member
of the A.N.C.
Cheetah's big
hand in front
of toothy smile

you are sleeping
fingers twitching
in the flickering
light, tiny
ghosts held
in the hand.

3.   clap hands, clap
hands, we all
fall down

somewhere
beneath the flesh
near the slim bones
of your hand
memory gleams

it lies close
to the blood warmed
by the clapping

look, look, shine
a flashlight through.

Kathleen Betsko Yale is an award winning, published playwright, whose work has been performed in the UK, and on some of America's most prestigious stages, including Yale Rep, New Haven; Mark Taper Forum, LA; The Public Theater in NYC; and at The National Playwrights Conference in New London, CT. Kathleen adapted her play, *Johnny Bull,* to an ABC-TV Movie of the Week, starring Kathy Bates, Colleen Dewhurst and Jason Robards. The movie won the Luminas Award for Excellence from the Women's Committee of the Directors Guild in LA. Kathleen is also a founding member of the First International Women Playwrights Conference and is coauthor of the landmark *Interviews with Contemporary Women Playwrights* (William Morrow & Co., NY, 1987). In addition, Kathleen has received grants from NYSCA, NYFA and CAPS for her plays and screenplays. She has acted on and Off-Broadway, performed in national road tours and in regional theatre, and has been seen on most of Buffalo's local stages, including the Irish Classical Theater, where, in 2014, she played the role of Lady Caroline in the critically acclaimed production of Oscar Wilde's *A Woman of No Importance.* Kathleen is also a proud member of the venerable poetry group, Women of the Crooked Circle.

TWO PARTY SYSTEM:
TAKING THE HOUSE

My window sill is packed,
Standing room only for
A murder of crows.
Gangsters in black,
They square off, hunch
Necks into shoulders,
Brandish stiletto beaks;
Cawing *fuck off* to each other,
Sharing dirty jokes, they joust;
This one draws blood,
That one thrusts his claw
Close to the face of another:
Hey, asshole--eat this!

I rap sharply on the glass, and
They become one in flight:
Astonishingly beautiful;
Despicably impressive in
Their unity; like Republicans
They circle thrice,
Shit twice on those beneath, and
Settle, each to their own limb,
In tall trees, high above the
Garbage and the weeds, behind
The gas station.

Now soft, grey pigeons
Take the ledge with
Careful sidesteps, and politely
Folded wings, and professorial
Rings around each
Blinking, wary eye; they
Mourn past losses, and they coo,
Vruuukuuuu...Vruuukuuuu...
Exchanging little pecks, and, after
Grooming lilac, iridescent necks,
Take a gentle nap.
How sweet...
How brief!
The gang of crows blasts back
With terrifying skill! And pigeons
All are forced (again) to cede
The crap-glazed sill.

They know who's boss.

UNDOCUMENTED IMMIGRANTS

(in which a fellow from County
Cork assists a lady from Germany)

You know, I'd a wee adventure, once,
On a certain stretch of Broadway,
Outside Shakespeare's book shop (a place
I was wont to browse but never spend),
Where I come upon a bag lady with awful bad legs.
Poor smudge of a thing she was, leanin' over
Her supermarket cart, moanin'
Ohhhh, such a terrible sound, like an old siren
Warnin' of an air raid.
So I says, *What can I do, me dear?*
How can I help? And she spits:
NOBODY CAN'T HELP DA DEAD!
Plangent as a bell, she was (and twice as loud):
DEAD TIRED! DEAD BROKE!
DEAD AS FOOCKIN' DOOR NAIL!

Not to me, Madam, says I.
And it must have sunk in,
For she stopped bellowin', and
Showed me her sufferin' legs, poor dear
Varicose veins, I'm tellin' ye,
Out to here...like a harvest of sore grapes
On a twisted, blue vine. And I
Don't know what kind of noise it was
That come out of me to see that, but
Somethin' worse than a wounded ferret,
For she starts to cry...
Not used, you see,
To violent empathy --
It weakened her.

OHH, MEIN GOTT, she weeps,
I GOT GET VUN HUNDRET T'IRTEEN SSTREET,
AND I CANNOT GO VUN SSTEP MORE!
Well, I'd treat you to a taxi, Madam, says I,
But, after a night I'd rather not analyze, I
Find meself....ehhhhm...in a state...ahh..
Of financial compromise.

I DON'T VANT NO CAB!!
ZEY DON'T LIKE MEIN CART!
IN HERE ISS MY LIFE!
THEY NO-GOOD, TAXI-BASTARD FOOKERS!

Ahh, bless her, she with her cab-cursed cart,
Hard-pressed to get to 113th Street, and me
With a sin or two in need of dispensation,
So I think, why not kill two sparrows
With one house brick?
If you'll do me the honour to sit upon
Your belongings, Madam,
I'll give you a ride, so I will! And I plumped up
Her plastic bags, and all the rest--just how
I hoisted her up is best left unsaid--but still off
We flew: Me, the unholy wings of her silver chariot;
She, clingin' on for her dear, auld life,
Through threat, through adversity, in the direction
Of that most dangerous den of thieves
In the whole, uncivilized world--
Columbia University.

I'd a skinful of Red Dog beer, so I had
And, therefore, sang to her all the way:
    Oh, would you rather swing on a star,
    Carry moonbeams home in a jar,
    And be better off than ye'are...
    Or would you rather be... a mule?
Ahhh, we must have made a wonderous sight
And all...kathump, kathump, kathumpin' along:
Yours truly salutin' the crowd outside
The Apollo Theatre; herself ridin' high,
Like an elephant boy in a howdah,
Swaying this way and that, lettin'
Fly some German I'm glad I didn't understand,
And cursin' me a streak of blue for bumpin'
Her too hard up and down the curbs.

Well, when I lifted her out (easier said
Than done) at St. John the Divine,
She held me in the vise of her one fierce hand,
And dug up the archives of her cart with the other,
(Releasin' remarkable scents as she went), on
Tiptoe, bunions peerin' through
Windows in her slippers, bent over, hose
Exposed and rolled to the knees,
She come up with a roll of Lifesavers,

PLEEZE, YOU TAKE!
Ooooooohhhh, noooooooooooo, I go,
You'll need `em for your own self,
Won't you, now?
But she kept her fist thrust out, and it
Was then I noticed the tattooed line
Above her wrist.
TAKE, she orders me,
YOU TAKE VAT I GIVE!
And so--one fugitive to another--I did;
I mustered me last shred of charm, and
Accepted that most coveted honour:
The Dirty Roll of Mixed Fruit Lifesavers Award.
And bowed, then kissed her
Numbered arm. Says I,
My *pleasure, Madam.*

RESURRECTION

Part 1)

One night
In the winter
After my daughter went away
But a full season before my son did
A lone tree in the field
Behind the house at Merienda farm
Was destroyed

I don't know
What caused the tragedy
Perhaps it was diseased
Or fell victim to
A strong wind or lightning...
Or suffered a fatal shock
From the dawn-splitting scream
Of the jets in the war factory
Behind the woods

Anyway
The tree split into three
Fell dying
One great limb

Sprawled toward the East
The other West
Like crucified arms
Black and knotted
Across the February snow

But the center of the tree
The core of it
Still stood
A wounded splintered spike
Jutting stubborn
Into a pewter-colored sky

Every day
At my window
Through prison bars of icicles
I mourned for that tree
At night I drew the blind
So I would not see its
Moonlit skeleton

(Part 2)

But one morning
Spring rolled in drunk
And very late
Careless that we had
Hovered at curtain slits and
Waited up for her all winter's night
Scanning and rescanning
The grave of last year's garden
And the maps of each other's faces
For a hint of life
A kinder season

No
Cool spring
Said it was none of her business
What we'd been through
And damn-well none of ours
What time she came in

But she stayed and
Humming all the while
Rolled up her frost-feathered sleeves
Did a full month's work overnight

Tore the plastic from cracks
And eyes of the houses
Sucked weeds from the earth
Threw acres of grass out of bed
And lifted the lid off the pond
For a beloved boy to
Tease the trout

(Part 3)

Alone
In the center of the field
The ugly fingers
At the ends of the tortured
Arms of the dead tree
Stirred in the mud
And sprouted apple blossom

Michael Boughn was born in Riverside, California in 1946 and moved to Canada in 1966 because of his opposition to the war against Viet Nam. He worked in the Teamsters for nearly 10 years during the 1970s. In 1986 he received a PhD after studying with John Clarke and Robert Creeley in Buffalo, where he started shuffaloff books, a peripatetic micro press, in 1988. He is the author of ten books of poetry, including *Great Canadian Poems for the Aged Vol.1 Illus. Ed.* (Book-Thug, 2014) and *Cosmographia – a post-Lucretian faux micro-epic* (BookThug, 2010), which was short listed for the Governor General's Award for Poetry in Canada in 2011. He has also published books for young adults, including the Red Maple Award nominated *Into the World of the Dead* (Annick, 2007), a mystery novel and a descriptive bibliography of H.D. He coedited Robert Duncan's *The H.D. Book* with Victor Coleman (University of California, 2011). He was described in the *Globe and Mail* as "an obscure veteran poet with a history of being overlooked." These poems are from his latest work, *City, Book One, Singular Assumptions* (BookThug, 2014).

I.3.iv - Economic reality
> "I don't need therapy – I need money."
> —*student saying*

You can't earn enough in most
lifetimes to pay for the poetry
required to explain economics
to reality. If words could be worn

out and used up, crinkled in small
soiled balls or left emptied
and sticky in hornet infested
containers, economic reality

would be its tractatus, its ode
on a Grecian liar
ringing through hulls of democratic
bluster from mouths in swollen

red faces determined to pull
bootstraps of every errant pilgrim
into gravy free enterprise
of incarnate logos saturated

dispensation's spiritualized
saving accounts. Who remembers
economics is to home as divine
life is to distant archaeology

of theological midden heap
may be prepared for sudden
showing forth of hidden door
into trans-galactic transfer of cold

words into apparition of deeper
encounter. Say, a parking
lot within the one you just left
your car in, a vast sealed tomb

vibe emanating into corners
and crevices while it gains
a reputation for ease of shopping
pleasure, free parking, and

authorized admission. Then economic
reality realizes the rent
is too low and moves increase of what
ever margin darkness brings to talk

of blue. Household debt, too
a mystery of subtle encounters
with manifestations of density
deficit, misses the train and winds up

trapped in some allegory of profligate
burghers astride equine
rectitude in the charge up
Consumption Hill. Gravy

as an elemental leads to formations
of fat cutting brigades and periodic
weigh ins designed to distract
attention from vacuous visions'

hallucinatory underground utopia
toward what people want and back.
What people want is an abyss
yawning with boredom and often

confused with questions of life
on other planets. Is it there? and how

many eyes does it have? Economic
reality is its human disguise

amid levers of power and stands
for distribution of terror and pain
beyond the usual kind, along with
accumulations and hordes, beyond

as they say, imagining, where all gravy
goes once it has been cut, or cut
loose, a true economic reality
awash in glory and righteous

affirmation of divine law,
or maybe just a general rule
or possibly an operating
principle, how fat always

flows, as part of the Grand
Design, up, which is where after all
it belongs, in immaculate
dough-re-mi ascensions.

I.3.vi - No further *adieu*

Having reached the end returns godly
reminiscences to originary impulse's

boundary fetish. Maybe not boundary
as breath on neck announces

skin – more like a fence through dappled
meadow, a real fence, no doubt, but reeking

of overripe metaphors. Relief of the end
is a kind of meadow and therefore

dappled, a state of interruption tumbling
out of trees, some of which are oak,

birch, and sugar maple, at least
in memory. Wind telegraphs it

and edges flutter, delight a question
best left hanging, a state suspended

in light of dappled meadow
which may take tautology to a level

of impertinent signals, the kind
that lose you or leave you overlooked

by the mainstream which is busy
reiterating pre-established cartological

conundrums ironically inflected
to indicate subtle distances and taste

for great literature. If it bids
awakening, it remains a silent

partner, though the stakes become
astronomical, translated into blue

light of stars whose distances wheel
along boundary *adieu* calls

to attention, to here, that supple
shift of weight yields the world

in spades. Anyway, it's a place to start
infrequent engagements with enormous

instances of lapsed, terminal nostalgia
thus getting on with it, no further

being a prod because certain limits resist
easy placement. Returning to delight's

surprising instance was ordained
by virtue of some difficult

to define authority often
omitted from lists of admissible

proclivities. But maybe further
interrupts it, leaves it behind

and delight is cut loose, maybe
no further's boundary leaves *adieu*

in the dust of a passage delight
claims to have elaborated in clear

flutters signalling another city
not so much beyond as within, the way

a dream is within the arms of nether,
a boundary of such disproportionate

nebulosity as to make a Bay
blush, 5AM, July 4th, two thousand

twelve, and then it *is* breath on neck
announcing skin even as the fence

continues to demand its dispensations
and formations, and the meadow

shakes off metaphorical implications
and dapples as if life depended on it.

Lewis Bowman was born near Boston in 1941. He later lived and attended school in Vermont and central New York. He attended the University of Buffalo continuously from 1961 to 1966, where he received a BA in English, and studied modern poetry with Le Roi Jones, Ezra Pound with Herbert Schneider, Yeats with Basil Bunting and creative writing with Mac Hammond. He also obtained some background in the natural and social sciences. He later took graduate courses at UB for a few years. During his student days, he came to know Gregory Corso, Allen Ginsberg, George Barker and John Logan, and also met James Dickey, Ann Sexton and Richard Murphy. He has a moderate number of appearances in print, and has worked as a college instructor, a musician, a music teacher, a technical writer and a salesman. He is now retired and living in North Buffalo, where he continues to write poetry and play music.

At Jekyll Island 3/31/66

I

There is softness in the landscape,
Sky becomes water, becomes trees, becomes land,
Contrasts are blurred,
A blend of colors free of brilliance, but the gentleness of the sea
In which big waves break far out, near the horizon,
And small lake like waves caress the shore,
Touching lightly, they show the tenderness,
Of lover for woman, in the favored moments of early night,
No anger here, fury remains distant,
As aspects become a one harmonious whole.

II

Ancient gnarled oaks stand on the shore,
With the greybeards of undisfigured age,
These trees were old,
When Sidney Lanier walked upon these shores,

And played his flute beneath the bearded branches.
And they were old long dreams ago,
When the first mariners walked upon these shores.
Their numbers grew, settlers came, brought slaves,
Then war and redefinition.
Metamorphosis becoming order.

III

Sing sweetly dear Sidney Lanier
And play your ghostly flute beneath the trees
Intone Baroque counterpoint and Schubert's lieder,
To complement your gently dulcet song,
Played to a love, with parasol and Crinolines,
As I sing of my manhood to her of tanned limbs and long hair.
I shall play counterpoint.
Perhaps our songs will then be part of one.

IV

Your flute now sings only in memory's echo,
Beneath the trees,
They are ancient,
But they may fall, burn or die
Or be cut by unfeeling muscular hand
That wields the axe and saw.
Seawater is filtered through sand,
The salt is lost.
Water of life remains
Water of the sea
Mother, maker and destroyer
Washing upon these shores
And redefining them
Beyond the bearded oaks
Trimmed with the Spanish moss, in the softness where time
Becomes too abstract to matter,
Next to the sea, benign here the sea our mother,
Next to the sea, past, present and the soothing blur of colors,
The guitar plays counterpoint to the flute
And the sea provides the muted kettledrums.

Sing a song of love and sensuous beauty
Sing harmony and order in flux
Sing of union in which different times and places
Become one, like waves of the sea
The song of the ephemeral cricket in the fields,
The song upon the shore of ageless waters,
The melody of sea change and constant matter,
Transmuted,
Only beauty and life force remain.

Nineteen Fifty Five

Jimmy Dean, oh wondrous
    angry young man
        who evolved on screen
Into spent, drunken Jett Rink,
Movies of my young days,
Fifty years and a little over
    three weeks ago
Donald Turnupseed turned
        into the path
Of your speeding Porsche
    Spyder
You turned, seeking to
    miss him on a quick trip
To the spirit world at
    age twenty four.
If it hadn't gone that way
    would you have done some of
        the roles of Newman and
            Redford
Or maybe even Dustin Hoffman
Hopefully aging gracefully
    while retaining intensity of spirit
Or would you have faded
Into the quiet, self-imposed

obscurity of Sandra Dee?
Do you still see Natalie?
Do you spend a lot of time
      with Elvis and Buddy and
         Carl and Gene talking
            cars and listening to rockabilly?
Would you like to still be
      here or is America now
            too messed up for those of
               a simple and gentler time?
A few weeks before you crashed
My family and I went to the
   Vermont State Fair, the day
         President Eisenhower would speak there.
He circled the field in front
   of the grandstand in an open car
And spoke in the open air at an
      open podium.
It was a time all felt so
   very safe, secure and peaceful.

 A time safe and somnolent
      but also seminal –
Nineteen Fifty Five

Emmet Till was lynched
      for looking at a white woman
Rosa Parks held her seat and
      stood up for her rights
And many, acquiescently downtrodden,
said, "Enough is enough!"
"A time is coming."

I met a Black preacher
         from South Africa
at my Vermont, small town church.
He spoke of injustice.
I, who had been speaking
   of my love for playing jazz said,
"This has to change"
"We can have a kinder and

more beautiful world."
And Doctor King, young, starting out,
Preached for change.
Even then I felt
No one should be treated
    as less than a full
human being.

And Allen Ginsberg wrote
    Howl,
Giving voice to those
        mocked by McCarthyite
            America.

The seeds were sown
A few years later the
    plants would begin
        to grow
In increasing profusion
    in a time of wonder
With small and separate
        beginnings.

Kastle Brill is a poet, memoirist, fiction writer, artist and editor, who has published two chapbooks, *One Night Stands & Other Pieces of Time* and *The Head*. Two of her paintings were used as the front and back cover art for *Earth's Daughters* magazine Issue 77. Her poems have been published in *White Pine Journal, Black Mountain II Review, Serendipityarts, Poetry on the Bus* and *Earth's Daughters*. Kastle has read as a feature with Joanne Kyger, Bobby Louise Hawkins and Sharon Doubiago, as well as at a NYSCA panel with Allen Ginsberg and Jim Carroll. She has done numerous readings in WNY for Just Buffalo, NYSCA, Artists' Gallery, Niagara-Erie Writers and Ujima Theatre Company, and also at Daemen College and Empire State College. Her monologue *...And the Beast* was performed at TheaterLoft. She is also a retired environmental lawyer and an active tai chi teacher.

The Flyer

I know how it feels to fly
not with wings but force of will
almost strong enough

an eagle seeking worms
inelegant but real as arctic
wolves for mice

close my wings to fall
dip to earth as in salute
to that which fed me

look up   look up
the eagle comes to eat
accepts the carrion

I catch   the air rising   warm
into the sun   search for currents
for my love   my rival

dropping to
rabbits   to foolish crows
who do not know they're food

dying for a mate
who has nothing but hope
and more carrion

mobbed by jealous black birds
hunched about my meal
like a greedy old man   like a

cartoon boy over a stolen pie

I pull the curtain of my wings
around the dead

Harry

My Brooklyn never heard of Land o' Goshen. We knew only
Land o' Lakes, sweet Jewish butter, and Harry Goshen my
father's friend.   Near the MacDonald Avenue El, where
houses are all born together and people live side by side and
up and down. Harry had a building -- a store on the ground,
ladies specialties: dresses, stockings, custom fitted girdles and
brassieres, an apartment over the shop and rentals above that to
pay expenses.

Harry lived in a land of women, wife, daughters, and a single
catholic "girl", who lived with all of them and worked in the
store and played bingo at the church.   The women took care of
the shop, the building, the meals the tenants, everything. Harry
dressed in tan suits and wore a matching hat, took his beige
Cadillac to the race track and drove them all to Florida once a
year.

The girls married, the family trips to Florida stopped and Harry
found another woman. He left his wife who gave her name and
life to the store, and Mary, the girl, who had also been his
woman all along.   My mother still bought our underthings from
the wife and girl. Harry no longer visited us. But my father still
claimed him as a friend, because they were boys together in
the New York City land of settlements; because they both came
from the land of boys.

Bioluminescence

cape cod mass

here we are
on the elbow of the arm
latest summer
the sun a switch
of season August
the day "on"
"off" to night's dark October

we are mad in our last days
watch the night sea
the bluefish hunt
the mackerel jump to escape
we will be caught too
in schools -- snatched
into life or not

we scan the sea
for the cold light
of another kind of life
Is it come? or
is it the reflected
glare of street?
the broken
mirrors of the moon?

to touch is to know
to disturb as sand
and wind does not
take off the shoes
walk into the wet
shuffle -- waggle a toe
see a glow
they are here
we take off everything

first the water is cold
then like winter ice
the wind with a hint of glacier
deeper our legs grow numb
lifting our knees we see
our skin glowing and winking out
like the night sky lights

when the clouds rush past
microscopic lights of other lives

and still we go
swimming out
fear against desire
to lower and roll into
the cold starry water
sinking into the sky
lights trail off our fingers
aquatic milky ways
friends a bright distant splash
dive with open eyes
a jellyfish a winking beacon
a larger tactile glow
from the colder deep
weaving through the
gentle dangerous liquid night

when we leave and walk
to the heavy shore
we carry on our bodies
and in our hair
the microscopic lights of other lives
the dead and dying stars
who traveled with us for a while.

Jennifer Campbell

is an English professor at Erie Community College and a co-editor of *Earth's Daughters* and *Beyond Bones*. She is the author of the full length collection of poetry, *Supposed to Love* (Saddle Road Press, 2013). Her first book, *Driving Straight Through*, was published by FootHills Publishing in 2008.

Recent work appears in *Common Ground Review, Sow's Ear, Fugue, Seven CirclePress, Saranac Review, The Healing Muse, The Pedestal, Earthshine, Bloodroot, Bluestem, Slipstream, Red Rock Review* and *Slant*. She has received the SUNY Chancellor's Award for Excellence in Scholarship and Creative Activities, along with an Honorable Mention in the 2010 *New Millennium Writings* competition and a Pushcart nomination.

First Born

Bewitching imp, at it again.
You cull my complete attention:
soft blue kiss of veins across your fair skin,
inky eyes pouring infinitely, never with tears,
feet unlined, toes curling onto my arm,
seeking heat and muscle, bone and blood.

From where did you come
and how did you magic me into light,
the curtains of my heart
drawn against your pure need?

The One Where We Dance Around the Pain and Suffering of the World

Jeremiah and Francesca,
Mohamed to gentle Sarah,
their names charting them as greats
in this year of the tiger,
spin their cyberwords skyward,
refuse to eat pepperoni pizza
(but only because it tastes bad),
renege on their promises
to not read *Twilight* or buy
Valentine candy. But they aren't
allegories or Biblical offshoots,
only community college kids
dripping sarcasm.

They may never lead us to answers
we gave up hoping for,
but I tend to think they'll one day
ache with caring, every synapse
firing tender meaning.

Then again, I ask the class to list
the greatest horrors of the last
one hundred years and they name:
The Holocaust. Katrina. Haiti.
Tom Cruise.

Sighing, I admit
it's all in the spin.

Nachtmusik

Salmon sunset, slashed through
with midnight blue. A matter
of sensitivity, what's best, and may not be
understood immediately.

Of course the kids sensed it,
the contrabasso of their father's voice
steadying mother's unconvincing
nightly trills. The word divorce

spoken only once, settling in the air
evenly and without a rise of emotion.
Keying the car was a surprise,
a man's m.o. Never predictable,

Cynthia had more tricks in mind.
No one expects a classy wife to risk
staining her silk suit with white spray paint.
She accented George's black mustang,

his one true love. Helpless friends
merely listened, the kids disappeared
into books, but the last movement
was already coming around.

Late in the summer, she slipped below
the bedroom window, performed her final
serenade. It's a symphony, really, the sound
of sugar grains being siphoned into a gas tank.

Late Frost

They say the mind opens best
when at rest, and it's true, I noticed
the tiny ice-drop ornaments when I was
being a tree, my yoga breaths rooting me
even as shards of distorted light caught
my eye, hail pounding the windows.
Forgetting the impossible slick slope
into the studio, I sunk toes into the mat,
clinging to the powder-white birch
of my childhood, branches lilting forward
with the in-breath, backward with each exhale.
But that birch was in the way, blocking
clean t-ball hits and batting down
our spiraling footballs with its big-brother palms.
It was a good safe for hide-and-seek,
a lousy second plate. Not much for shade
in the bright white summer, barely enough
for the collie's lavish nap. We were sad
when it came down, bacteria a disappointing
thief. That, and mother's redesigned
landscape. A poor end for our lanky bully
who played by his own curious rules,
an odd distraction from this current pose.
Willing an answer for the intrusion,
I turned Truth over and over in my hand
like a lab-created diamond, held films
of its secrets to the light, but none of it
warmed me as much as memory's
cunning path. Its shrewd reveal.
I suppose we've all seen enough
cold-glazed beauty. A dip
of June flame would suffice.

The Way I Saw It

Trailing over the surface
of the same old fight, I struggled

to wrap my fingers around one strand
of substance. We both knew what hid

beneath the reflective lake, considered
reaching in for one weed and pulling it,

hand over hand, the extension and depth
of our sunken love. But it was her name

that kept surfacing, and you, open to questions
I'd tired of contemplating. I only wanted

to hear you loved me more, lower
the anchor back into the wet.

Some things went unsaid that night,
nagging pains, phantom ripples,

but I'm content to have thrown them back,
someone else's to salvage or set free.

Don't forget: I've watched you sleep,
give in to my protective gaze.

Like a child crying out in dreams
to a fear he can't articulate,

your eyes sought mine amid the failing light—
no words left until the next day,

when the moment's passed, the bench
beside the still water empty.

Charles Case resides in Buffalo. He is a writer and an attorney. His poems have been published in small press around Western NY. He was included in the Fall, 2011 edition of *Beyond Bones*, an anthology of Western NY poets. He is a winner of the Marita Hobkirk Memorial Poetry Prize.

Charles' poetry is influenced by modernist poets such as T.S. Eliot and William Carlos Williams, as well as everyday speech. Blues and folk music also have been a source of inspiration for him. This music often has absurd story lines and larger-than-life personas that inhabit their own reality. It has its own history, theology, science and morality. The musicians who have carried on this tradition have inspired him to trust those alternate realities. Charles often begins poems in fragments and tries to trust the strangeness of ideas that initially may seem mundane in order to find those fragments a voice.

Poetry Chores

Allen Ginsberg never helped me do the laundry
as he talked away in long discourses,
pausing to breathe only at the end
of each thought. He made it exhausting
to separate the colors from the whites.
I tried to measure out a little less detergent
than I needed, so I could save some money,
and he questioned why I must be so clean.
Why must I wash my clothes for the capitalist swine herd?
Don't be the sheep to the hogs! He was incensed.
I resented his implication, but he kept talking
as I cleaned the rusty dryer's lint trap.

I have a howl of my own I tell him.
You will hear it when I take the dog out at night
and the rain drizzles along my shoulders, stooped
forward in the dark. It's the sound of my hands
rustling in the pockets of my windbreaker,
that settled moment when I don't reach for your book

or when I cease wondering why I ache in the cold.
You have to listen carefully, but before I call the dog
to come in the house, I puncture the universe
with the gentle slide of my hands over nylon so rebellious
it refuses to let in the breeze.

I've toasted anarchy, too. I've rolled for days
in another's sweat and stale air as our half-crazed limbs
fought fatigue in between conversations about drugs
and liberation. I've allowed my words to go on and on
without end, and I have chastised everyone
who didn't listen to me. I love your book, but
sometimes the dog jumps up on my pants
with muddy paws, and I am afraid that
in the daylight, I won't be able to hide the stain.

Afternoon

I put my ladder against the window ledge
and watched afternoon undress. I felt strong
watching her bare skin, and the hair shaking
between her legs brought me peace of mind.

The curve
where her back and waist came together
revealed that each preceding day
led to this moment.

As a child I looked out the window
on rainy afternoons,
watching the water pool and flood
the road in front our house.

I imagined the rain would walk
into our living room and, looking slightly confused,
would ask me to play. I imagined that it was not as bad
as my parents said to get caught in the rain.

But when it came it came with chaos
and admonitions.
One day, the city came, too,
and fixed that road.

I have seen days collapse
under their own weight causing time to disappear
without the universe
ever making up the difference.

I have seen days dressed in black,
and I have listened
as their funeral hymns
trailed into endless silence.

Like the day they finished the road. Morning
split in two, its gaping halves held together
with a few strands of tissue and dangling flesh
that looked like threads;
                                    there was blood.

Its jagged edges spread apart,
the entrails stretching slowly from the top.
She was born into the world,
and I saw afternoon for the first time.

Her left hand emerged first from the void,
then the other, and she felt the uneven edges
of the house as she pulled herself
from the entrails and bile.

She moved slowly at first, but when she realized
that everyone else was overdressed,
she leapt and twirled about the room,
slender and bare.

It was nearly two o'clock,
and I was working at something so important
that I barely noticed my dreams
walking backwards into obscurity.

I barely noticed the naked afternoon
dancing as if no one could see.
I still look in on her when I need to pretend
that out of place things are innocent.

I never knew what was so important
that they had spent all that money.
But I know there is nothing like naked
to shake ambivalence off.

I know, too, that money can fix
a road, but never mend broken memories.

Elaine Chamberlain taught English, Creative Writing, and Art, and has done volunteer nursing in Southern Mexico. She likes to write about growing up in Seattle, about the Mayan people who were her patients in Chiapas, and about travel on the cheap. She has ridden chicken buses in Mexico, Guatemala, Costa Rica and Bolivia. She's biked and ferried in Nova Scotia and traveled by train, canal boat and bicycle rickshaw in India and Nepal. Recently, she retired after twenty years of work as a mental health counselor. Her current passion is the art of collage and diorama.

Departure

You wanted to leave at dawn
but I turned off the clock
and held your head in my hands
remembering with my lips
your ancient, heavy eyes
and how your brows grew together.

I was Lot's wife
looking back for the last time
on the nests your fingers made for me.
On the gentleness of your body.

I climbed with you to the mountain.
I wanted to give the flood.
But in the end I gave nothing.
When you left there were no words.
There was only rain.

Mexico City

In the court yard a caged canary twitters.

Ignacio Mauriscal Street. Paradise of smells.
Grapes. Tomatoes. Tamales. Hot roasted corn.
Heaven of sounds. Children leaping. Dancing in pairs.
The grumbling hurdy-gurdy. Newspaper vendor's plea.
Shriek of the scissor man. Clank of the milkmaid's can.

The sky is memory blue.
I find myself falling into it.
My breasts and belly are cloud.
My pelvis is the sun.
And you are
a wolf loping
toward me.

Or, you are a child
running with outstretched hands.
I shower your hands with pebbles.
An egret flies from your hair.

Now the sky is smoldering.
From its darkness comes
your heart bitter, white and hot.
I turn my back. You are mumbling.

Why must I always return to this city
with its melancholy and intractable filth?
Why must I return to its rutty roadways
and its ghostly all too familiar creatures?

Because. I love the blinded beggar
teasing his small, sad guitar.
I love these odorous shops.

I love the dark faced women
selling chicken
in bunches
like flowers.

Huertas Delicias

I.

In this blurred Cuernavaca photo
you and I were extraordinarily young.
Your beard was red.
Your waist was a boy's.
And my legs were strong horses.

We were green as the grass we postured in.
Poinsettias bloomed like pelicans,
like flamingos, like storks.
The mispero delivered her fruit.
Remember it.

This other photo is unclear.
Valerie took this.
There is her finger;
a blotch in the corner.
She refuses to develop.

Valerie.
Chestnut hair.
The color of nothing
in the tropics.

II.

I believed in happiness
and it was misery
beneath the grace of volcanos.
Popocatepetl
lay beside our window
delicious and unreachable;
more feminine than legend
and perfectly asleep.

At noon, Brahman cattle
lumbered up the hill
to feed in a hot palm shed.
At noon, where everything is fed.

The sidewalk shoe man took his rest

under speckled bougainvillea
and a caged centzontle sang.

The milkman clattered home
under a mountain of cans

steaming tortillas
balanced on his hand.

The horse was roan,
almost the color
of Valerie's hair.

III.

The milkman
offered his horse.
I wanted to buy it,
believing beauty was for sale.

Happiness was owning
and so I never knew it
when it lit upon the palms,
when it clattered with the birds.

I could not feel it
as it curled like a cat
in the unused, outdoor oven.
I ignored its swaying
in the genital, green papayas.

I did not recognize its scent
in the narcotic flor de nardo.
Bitterness lay beside me
and grew.
Like a child
with wild
persimmon hair.

Lynn Ciesielski has an MS from SUNY College at Buffalo. She taught for over eighteen years in city schools. After taking an early retirement, she turned most of her attention to writing. She has been featured all over most of New York State, and twice in England. She currently co-hosts the Circleformance Poetry Series in Buffalo and The Screening Room series in Amherst, NY. She also hosted the Stop, Look and Listen Series at Impact Gallery and Buffalo East. Her poetry has been published in *The Buffalo News, Iodine Poetry Journal, Wild Goose Poetry Review, Obsessed with Pipework, Nerve Cowboy, Slipstream* and many other periodicals. The chapbook, *I Speak in Tongues*, published by FootHills Publishing in 2012, is her first collection. Her latest book, *Two Legs Toward Liverpool*, was published by Main Street Rag Publishing Company in 2015.

Pizza Again

Your hips are at least an hour long
and those firm slender thighs
more than thirty minutes from the outside in.
Love with you makes the ticking
of the clock disappear
as the potatoes over-bake.
Dinner is burnt once again
but we don't care much.
We'll just order out.
The pizzeria profits on our passion.
Mr. Todaro celebrates our expressions of amore.
If this keeps up, he smirks,
that trip to Miami won't seem so out of reach.
He sprinkles on the extra cheese
and thinks tenderly of his own wife
waiting at home patiently for the restaurant to close.

Sticky Decisions

In the beginning
there was always enough
to pay bills
and a little extra.

For us it was the extra,
the gumdrops between our teeth
that made it hard
to talk about
how to spend it.

We still chewed, never mind
that the gas wasn't paid.
Candy replaced warmth.
What was extra
became all we had left
for meat, milk, a roof.

But it was only pennies.
Gumdrops were greedy.
Finally we couldn't
pay the dentist.

Chain Reaction

The multi-colored skylight captures
voices, shuffling feet, gasps.
Sun splashes prismatic triangles of warmth.

But the window threatens to rain brilliant shards
on the man-messiah who graces the altar,
to shear him even as he bleeds on the cross.

Cloth drapes the marble, waits to absorb blood.
Bouquets of chrysanthemums adorn the scene,
brush it with white prayers, pure as a sea breeze.

Let the Whistle Blow

Let my ashes tumble gently
in the whistle roll.
Let those soft gray charcoal memories drift
along the splintered tracks.
I'll be crushed to specks of dust
on rolling metal wheels
that travel steady, rumbling on their way.

Let me be the powder on wood and steel bed
that lies along the factories of my youth.
I'll go from blue to black to gray.
My life will cycle death, then round again
to roll the other way.

I'll be the powder that rubs footfalls
of worn out working stiffs
who cross the tracks to get home
after long twelve hour shifts.
I'll be the powder that scents bodies
of dead factories that lie vacant
at funerals where we honor memories
of bonuses and profits.
I'll be the dust that smoothes the edges
on my mother's harsh, sharp words
when she had to leave her home down by these tracks.

I want to hear the bodies heaving
those constant belly laughs,
like those I heard when I played on stage,
the jolt of each car rolling, rolling till it stops
just long enough to switch its riders over.
They'll leave a bit of me in each town
among groups of restless teens
who sneak hidden sips of beer and stolen kisses

And I will sleep each night and morning
in the gray, in the gray of my body and the sky
to the clunking rattle sound
of fierce and storming godforsaken giants.
The rails will continue to guide my steady gait
And the rain and the sky, they will play, they will play
in my time-worn, well visited backyard.

To the God of Song
after Leonard Cohen's "Hallelujah"

We dwelled together
at your core,
deep in the earth;
we were bubbling hot,
magma.

Now we concede
to surface touch,
weak messages,
quivering whispers.

If God is love,
love will save us
make our songs
bellow out,
our embraces clutch.

Marten Clibbens was born in England to Welsh ancestry and moved to Buffalo in the 1980's to study with Robert Creeley, an experience which encouraged him to begin writing poetry. He has published five slender volumes of verse: *Sonet* (Leave Books, 1995), *Triplet* (Starcherone Books #3, 1998), *Sequence* (Lost Pages Press, 2006), *Veterans Day* and *Three Forms* (both from the Buffalo Ochre Papers, 2010 and 2012, respectively). He has also collaborated on works of visual poetry with several artists, including Edward Gates, Richard Scharff and Anne Reed.

Refugee

1

I become accustomed
to this or that severe
determination of shores
not home and stations
galore with statutory
criteria of patrol

2

In bars without familiar
I become a solitary voice
the self a reflective surface
is contrived by the duration
and protocol of the foreign
which traduce its borders
and define the curriculum
of its tongue

3

I do or does not become
accustomed to this or that
anomie of its tongue: the
austere alignment of doors
the glide of diphthongs not
home and nor is the memory
of waking to a scullery hung
with partridge and pheasant
poached by an uncle not uncle
whose village provides remote
idyllic if transient refuge
from the bombing

4

                    If
the furious history I am
become. The mewling child
prodded from trams and tugged.
Loyal to the secret places
the fields of mustard and rape
whose leaves are fodder.
Avoid the document. Airports,
harbours, safe houses are not.
Cell phone, telegram, e-mail
a treachery of traces.
Aphasia a vault of echoes.

5

                    I was
mistaken and admitted you into its confidence
in error: home is no more the fluctuating hills
than the multiple silences of the ocean, no more
the flood plains than the burning stubble: a frail
compendium of disingenuous shibboleths: a passing,
a robe of deeds: a fleeting cognoscenti, as light,
the evening flit of the pipistrelle, or the gliding
pounce of the harrier, brief as pulse: a syllable,
a metrical unit, singularly not an index of ethical
complacence any more diligent than a scattering
of leaves is an apt conceit for a self.

6

The fragile conviviality
   of a tacit and furtive
community as relative
   to home as the ritual
dislocation of public
   from private allows.

7

I do not inhabit
the shires of my breath
the blade and legerdemain
of my tongue in flight.
The posture of my body
is dictated by cricks
determined by labour.
Memory is a prospect
of shale and scree.

Sandra Cookson is Professor of English at Canisius College in Buffalo, New York, where she teaches writing and literature courses, specializing in modern and contemporary poetry and poetry by women. Her PhD Dissertation is a study of the poetry of Louise Bogan, and she has written extensively on Bogan's poetry.

She has been writing poetry herself for a number of years, interrupted at various times by marriage, children, school, singing and music. She has divided her life between Chicago (where she grew up); rural Connecticut (where she raised her three children and a variety of dogs, tended a lot of perennial gardens, and earned BA, MA, and PhD degrees at the University of Connecticut in Storrs); and, for the past twenty-five years, Buffalo, as a faculty member at Canisius College. Her poems have been published in a variety of literary magazines, including *Passager, Karamu, Common Ground Review, Rhino* (Chicago) and July Literary Press anthologies. Her chapbook, entitled *Two Loons Taken for Vultures*, was published by Finishing Line Press in 2011. She is a member of the Freudig Singers of Western New York, a chamber chorus, and also of the choir of St. Joseph's Church in Buffalo.

Nocturne

The seal knelt and bowed his glossy head;
that cad desire roused himself again.
From a nearby room with door ajar
a shower of mist rose from the lovers' bed.
The mixed and crossing currents of the dream
dissolved in a cacophony of voices
hustling up their business as in life;
subsiding, left a residue of silence
in which the dreamer woke up satisfied.
Something in the mix of speech and feeling—
the waking life, the business of the day—
injected in the landscape of the dream
seemed right: the music of the hurly-burly
above the suave continuo of night.

Venue

In dreams one stays the night,
  loses one's clothes,
gets lost in the house;
  sometimes a word reiterates:
"Venue," from a board meeting
in that other life, makes its own little joke
  of my disdain for it (stiff
cliché of the marketplace),
  makes itself the center of my dream:
"Finding new concert venues."

Venue. Strike the word from the language.
  I waited for the meeting to end,
gazing into the next room, trying to decipher
  the figure in the wallpaper--fruit or bud?--
noticed that the wainscot looked newly restored;
  so I didn't see his harpsichord, camouflaged in the wood trim,
its refined shape flowing from itself to the center of the room,
  until I had to walk past it; awed a bit, pretend I'd seen it all along.

When in a dream I journey through a house
  I know is the composer's house
I climb up flights and flights of stairs;
  I am searching for something.
Finally an enormous space opens above me,
  with a catwalk all around it,
and a domelike ceiling soars above my head.
  As if music were my home, I recognize its architecture;
the dream repeats: this is the perfect venue.

Four Songs of Desire

1. *I Willed Desire to Leave*

I willed desire to leave;
it left my heart a stone,
eaten by bitterness and shame.

Then like a sternly but lovingly chastened
favorite child, it crept back in again
to inhabit the shallows.

Clever fish, my desire,
silvery creature of the intellect,
having slipped the body's net.

2. *Far Removed from My Desire*

Not love, but its antechamber,
my desire is like the sea,
a many-tentacled muse.
Its power only ripples the surface.
The night is calm, the sea pulses.
I am a small boat borne out on endless waves,
free though I want to be bound.

3. *From My Body I Rooted Out*

From my body I rooted out the nugget of desire;
I probed it in the body's tongue,
seeking a truth that could not be ignored.

In another life we would have sought it out
together, the source of love in one another's deepest parts –
not to destroy – to hold up to the light.

But you told me another truth: the one I knew,
that talk obscured, and desire made me deny.
Now let my heart become wise, as my body, wiser, instructs it.

4. Love Song

Tell me what's true and I will be it.
If it lies in your silver eyes
or in the softness of your hand,
I will embrace it forever.

If, like an emerald on the beach,
it is there one day for the taking
I will take it and wear it next to my heart.

If what is true is the body's lust;
if this is separate from the soul's,
I will marry the two in your presence.

If to be true is to be faithful,
I will stay by your side.
If it is to part from you,
Heaven help me.

Late Quartets

Tall pines, inexhaustible depth:
a primeval forest of feeling.
Bears sleep there; and all the power
we can summon for beauty and terror
has its source in such a place
that is not a forest or any place on earth,
but is as infinite as the soul,
and finite as the cadence, brief and tender,
righting the world for the moment, saying:
It's over for now, and life may treat you well.

Prospero's Sacrifice

I loved this island, my house, my little son.
I was the Prospero of my post-nuclear world
until the hideous noise filled the skies
and flattened the grasses in its passing.
Then I stepped ankle-deep into the ooze
and howled to a god I hardly knew;
I bargained everything away to save them.
We were a family of players; each night
we made new worlds on stage; each night
we donned new faces and destroyed them.
Now my plays are all of sacrifice;
whatever the postman says—my fool, my master—
I'll do to save them. Burn my house, swear
myself to silence, build and burn again.

After

The world falls from your hands
and the great cities sail away,
taking all traces of you with them.
Even your museums and jukeboxes
are time capsules that will never open
to the things you were famous for.
Uncounted pages leaf past and are swallowed
up: the tiger and the peacock,
the book of warblers no one has heard since.
The ugly burnt-out hulks finally crumble;
rising deserts color the horizon no color ever known.
Plastic and ocean remain. Blue was the color,
but there is no one to remember what it was for.

Martha Deed, PhD is a retired psychologist who received her PhD from Boston University. She is also a poet and web artist, and the mother of Millie Niss, also a poet and web artist, and a mathematician, who suffered from Behcet's disease, and who died of hospital acquired infections following Swine flu in November 2009. She and Millie collaborated on many projects combining poetry and art, and she has written the history of their collaboration, "From Fluorescent Cocktails to Pure Cement" (2010), for Poemeleon, as well as the story of Millie's final illness, *The Last Collaboration* (Furtherfield, 2012).

Martha's poetry appears in *Shampoo, Unlikelystories.org, Edifice Wrecked, New Verse News*, and many other venues. Her work appears in anthologies published by Red Hen Press, Iowa, Mayapple and others. Her chapbooks include *#9* (Furniture Press, 2004), *65 x 65* (small chapbook project, 2006), *The Lost Shoe* (Naissance, 2010), and *This is Visual Poetry* (2010) and *The November 2010 Project* (2011), both from chapbookpublisher.com. She curated and edited *City Bird: Selected Poems (1991-2009)* by Millie Niss (BlazeVOX, 2010). Her collection, *Climate Change*, was published by FootHills Publishing in 2014.

As a psychologist, Dr. Deed was active in patients' rights, domestic violence intervention and child custody issues. Her research was sponsored by grants from the Violence Against Women Act, NYS Bar Foundation and the Baldy Center for Law and Social Policy at SUNY/Buffalo. She is affiliated with Consumer Union's Safe Patient Project network of patient advocates. Her website is www.sporkworld.org/Deed/

Poppycock

Leave your common sense
outside the door
do not speculate
what I say is not evidence
the judge will instruct you on the law
when I shout at the murder victim's mother
do not hold it against me
or take it out on my client sitting here
in prison pallor, gray suit and tie
so you will not know he is in custody
I am only doing my job
even a dead child's mother can lie
wouldn't you agree   her lies
could put my client behind bars

his freedom is at stake   his innocence
so important I will tell you what to think
which facts you should ignore
do not speculate I say
leave your common sense
outside the door

Checkpoint on the I-10

This isn't Naco, you know, Maybelle said. And Fred knew she was on a rant again, so he just hunkered down over the steering wheel, flexed and unflexed his knuckles, ducked his head below the cannon fire, and drove on toward the mirage up ahead. A mattress under a trailer is not for me to sleep upon, worse than the Comfort Inn in Cleveland, I can say, though no more dangerous either, but not my cup of tea – nor the sanctuary of a hard pew in the mission church, Maybelle continued, undeterred by the lack of argument from Fred. You see those lights? red and green snaking across the road? cobra of the desert? Does that not offend you – a free American and hence free to travel – to be stopped by officers in the middle of the day on a major godfearing highway to Florida? It's not a toll house, you know, it's a goddammed customs house in the middle of the desert with folks that have nothing better to do than to ask you where you spent the night, what is the purpose of your trip, demand to see your i.d. to hear you speak, lest you are hiding some accent beneath your tongue. It's a damned affront. I don't care if they build the fence with trash to keep the migrants out, but stopping Republicans in a Lexus is ridiculous unless we left our license plates at home. I mean, we're New Yorkers and proud of it even if it means we can't eat lunch in Altus, Oklahoma, all those pickup owners staring us down and shifting in their seats until we leave. It's freedom that we crave, Fred, and freedom that we've lost. . . Fred, are you hanging on to my every word? Look up, stare those officers in the eye, but not defiantly. Here's checkpoint charlie coming up

Day 19, Texas and New Mexico

The Stubbornness of Chocolate

The chocolates were a stubbornness detached from intellect.
Marianne Moore (1997) *Selected Letters*. New York: Penguin. p. 502

Death, the final miracle
incomprehensible
the body holds tight its secrets
slipping away
the warm hand not squeezing
heart beats slowing
eyes closed
left arm raised and lowered
the one you haven't moved for days
no urine
the transfusions
blood pressure slipping down
the pressors not working
and then the creamy foam between your lips
the x-ray – yes – a wounded lung
punctured in the act of saving you
for this hour – we touch your hand
with our gloved hands say we love you
leave the room for the surgeon to place
the chest tube
scarcely reach the waiting room before we hear
code blue icu
and we know it must be you
and we sit
we wait 30 minutes until
the nurse tells us the doctor wants to talk
to me – no pulse but she is young and so
we tried for longer than we've ever seen
a person emerge and leave the hospital
your brain ruined beyond all repair by now
your heart like chocolate has lost its stubbornness
detached from intellect
after –
we see you
say we love you
we touch you still warm
we kiss your face with forbidden naked lips
but you are gone
and when next I sleep
I awaken to an emptiness so profound
so tangible its shape
fills the house with absence

Duplicity of Sand

I never thought of doorsills
the height and width of them
the possibility of splinters
before I had a child

the diameter of a doorknob
the ease of a doorhandle
the trickiness of grass
the duplicity of sand
the danger of dishwater

before I had a child
I never contemplated
the mental gymnastics
involved in sitting

before I had a child
I never comprehended
the significance of electric outlets
measured against the diameter
of baby fingers

I never foresaw
the pleasure
memories of her childhood
could bring

for in those moments
she is still alive

Morris Island Mockingbird

The Mockingbird on the road to Morris Island
does not sit on a fence, but rather on a metal
lobster trap though if there are lobsters off Cape Cod
I am unaware

Unaware of this bird's ancestry
socioecomic status
party affiliation
or its reason for perching near this road
on the way to a military installation
or whether it is on Homeland Security's
No Fly list

It does not fly when I approach
document its presence on top of the lobster trap
which in turn sits on a pile of gravel
the *provenance* of the gravel
also unknown

But the mystery of its age
clears with the wind
that ruffles its feathers
exposing the down underneath

too young to carry a gun
but perhaps old enough to mimic
the auto alarm sirens on Clinton Avenue
as sung by its long-dead relatives
in South Nyack, New York

Mimus polyglottos, 10 in (25 cm)

Alexis De Veaux, PhD is a poet, playwright, short fiction writer, essayist and biographer whose work is nationally and internationally known. Born and raised in Harlem, New York City, Ms. De Veaux is published in five languages-English, Spanish, Dutch, Japanese and Serbo-Croatian. Her plays include *Circles* (1972), *The Tapestry* (1975), *A Season to Unravel* (1979) and *Elbow rooms* (1986).

Ms. De Veaux's work has appeared in numerous anthologies and publications, and she is the author of *Spirits In The Street* (1973); an award-winning children's book, *Na-ni* (1973); *Don't Explain* (1980); *Blue Heat: A Portfolio of Poems and Drawings* (1985); *Spirit Talk* (1997); and *An Enchanted Hair Tale* (1987), a recipient of the 1988 Coretta Scott King Award presented by the American Library Association and the 1991 Lorraine Hansberry Award for Excellence in Children's Literature. She also authored *Warrior Poet, A Biography of Audre Lorde* (2004). The first biography of the pioneering lesbian poet, *Warrior Poet* has won several prestigious awards, including the Zora Neale Hurston/Richard Wright Foundation Legacy Award (Nonfiction), 2005 and the Lambda Literary Award for Biography (2004).

In other media, Ms. De Veaux's work appears on several recordings, including the highly acclaimed album, *Sisterfire* (Olivia Records, 1985). As an artist and lecturer, she has traveled extensively throughout the United States, the Caribbean, Africa, Japan and Europe, and is recognized for her ongoing contributions to a number of community based organizations. She was named Best Literary Artist for 2005 by Buffalo's *Artvoice*. In 2007 she was awarded a Literary Legacy Award from Just Buffalo Literary Center for her lifetime commitment to literature and literary advocacy. Ms. De Veaux's most recent work, a critically acclaimed novella called *Yabo*, was published by RedBone Press in April, 2014, and won the 2015 Lambda Literary Award for Best Lesbian Fiction.

A VIA CURCIS do CORPO/THE STATIONS of the BODY

(after Clarice Lispector 1925-1977)

I am a creek, on my right side the current slows, rushes; hits a boulder of

muscle, perhaps tendon; once I rode a bike

like a kite, fell; split the earth of

my thigh and simply kept on going, I was younger then;

when I became older my body hid its creek in plain sight, as these banks do;

we hardly notice smaller bodies of water, not full of the lore

of oceans and the seas, their mysteries more transparent, it seems, like

quadriceps; this ambling water talks to water I walk through

in the bay's low tide, the future and the past are talking too;

a fog horn coos to the shore and passing boats

going and coming the day long as these prints

of paws and feet, evidence of what matters, in the sand, the natural body;
links us

this is the question:

if I had only one sentence today;

some creeks listen, others interpret

the curve of aging,

 I swallow drugs to drown pain

ashes to ashes, water to water;

in the gutter above the window, the dove

is still sitting on her eggs, this morning

we walked miles over the breakwater, jagged as ache

the tide eavesdrops

a lighthouse winks in the sun, shimmers

I wait for you, love, coming with the ferry

my body's promise;

I will go down to the bay again

HOUSEWORK
(for Tillie Olsen)

I have 3 brooms:
1 for dog hair
1 for dust
1 to sweep evil

my mother waxed years off
second hand linoleum
plastered cracks
kept shiny
a tenement kitchen fixed broken lamps
a used iron
and did her nails
red
always
red red

sweep your own porch
before you sweep the neighbor's yard

when light and dust
conspire
I shed pretense
staircase to staircase
water bucket
mop
mop
water
bucket
bleach

my grandmother's life haunts
me 48 dollars a month and
she practiced cleanliness
next to godliness
on her knees
1 broom
what is the color of white
dirt
a lifetime

linty words
in the vacuum cleaner
no lost poems
a typology of days my mother's headrag

my grandmother's
mine

I cannot barter
haunting
what privilege will not soothe
I clean my own house

MIGRATE
(for Beth, George, Georgie)

To.
To leave behind, to take
lightning; or that favored rug,
a shadow of light, color, these cups
of phone calls, answered, long words
to friends, to family, to there;

to become;

 I am writing this
quick, too quick perhaps,
I cannot race a sunset,
I cannot language feeling
of an axis,
or sound of earth
turning; I have discovered
more than one life
living this one

SNOW: December 2008

A shower of blue light fixes the footprint going and coming; a crossword
puzzle: 6 across, two words for meaning, 6 down, the soup of yearning boils,
boils, the stove cools winter's naked, brands tenderness, what dies; the aurora
borealis, the heart;

Perhaps this is a world disintegrating, we shovel it out of our way;

I am snowing; if everything alive speaks, what is this saying?

Morning yawns, returns to sleep; the agony of wonder fills the veins, its
coupling and uncoupling;

Stars attached to night's purple, alive and dead in their own light;

How marvelous the human eye, to see across perfect blank boxes, words; we
learn to print then the tyranny of the alphabet;

Those white roses bloomed, vased, in red eucalyptus, you were mistaken, I
meant less to seduce than to mourn your leaving; it was magical,

 that planet we lived on;

Christina Woś Donnelly is the cofounder and former coeditor of *Not Just Air* (Sundress Publications), as well as the author of two chapbooks, *Venus Afflicted* and *The Largely Unexpurgated History of Scheherazade* (Moon in Blue Water Productions). She finds kinship in women's stories from scriptures, mythologies, classic texts and modern media, and in the daily lives of women everywhere. Her poems have appeared in *Pearl, Nimrod, Earth's Daughters, Lilliput Review, Moondance, Slipstream, The Buffalo News, Beyond Bones* and *Persimmon Tree*. Her work has also been included in eight anthologies, including *Susan B. & Me* (Big Kids Publishing), *Silver Boomers* (Silver Boomer Books), *Off the Cuffs: poetry by and about the police* (Soft Skull Press) and *Common Roots, Common Ground: Poetry of Cultural Diversity* (Salt Winds Press).

Christina has been a semifinalist for the 2008 Pablo Neruda Prize, a recipient of the NYFA Strategic Opportunity Stipend, an *Artvoice* Artist of the Week and a *Blaze-VOX* Buffalo Focus Poet. Her poem, "Recessional," recently won the Prize for Best Cadence in the The Binnacle Tenth Annual Ultra-Short Competition. She twice guest-edited *Stirring* and served as poetry judge for the 2009 Abilene Writers Guild Annual Contest. She has been featured widely at Western New York, Baltimore and Washington metro venues, including the Library of Congress. The Niagara River flows past her windows.   http://www.pw.org/content/christina_wos_donnelly

---

Let There Be Silk

Let there be silk
that we may have beauty
as a flutter of blush
or peach and perfume
in women's passing.
A spilling from the crooks of arms.
A draping over shoulders
and beds. An artless falling
open (maybe artful).
And beauty in the eyes
of men who, gazing, soften.
And to give them words for powder
and the whisper of thighs.

Something Like the Truth

Something like the truth lies
in wait, firm and dense as lard,
threatening to ooze and run
when things heat up, staining
your dress, dripping
to the floor, seeping
under nails, soiling
your hands.

Something like the truth
does not taste good
when sucked. Slides
thick and unctuous
down the throat. Coats
like semen, can't be vomited up.

Something like the truth lurks
in doorways, lowers in alleys,
strikes from behind. Clamps
the chloroform rag over your face.
Drags you limpid backward, losing
a slipper never recovered.

Apology for Mrs. R

"Mrs. Robinson, you're trying to seduce me.... aren't you?" – The Graduate

She never looked
like Katherine Ross, not even
when very young. Boys touched her
only with their scraping gaze,
spoke to her from far across the aisle
or street, pelted her with spitballs
and words carefully calibrated
to impress each other.

When her breasts bloomed
sudden as stigmata, men with curly hair
on their knuckles and a tan
line on the third finger of their left hand,
clustered on her like blue bottle flies
on a bruised apple.

In college, losers with problems
deeper than philosophy, too deep to drown
in pony bottles of Rolling Rock,
sought to lose consciousness
in the wetness of her crotch, in tresses
of pubic hair. And public places
were no impediment. Even her "Don't!"
was translated, "*Do!*"
But that she seldom uttered for fear
of wounding with some cruel truth
like, "I don't find you at all attractive."
She could not say, "Brush your teeth,
then maybe we'll talk," or negotiate
a tactful retreat from the backseat
where his round-shouldered,
stick-figured frame pinned her down
with pity or guilt at his blue-balled arousal.

"So old Elaine Robinson got started
in a Ford" by a premature ejaculator
impotent at thirty-four. And so
the girl became the Mrs.,
sought out consolations,
learned spells. In middle age, she casts
a nyloned gam across their line of vision,
conjures up her recompense
with a vengeance.

Cassandra in Captivity

Grateful acknowledgments to Euripides and Pierre Grimal

I came on deck to vomit not to weep,
to purge myself as best I can
of Agamemnon's seed. He's filled and refilled
every orifice. Would that I could void
my battered womb. My lord victorious
is randier than Priam's goats in rut.
Boasts he will make a bastard on me,
a grandson of his old enemy
to empty palace chamber pots.
I will not live to see that indignity,
nor to clean his wife's fingernails,
launder her menstrual cloths.

Even as he wrenched my legs apart,
I saw still more blood: my throat slit
over his draining corpse, Clytemnestra
spattered with my blood, gloating
over both our bodies. While he rammed me,
I was in too much agony to force
my screams to words, to prophesy
this new horror. I would have if I could,
if only to spoil his pleasure in my pain.
He would not believe me now.
He'd say I made it up for spite.
No one in Ilium believed me.
No one ever believes me. Visions are no gift
to such as I, nor being most favored.
Apollo loved me once yet changed his mind;
then the army chose me, "flower
of all the captive women", alone
choice enough to honor their commander.

The deck heaves! I stumble.
(They always said I was "unbalanced.")
Past time to weep for Troy or glimpse my home.
The stench of rancid smoke still fouls this robe.
I weep now only to unseal my eyes,
to cleanse the semen from my lashes,
that I might see more clearly
our destiny and take what satisfaction
I can find in thus commingled blood.

Nava Fader is the author of *all the jawing jackdaw* (BlazeVOX, 2009) and several chapbooks. Most of her poems begin with a line by somebody else. Recent projects include a manuscript of false translation from Dante's *Inferno* and a chapbook derived from Michael Basinski's *Trailers*. She received her master's from SUNY/Buffalo's Poetics program, writing her thesis on Adrienne Rich.

My hunger, Anne, Anne!
Flee on your donkey. (From Rimbaud)

On the enormous boulevards with the saints above the cash machine, there is your temple.
Which Brahmin to interpret the proverbs for you.
I'm weeping and croaking encore to those bastards.
My martial heart would fly to South America and its silvery sun.
Let's learn the names of the flowers en espanol.
My campaign is down this way, with a machete, my epaulettes, and my nose.
They are devout, the peppercorn dancers, down on the plains.
This is my messenger through enemy lines, carrier pigeon, pecking out and in again.
My brain, hummingbird, beating.
Those exiles, the witnesses, placed at the scene serving hors d'oeuvres and vignettes, the history of dramatic literature.
I have indicated the richest pastry.
I have observed spooky stories and talk of treasure maps.
Your face, with calculated stupidity hangs on its scaffolding.

And so it was I entered the broken world (H. Crane)

a common laborer
in a munition plant
and a shipyard on the Lake

South of Cuba my grandfather
set the cows out milk and lemon
the grass sticky on the fruit ranch

is it that you can not remember the difference between gravel
and tongue once
the wound in his thigh was fatal
or the headache she jumped from

the bridge gleaming expansion of the still
milky iron whetted the cable string trembles
and the world

once was hollow whole the blow
of the traffic pedestrian forge its echo

pappi ran the candy factory and I worked the lever. The chocolate creams
shine secret: vanilla tangerine maple anise mint the leaf stings is medicinal
bound layers of sweet and semi dark in tombs or thrones take ease.

False translation of Hunger, Rimbaud, A Season in Hell

If it's the gout it's not the war
that pours to the earth like clowns
In June the troubadours of the air
of rock of charybdis of fear

these amuse, turn about. Prance, tickle
pray on the children
until the cats come
with whom they have an appointment

Mangy the caterwauls for the sake of the bruise
small hairs are fooling the egglets
winds are older than floodings
pain always dancing in the greasy valley

the winding one is birthed under the fumes
in the cradle his belly grows plumage
of the old ways, of flight:
come to the luau, we'll take a taste

do it with the lettuces and fruits
no one's watching what you do with the blade
how you lay your pubic hairs
not tangled among the violets

what a sleep! what a stew!
by the axes of Solomon
gold bouillon cuts below the ruddiness
and the honey sinks to silt.

...fossil ribs and saws embedded there (Ciarán Carson)

let's pretend we believe in archaeology

revealed, the thing changes just as
infrastructure knock knock the bone is living
instead of chalky cleaved unyielding until crack
chisel extricate me from my bones—impossible
the skeleton of buildings before
raised giants metal heavy all eyes and blank
eyes downtown neon miller beats

bread for the morrow dust
at night Formica
might live forever poor millie's
fingerprint the cornstarch
so early in the morning This is the way

leave it to rise in the night
kitchen and sing
under a blue
bluemoon blueprint plan
the parthenon (let them eat it
aerial view and some parts
still standing Inhabit

my bones (painted columns nothing
unusual I've never seen
a skeleton key
or known or wondered what skeleton cities
this way—through triumphal archways lie.

Irving Feldman was born in Coney Island in 1928 and grew up there during WWII. The questions raised by the war and the Holocaust have echoed in his poetry throughout his life. He worked his way through college as a farmhand, merchant seaman and factory worker, and received his BA from City College of New York in 1950. He completed his Master of Arts degree at Columbia University in 1953, and after that, received academic appointments at the University of Puerto Rico and the University of Lyon in France. After returning to the US in 1958, he taught at Kenyon College until 1964, when he was appointed professor of English at the State University of of New York at Buffalo. He was eventually appointed Distinguished Professor of English, and retired from teaching in 2004.

His collections of poetry include *Works and Days* (1961), *The Pripet Marshes* (1965) and *Leaping Clear* (1976), both finalists for the National Book Award, *Magic Papers* (1970), *Lost Originals* (1972), *New and Selected Poems* (1979), *Teach Me, Dear Sister* (1983), *All of Us Here* (1986), *The Life and Letters* (1994), which was a finalist for the Poet's Prize, *Beautiful False Things: Poems* (2000) and *Collected Poems, 1954-2004* (2004).

He is the recipient of a National Institute of Arts and Letters award, as well as fellowships from The Academy of American Poets, The Guggenheim Foundation, The Ingram Merrill Foundation and the MacArthur Foundation. He has lived in Buffalo for almost 50 years, and is one of Buffalo's most revered and popular poets, bringing amazing life, depth and precision to every experience he writes about.

Apocalypse

At the end of Forty-second Street
A broken sun goes down in squalls.
The wind-bewildered twilight
Is blasted on the cracking walls.

The bells begin, against the stone
They butt their swollen volumes of doom,
The auto horns cry out, Atone! ---
From their jobs the poor go crowding home.

Ragged glory of the day's
Dying; winter riots on the drum,
Summoning the poor to their patience.
Salvation is a growing numb.

The bells are pounding the last glint.
Where Seventh Avenue makes a cross,
Grazing on the shores of print,
They await the coming of the bus.

The Dream

Once, years after your death, I dreamt
you were alive and that I'd found you
living once more in the old apartment.
But I had taken a woman up there
to make love to in the empty rooms.
I was angry at you who'd borne and loved me
and because of whom I believe in heaven.
I regretted your return from the dead
and said to myself almost bitterly,
"For godsakes, what was the big rush,
couldn't she wait one more day?"

And just so daily somewhere Messiah
is shunned like a beggar at the door because
someone has something he wants to finish
or just something better to do, something
he prefers not to put off forever
—some little pleasure so deeply wished
that Heaven's coming has to seem bad luck
or worse, God's intruding selfishness!

But you always turned Messiah away
with a penny and a cake for his trouble
—because wash had to be done, because
who could let dinner boil over and burn,
because everything had to be festive for
your husband, your daughters, your son.

Immortality

The tropical, vast, velvet, star-struck dark.
The surf, black to white, against the seawall.
San Juan. Between Christmas and Epiphany.
The Casino's creamy, moonlit premises
—Spanish tile, marble, marquetry, high wooden beams.
And here the august Academy has convened.
On the swept parquet (where last night's happy hundred
debutantes salsa'd the sun up from the sea)
are forty folding chairs (metal, gray) on which
are old friends, the old wife, old lovers of
the old poet, the lone inductee, standing on
a little low stage —Don Ernesto Pla, once
Romantic-Marxist-Nationalist-Christian,
now abstracted by age to a shrunken gesture:
this last of the octogenarian magi
blinking, smiling in perplexity
at all the kingdoms lost along the way.

Easier to bring a dead man back to life
than make an old one young? But if he's not
rejuvenated, he seems juvenile, at least,
with that tremulous certificate he clutches,
a large, important, parchment report card,
its message from muses to mamas
saying, "Your little boy's doing just fine!"
—whose text, in full, is being cabled to
the *Times* of Jupiter and Saturn's *Evening Post*
and other shining capitals of heaven,
because, as everyone knows, knows too well,
the ceremony is pre-posthumous,
garnishing the florid necrology
with one sweet ultimate puff, one bloom, one blurb
to bear in hand up to Helicon's gate.

Her smooth brown hand poised above the ivories,
María Vargas at the upright is ready.
Refugee three months from Castro's Cuba,
she's ardent, patriotic, eager
to pulverize the keys to divine confetti
in honor of her newfound home, her country.
Now from the sack of Uncle Santa's heart
she hurls down avalanches of Recessional,
pseudo snows of yesteryears that never were.
Thunderous tinkling riots there: it's "Jingle Bells"
rollicking so fast it's running out of sound

—as if ghostly herds of Bobtail rose from nightmares
of knackers, and ran ran ran in the traces!

Now here's a pretty kettle of kitsches
—all bubbling along with evident good humor,
while inducing moral motion sickness.
Everyone's getting a little queasy
from all this heartfelt inauthenticity.
It's so provincial, really—so colonial!
It's embarrassing, it's disheartening
to see the here-and-now is, here and now, *nowhere,*
not for real, doesn't count, unless, until
the Eagle's lime comes down and whites it out
in whirling blizzards of his being there and then.

Oh, but at this killing tempo, even
the piano's begging to have a heart attack.
Stop her, stop her! everyone wishes.
María's indefatigable, oblivious.
But look at Don Ernesto now—he's dancing!
Oh, it's not the tedious Eternity Mambo.
And it's not the sad Mortality Tango.
It's something else, something else entirely!
—something grotesque, perhaps, no, uncanny,
a halting hop, sort of, a hopping shrug,
or lurching shuffle, a kind of stumble *upward,*
as if, thigh-deep, sinking, he fought huge billows
of this jolly white plague of musical sewage
—up there, in New York, treated as "camp," surely,
and yet on him descending here in all
the fury of its raw banality!

No. Don Ernesto Pla does not break down.
Not in helpless weeping, or hopeless laughter.
He goes on being faithful to the farce,
in courtesy to María, to everyone,
granting as a grace what his moral weight
—his mortal history, his life lived out to be
this decay, this dying—rebels against.
Yes, he goes along with the music, he does more,
inventing the dodder-dance-and-stumble-walk
that keeps overcoming its own refusals
down the little staircase's six enormous steps

one by one by one by one, not swept away
but giving chase very slowly —until
then and there on the snowy parquet before

his white-haired cohort Don Ernesto catches up.
He reins in María's runaway piano.
He silences the tumultuous black box,
the hissing runners and muffled hooves
right at the black and crumbling brink
—silence the audience crushes between its palms,
then lets fly up toward the rafters, and up
and up to the heavens significant with stars.

Malke Toyb *

When she was still a tiny girl,
well, not so tiny, a *little* girl,
one day her mother's lips were speaking
and saying nothing, birds were mute,
she saw her father clap hands at her
and shout no louder than the sun
cries out crossing the heavens. That night
the lightning stroke buried itself
in the sand as silent as a snake.

She grew. She grew. And heard no better.
Grew. And heard no more. And understood
she must be so always, forever.
Now she knew: God the righteous one
punished her for something she had said,
said or heard—did it matter which or what?—
something bad, for sure, for God is just.
Nothing less could justify the God
of this affliction that took from her
her mother's dear voice and the voices
she had never known—nor ever would—
of her daughters. And yet she heard
well enough her own voice saying
always within her, "Punished. Punished."

An old old woman died, and brought
her faith into the presence of
the face of God, which was kindly
and spoke to her so, "Malke, dearest,
you've suffered grievously enough.
Shall I restore at last your hearing?"
But Malke was humming, humming.
"Malke, beloved child," God's voice grew

more tender, gentler, more urgent still,
"let me restore to you your hearing."
But Malke went on with her humming.
"Malke, please," The Divine One whispered,
"just a taste of the honey of hearing
—surely, one little taste can't hurt you."
And Malke was humming, humming,
"You forget, dear Lord of hosts, I'm deaf.
I can't hear a word you're saying."

And so for all Eternity
The Divine Lips plead and Malke answers.

*Deaf Queenie

Kenneth Feltges is a talented teacher, poet and photographer. His teaching career spans 45 years, first at Kenmore West, and most recently at Mt. St. Mary Academy. In 1988, he was selected as Teacher of the Year for the eight counties of Western New York by the Western District PTA and has been named as one of 25 Teachers of Merit by *BUSINESS FIRST*. A few years ago, Kenmore West established the annual Kenneth Feltges Poetry Award, which is presented to gifted young poets at the school. Ken is a past winner of the Just Buffalo literary competition for writing original poetry, and he was named a Western NY Writer In Residence. His collection of poems, *Before Things Change,* was published in 2012. People often comment on the strong visual—almost cinematic—style of his poetry. This may be grounded in the fact that Ken is a highly accomplished photographer, whose work has won several awards in area art shows, including first place in the prestigious Lewiston Art Festival. He has been married for 45 years to his wife, Trudy, a former English teacher. They live in Williamsville, NY.

---

if I told you

if I told you I still loved you
would you stab me in the face
with a fork?
because that's what happened last time
a fork in the face

wait don't get mad
let me start over
I waited almost two months to come back and see you
because now I'm lookin more like myself
the stitches are out and the scar looks a little better
not as red

you and me we could still be a team
you know
do real things together
take walks
listen to music
talk about what's important
sometimes go to the movies
get married even

I'm too old to be a kid for the rest of my life
drinkin
workin nowhere jobs
sleepin late
all my days runnin together like I don't know what
God sometimes I don't even know what month I'm in

I'm almost twenty-three years old
and I'm a nobody
let's face it
a nobody
all I got is three tattoos
an old banged up car
and a bedroom in my mother's basement
five feet from the sump pump

it's way past time for a change
so I went out signed up for night school
already been to the first three classes
I'm one of the oldest ones there
sometimes it feels like a kindergarten for losers
don't look at me like that
I'm not complainin
gonna get my diploma
then maybe community college

I listened to you
about changin things
then I listened to myself
and guess what
we're both sayin the exact same things

so back to what I asked before
what would you do
if I said I still loved you?
another fork in my face?

relax, don't say anything right away
you and me together again
like bread and butter
like bacon and eggs
give yourself some time to think about it
then maybe we could sit down and maybe have
some coffee or soup
stuff you can eat with just a spoon
doesn't hurt to be careful
if you know what I mean

Daddy-time

Saturday morning 10:30
and her children scatter like loose change
battling for a front window position
a crunch of faces fogging the cracked glass

It's almost Daddy-time

Defeated by the sameness of bread and butter schedules
the every-day mother retreats to another place

Then He is there
invading home territory
bribing her children
with new toys and a hundred kisses
still calling them His little mice

Almost invisible in a flannel robe
the every-day mother
drifts from room to room
pretending not to spy
but it does not matter
she has already lost

but she cannot surrender

Climbing to His shoulders
hugging
pulling hair
the little mice capture their once-a-month Daddy

Later He swings them one by one
round the room
dizzy with delight they squeal His name
"Daddy! Daddy! Daddy!"
(How can they say that word?)

Unbusy
dusting furniture
she tries not to hear their loud love
tries not to count giggles and screams

Suddenly they escape—Daddy and her children—
to the park
to the movies
or to the zoo

Alone
arms wrapped round herself
an empty hug
for the every-day mother
defenseless against Daddy-time

but she cannot surrender
she will never surrender

need

you need to find yourself lost
to disconnect the straight lines between your life and your dreams
you need to wander with passion
past schedules
that promise only to get things done on time
you need to write your name on a kite
and sail it so deep into the sky
that your mother can finally know you
you need to dance (perhaps a waltz) in supermarket aisles
while juggling cans of cat food and bundles of pork chops
you need to make school day lunches for your son and daughter
and allow them to re-discover their father
you need to find yourself lost

to angel float

through ancient fields of forgotten friends
and gather them up like crystal flowers
you need to phone your older brother
who was always younger than you
you need to die at least twice
and resurrect a better love for your wife
you need to uncount all the things that you think count
you need to shine your eyes early morning bright
and watch slow-motion reruns of your childhood

listen!

you really need to find yourself lost
and when you ask for directions about how to get home
people will cry and smile and say

"It's all right. It's all right.
You're already there."

Sally Fiedler was born in 1939 and grew up in a small town in northern Illinois. She began writing poems as a little girl. She received her PhD at the University of Illinois (Champaign/Urbana) in 1967, and stayed on there to teach in the English Department until she met her future husband, Leslie Fiedler, in 1971. They married and she moved to Buffalo in 1973. She had two children, and he had six. In Buffalo she taught at SUNY/Buffalo, the Poetry-in-the-Schools program, Nichols School, the Buffalo Seminary and D'Youville College.

She has given many poetry readings in locations around the world, including Vassar College, Black Mountain College Festival, Temple University, University of Hawaii, University of Southern California and Urbino, Italy. Her poems have been published in approximately 80 magazines, journals, newspapers and poetry anthologies, including *The American Poetry Review, Wisconsin Review, Texas College English, Folio, Spirit, Earth's Daughters* and *The Buffalo News*. She has published five books of poetry: *Timepieces* (1971), *Skin and Bones* (1972), *To Illinois, With Love* ((1975), *Eleanor Mooseheart* (1992) and *A Trick of Seeing* (2007).

No Mercy

Finally Eleanor decides to kill her houseplants.
She just can't take their dusty green hands
held up to her, pleading for love.
She has read somewhere that they like music,
that they scream when they are cut,
and wish to be moved about gently.
They are terribly sensitive.
So she thinks she will try
to make the end merciful, somehow.
In the late fall, she sets them
out in the yard, in dignified rows,
then runs back to the house, shuts the door tight.
"Tonight they'll freeze", she thinks.
"They'll fall into a nice green sleep.
There will be no screaming or carrying on.
Just a nice sleep."
Then comes Indian Summer--warm days
and nights for nearly two weeks.
Eleanor is miserable; the suspense is awful.
She wants it to be over fast,

like the electric chair, like most hangings.
Defeated, she brings them back inside,
sets them in their regular places,
gives them a little drink,
and a dirty look.

Griffith Court

To get there you have to go home
to the junction of the Fox and the Illinois
where radioactive water churns
under the new bridge
and then a mile east
past the township high school
and the worn little houses
in rows like broken teeth
the slump of shy old elms
and the sickly flowering locust trees
to the edge of the Clay Beds
abandoned brick mine
aslop with ragged ponds and woods
cattail and prickly pear.
Perched on the slope of the Beds
is a tiny house where once
a great tree stood shading the porch
shedding its leaves in full fall bunches.
On this spot you were happy once
raking up the leaves and shaping
them into floor plans for a little house
straight lines with spaces left
for doors and windows.
You were alone in the sun and shade
making forming singing song
thinking of nothing.
Just there, raking the leaves.

Unfinished Business

I remember looking back at you
where you stood still
clutching the garden gloves
and the delicate green cucumbers
grown from your own sets.
You are there
and I am going away
but I have to stop,
turn the dusty car around,
pull in next to you again
and climb out shyly
to kiss you once again.
I have to do this,
I cannot move away,
any more than I can sever
the nose from my face.
Afterwards, after that last kiss,
I drive into the late afternoon
and think that I will see you
again, but I won't, You will go
wherever the dead go
and I will be over here
and find it very difficult
for the rest of my days
to say farewell to anyone
without going, back, back.

The Poet and the Painter

For Catherine Parker

(On a painting on a poem by Neruda)

Isn't it odd that the artist
who doesn't write poetry
plumbs the words better
than the poet who can't paint.
What is the center? I ask.
Miasma, she chooses, and
creates a luscious swamp,
a bog of nervous portent.
In the foreground blue water
with bubbles rising,
peace lilies and their pads,
rose flowers of uncertain genus –
all surging sensuality, sunlit and strong.
Farther back the threatening trees,
whisper, *In life we are in death.*
And behind those, the line of red blood birds.
How do her hands know to do this?
What line of nerves runs from her
brain to her heart to her fingertips
while the rest of us simply
hew the wood and till the soil?

All is Real Here and Clear

Half of what happens to Eleanor
happens when she is asleep:

Perhaps it's a picnic
with someone she loves
who's dead now
but no matter.
How each petal in the field
of buttercups stands out,
defined against the damp grass.
She can stroke the hair
of her beloved's beard,
kiss the little creases
in his smiling lips.
Eleanor hopes that
when she is gone
those she cares about will see her
this way, that sometimes
at night there will be picnics.

To Continue

I find it thrilling that we are survived
by our particles.
Odd that I may just have brushed
a bit of Chaucer off my sleeve,
that Grandma Maud and Hitler
may lurk together under the nail
of my right thumb.
Odd to inhale a speck of field
mouse from two blocks over.

This immortal world is a democracy,
good and bad are deeply joined.
All that is and ever was
makes a sort of pudding,
a mash, a mulch of the real,
signs that we will go on,
ever and on.

Gail Fischer was born north of Buffalo, NY and grew up in Niagara County near Lake Ontario. She earned Bachelor of Arts and Master of Arts in Humanities degrees at the State University of New York at Buffalo, where she studied poetry with Mac Hammond, John Logan and Irving Feldman. She shared a special issue of *Audit/Poetry* with Thomas Frosch, and other work by her appeared in various little magazines. Her first full-length volume, *Red Ball Jets*, was published by the Outriders Poetry Project in October, 2011. Ms. Fischer lives on 97 acres of reforested land dedicated to the protection of song and woodland birds and other kinds of wildlife.

The Mob of the 21st Century

Scum of the earth have the run
of the earth
                              a wilderness, *maquis*, a
brushed edge of woods crushed against the clouds
scans by an urban peregrine. The falcon fists, dive
bombs toward quarry, hits stunning it and
clasps the draining carcass carried up, floats
navigating on the bronzed *Consolamentum* of its eyes.

Paper and water, warmed, would breed brown mold
and the spore-rise penetrate predawn; disaster—
the commonweal, vellum and vocables, will part.
Arriving, vehicles and light ungild
the gothic canyon, let dim figures slam then
shrink against streaked marble monumental slabs
where anger is vapor as solvents consume
the generations of graffito'd scrawls.
Not discerning cable guttural, turnkeys, tension,
battery and tunnelhum—invisibles, slouching
mobile vulgus, drag in to make a city run.

Like *pi*, slipping continually through revolving
entrances, they lug their decimals in attachés

and press and wait to elevate to dells
of wallless cubicles and doorless rooms—
the antitheses of old architecture. That
accommodated eavesdropping in secret
space—vast ceilings, vast maneuvered tapestries
hung to muffle footfall and a coronary pound.
And now, they're sorting out to lavatories
(markered once, little *Dulls* and *Buys*) where men
shake off each other's measurements, women
are making ageist comments from the stalls.

They perforate the air, returning, round
an S-curve through thorny desktop tumuli, hear
a unit head—Stampede of One—charge down
the corridor. He wants an audience, waits, then knocks.
Incarnadine, her wide computer screen reflects
a tidy universe of files and cactuses, a cache
of European shoes she leans above and chooses from—
her snakeskin pumps. She is all bully by wardrobe,
perfect poster girl for *Schadenfreude*—White Female
condescending to his entrance. On autopilot
she is dumbing down. He's sucking up, attacks
a rival, compliments her ravenous insight.
Her bookshelves shimmy up the wall she shares
with floors above and a commissioner—Feral
Buckslip (busily reinventing government
by gossip) who's surrounded by a moat
of liquid and ambitious blondes, hired to repel
but magnetize. (*Outspent, those watchpuppies
will have to let her pass*.) Her green eyes
complement the glass proscenium behind, glance
back to a dark and goaded raptor preening
the feather treble clefs that glyph its neck—
which dips and lifts between cathedral finials,
then bates (*how he is fidgeting!*) yanking
at the jesses of metropolis, a captive
masking-taped to where its food is found.

His mouth run out of coins, dismissed.
Storming, the unit head splits a sanguine klatch
of keyboard specialists (*the sycophants and sluts*)
whose whispering moans to this onrush of corporeal
Doppler effect, distorts a turbulent clot of ignoramuses
(*foetid!*) still fanning that administrator's
fondest praise. Hired is wired. A silent theatre

of backs of heads, hooded and tranquilized
under incandescent hoops of light pooled down
on plastic terminals, defaces the machinery
that molds and presses out and stamps
a product ghost. For seven hours they sit
and tan—stare directly into ersatz daylight—the more
lustrous the more deeply bronzed, depending
on the pecking order of how many megabytes;
or, in the polished fenders of the big hardware
acquire real neon. Passcodes are dangled, and encrypt,
and they log on (*and take their hits, at:*
*troubleyoutroubleyoutroubleyou*BACKLASH
BACKLASH*Cathari*SPLAT*blazesowell*NOT*calm*)
to anything, and to be culled and counted no one
needs to speak, is what the deal is—this virtual
venality. Agree with anyone, to put a signature
to paycheck, with their Lascaux script.
He will also sit and worship at the altar of technology—
he'll make her scaperodent, scaperabbit, scapechick—
banks at his office opening, and lands.
Grinning a sarin smile, he glares into the cave fire
casting shadows on itself, and warms his fingers
with the alphabet (*this inquisition will be C-SPANish, and*
epithets will splash the network's mean dim suites, the chips
will hit the fan!) and, gazing beyond a field of icons
to blue sky and overlapping *cumuli*, he presses "send"—
his message soars and flies (*I think, therefore I scam*).

Resisting broken slow descent, incongruent
muscles of the Otises stress in the wells
of their vertical routes. They lock, and square
after square plot of little crowds spill out
onto the basement's black terrazzo, looking for
D & C, the double meeting room, and spot
red arrows and "RASA" signs. Fluorescence
leaping at their entries fingers them in
with whole façade and pores exposed—females shield
the chest and solar plexus with their notepads, males
come in swinging Handhelds in their leather fists.
Voguing in erased couture, they all wear mall clothes
and set down Big Gulps or cups of steaming Styrofoam
so the rectangle of tables populates and sweats—
then spread a sycophantic hush for the big boss
Garry Factman (a *papiérivore*) who's infamous
for popping paper pills; he slowly masticates
an acid-free and lignin-free *parfait*. And he

pursues agendas with cunning acumen, targets
the item offered by some *altruiste*, her White Paper.
Tom, the Demoblican, is at the flipchart (*smirking
from the jaws, tall, a viable hometown opportunocrat*)
facilitating with Ms. Chevron-Voleuse
(*mask mixer, narcissist, mistress of sulk, who
cries and defames to be attended to*) her back
to the bare wall that blisters with mail room sorts
and clerks—the dim, the scared (the *null*).
Stampede bursts in late (*on schedule*) and sits
across from *Schadenfreude*—soon the two can
salivate in syzygy—on time to see the *altruiste*,
his immiscible underling, about to be attacked.
Mauronorola leads the pastel pack—pummeled
all their lives by fathers, brothers, priests, husbands,
sons, they'll play it safe and only plot against
a boss with breasts—she flaunts her rapport
with Dan, war buff and Re-enactor (*his sheets are
Izod shirts, his spurs his ecru golfing shoes*) who takes
command and charges with the boys, the batterers.
This sturdy sixpack signals to their leader,
Rob the Fifth (*the corkscrew his cathedra*) who then flashes
back a blessing with his brutal wit, emboldened
by the synod's dry imprimatur: The outsider is
fair game (*great sport*) and here was someone's work
to mash and spit. Concept after concept sharpshot
down—one sets an open switchblade spinning, skimming
the table veneer (*excelsior!*), another scissors coat linings
to shreds and another smashes windshields while
the wires are cut, another picks locks and the looting
starts—psyches (*emerging deep from micro sleep*) slam,
incise and bruise, corrode, engorge, and twist
out of control in this emotional mosh pit.
Words, *faidits*, those dispossessed nobility
—fractals splintering in the ear, mere
mirroring esoterica—stunned out of voice, run
where text's maimed ovum, maiming, lodges
like an apthong. To the incinerators—paper and flames!

Crouching on eggshells, those last
hired have the pallor of mushrooms.
Their lungs dulled with spores' damp chemistry,
roared hoarse under their deep reserve, some
must go up for air. They've seen the soul
summed down to its *planck length*,
admonished and diminishing, resolve:

And here, and now, I wash my hands
of *quid pro quo*. And turn—
to the aeries! and the *Endura*'s terminus.
A germ of good, the scent of home.

Lisa A. Forrest served as an Associate Librarian for SUNY Buffalo State from 2004-2013, where she founded the school's Rooftop Poetry Club. After twenty years in Western New York, Lisa recently accepted the position of Director, Research & Instruction Services at Hamilton College's Burke Library (Clinton, NY). Twice nominated for the Pushcart Prize, Lisa's creative writing has been featured in *Artvoice*, *The Buffalo News*, *Damn the Caesars*, *ecopoetics*, *elimae*, *foursquare*, *Hot Metal Bridge*, *Kadar Koli*, *Lake Affect*, *Not Just Air Literary e-Journal*, *Scythe*, *WordWrights* and *Yellow Edenwald Field*. She is the recipient of the National Public Radio News Directors Incorporated (PRNDI) Award for her radio commentary, "And So This is Christmas," which aired on WBFO, Buffalo's local NPR station. Lisa's first collection of poems, *To the Eaves*, is available from BlazeVOX. Her debut music album, *Oh Lake Erie* (2011), can be heard on iTunes.

Field Song
For Charles Burchfield

Listen long
to the song
of the telegraph

weird
beautiful
moonlit dawn

star muted
morning
sorrow

March rutted
rows & seams
wind harp spring

knotty eyed
crow edged caw
bird blue halo call--

old yearning hums along the wire

An April Mood

No stopping
good God's
Friday mood

hemlock low
anger winds
winding

creek's
sodden
risen shore

veiled iris
& buttercup
hidden

wet skinned
saplings dangle
lifeless—

White-breasted Nuthatch, Singing
-Written after Charles Burchfield's *Autumnal Fantasy*

Today's charm
lies in tonight's
back porch moon

gazing &
holy
wondrous

darkness
steels down
our days

unnoticed
pin-oak
frost edged echo

cavern glistens
bleating
heart bright

gnarly woods brood
shaggy barked
nuthatch
cries

gnarly woods brood
shaggy barked
nuthatch
cries

Of the Hill

No house should ever be built on a hill or on anything. It should be of the hill. Belonging to it. Hill and house should live together and each the happier for each other.
– Frank Lloyd Wright

There's a grave
out back
I'd fit across

scarred
soul in need
of saving

give us
room enough
to pace

desire nothing
but endless
distance

Written in Fall 2009 on the occasion of viewing an installation by the late David von Schlegel at the Connecticut home he shared with Susan Howe.

Eric Gansworth (Onondaga) is Lowery Writer-in-Residence at Canisius College in Buffalo, NY. His books include *Extra Indians* (American Book Award, New Atlantic Independent Booksellers Association Trade Book of the Year) and *Mending Skins* (PEN Oakland Award). He is also a visual artist, and has had solo visual art exhibits at Colgate University, Niagara University, Bright Hill Center, SUNY/Oneonta and Westfield State University, among other art spaces. His collection of poems and paintings, *A Half-Life of Cardio-Pulmonary Function*, was voted to the Number 3 position on the National Book Critics Circle's "Good Reads" List in 2008. His play, *Re-Creation Story*, was selected for the Public Theater's Native Theater Festival in NYC. His multimedia performance commission, *Home Fires and Reservation Roads*, was mounted in 2011. His written work has appeared in *Kenyon Review*, *Boston Review*, *Shenandoah*, *Poetry International*, *Third Coast* and *Provincetown Arts*, among other periodicals, and has been widely anthologized. His latest book, the critically acclaimed *If I Ever Get Out of Here*, a Young Adult novel, was published in 2013.

Dusk to Dusk

And the way some people tell
our Creation Story, after he covers
the dirt on the turtle's back with grass,
the Good Mind grows
a sunflower next to his lodge,
as a means of lighting
his small place in the world
embracing the state of his needs,
modest to a fault.

Of course, because the story leaves
some aspects of itself open
to interpretation or maybe leaves
holes where details are irrelevant,
we don't know how he comes to grow
the plant here. Did he find
the seeds in the folds
of his grandmother's dress
the way some tell it, the seeds
she carried unknowingly from her place

in the world before this one,
or did he will them into existence
with the strength of his need?
In the world in this time,
things like this are still possible.

And when his place to live
needs little, this flower
is enough for him to find
his way home, lighting
his doorway for some distance.

And when the world grows
too big for the meager ambitions
and good intentions of the flower,
as we all know our worlds
become, despite our own efforts
and intentions, the Good Mind
is offered a solution from the sky.

His grandmother's Elder Brother,
waiting in the clouds for recognition
says he will burn brightly,
attaching himself to the underside
of the Skydome and travel its surface
every day, spreading light for hours
then allowing for darkness to seep in
and govern the sky, balancing his movement.

The Good Mind, in appreciation,
acknowledges that the sunflower
will remain in his doorway,
and with its head, follow the path
the Elder Brother travels
across the sky, sharing light
and the possibilities of life
for every growing thing
on this turtle's back.

And when I think this story
has less and less connection
to me and the places I have lived
and the way the sun traces its arc
away from us and then back again,
a promise kept every day, I remember

a friend's garden, and the haphazard
pattern of sunflowers, like constellations
in the rich soil, and I asked,
in the setting sun, when the flowers bowed
their heads in rest and resignation,
why he had grown them that way.

He said he had grown a couple sunflowers
the previous year, because he liked
watching the way they observed
the sky's daily history, but it turned
out the birds loved the sunflower
as much as he did, perhaps more.

And in taking seeds
from the flower's heart
to feed themselves and likely
their young, they dropped some
along the way, that he neglected
to notice until they were grown
tall enough to be identified,

and as he had come here
from another place, himself,
he knew the way seeds could fall
in places they had not expected
and still survive, growing
into the beings they were intended
to be, chasing the sun
from a different point
beneath the sky, sending seeds
themselves when the time came.

While Hendrix Played a Solo: "Burning of the Midnight Lamp"

Above them, locked by thumbtacks
to the walls of a Lower West Side
apartment, ignoring the topless
woman pinned to the next wall,
lighting Monterey on fire with a fret
board and strings and those wondrous
fingers, Jimi filled the night
with a haze so purple it rivaled
the wampum beads these two would know
as surely as their own names,
tracing history, culture,
treaties that mostly document
violation—they knew Purple Haze
in their tissue, organs, blood.

In a chair designed for a single
body, they sat together, Skin to
Skin, she wearing Janis Joplin
glasses to see the world
through, he letting his hair grow
into history and toughening up his bare
soles, for the long haul,
testifying that they were
not like those Indians
Edward Curtis imagined through his lens,
they were not vanishing, not going
anywhere—the West Side still
within the territories
they had guarded for centuries.

The western door behind
them, they look at one
another, confident before
the photographer, that this is
the way they want to be recognized,
recorded—hand in hand, knowing
as Jimi did, that "The Star
Spangled Banner" could
bring tears to one's eyes
for a variety of reasons
and that their responsibility
was to hang on as all the other
Indians had before them
surviving to tell the tale, together.

Geoffrey Gatza is a widely published poet, and has received awards from the *Fund for Poetry* and a *Boomerang A-ward*. He is the author many books of poetry, including *Secrets of my Prison House* (BlazeVOX, 2010), *Kenmore: Poem Unlimited* (Casa Menendez, 2009), *Not So Fast Robespierre* (Menendez Publishing, 2008) and *HouseCat Kung Fu: Strange Poems for Wild Children* (Meritage Press, 2008). He is also the author of the yearly Thanksgiving Menu-Poem Series, a book length poetic tribute for prominent poets, now in its thirteenth year. The poems in this anthology are from his 2012 chapbook, *House of Forgetting,* which appears in its entirety in his book, *Apollo* (BlazeVOX, 2013), a concept book length work based on the ballet, *Apollo,* by Stravinsky.

His visual art poems have been displayed in gallery showings, including OCCUPY THE WALLS: A Poster Show, AC Gallery (NYC, 2011), *occupy wall street N15 For Ernst Jandl - Minimal Poems with photography from the fall of Liberty Square,* and in LANGUAGE TO COVER A WALL: Visual Poetry through its changing media, UB ART GALLERY (Buffalo, NY, 2011/12) *Language for the Birds.*

Geoffrey Gatza is the editor and publisher of the small press, BlazeVOX. The fundamental mission of BlazeVOX is to disseminate poetry, through print and digital media, both within academic spheres and to society at large. He lives in Buffalo, NY with his girlfriend and their beloved cat.

http://www.geoffreygatza.com/
http://www.blazevox.org

From: **The Twelve-Hour Transformation of Clare**

for Dorothea Tanning

Fifteen Hundred Hours

The afternoon sun bathes the thousand miles of addled tranquility.
The birds chatter away, marking no disturbances in the garden.
The mournful cry of a red-winged bird, flying lost in the blue skies.

Plotting, planning, exploring. What was next? What am I? What was I?
Curiously unfeeling her shade eyes look over the possessions of her home,
Attempting to discern what was absent from these seasonal necessities.

The consciousness that bound all of these obscurities and clichés together
was overgrowth, a hermit woman who escaped her life in the words of others,
who loved too much, loved too little; an unborn child swimming in springs.

Her midnight immateriality was in itself an icy success of accumulation.
A life of summer trees obscuring the war rallies her country entertained.
A severance of the self from painted still life, an ice cream and its cone.

Looking at the red trees she loses track of the looming presence
Of invisible gases rustling in temperature and pressure fluctuations.
Fusion, manipulation, questions of failure or success, fashion choices.

The scent of sarsaparilla, coke-bottle eyeglasses, allowances, space;
Winter. The weather is already warm, the ground should be frozen.
Fallen leaves on the pathway to the home of one no longer there.

Eighteen Hundred Hours

Her dark hair is a tangled thicket of possibility.
A madwoman of the woods, a queen of trees.
A murmuration of starlings lost to the exaltation
of the moment, alighting towards the moon,
struck dumb with love, hushed in place, a snowstorm.

Clare bares her specter wings open to nothing.
To white doorways leading her feet into rooms
Housing the shreds of ordinary human existence.
A drowsy future embodied in her visions of sleep,
Cannot now remember the unkindness they retain.

Her shape is malleable to her cerulean mood.
Words discovered as a wellspring of flowing
Shrewdness, a parliament of self-governance,
Ghost dances, her reception ballet; a lost monarchy
Of banishing perfections performed for mannequins.

A coronet of equal moral autonomy rings false, an untrue clang.
A hollow note her mind discerns, plucking out as times tables,
Recalling the chords of peerless sounds hanging in the sparking
googolplex of living words; the life sentences of the long dead.

A fleeting success inoculated against
the aphrodisiac of supreme power,
the holy vertigo of consciousness.

Her age of impoverishment nourished
in requiems, oaths and magic charms
Stories of intrigue spelling her far away, adieu,
Over walls of her upbringing as her song fades.

What can grief achieve, that the aureate words of failure cannot.
Limitations define us everyone in associative nightmare visions.
Beauty is the core of the anesthetic that quells painful outrages.
How can we all still be alive after all we have lived through?

Twenty Three Hundred Hours

Clare could not live in a place where she died

Her pleasure, her beauty
Is a peace, a love
Found in music and
Words. Afterthoughts.

This was, is a comfort
Glad, if that is the word,
For her to have died
Without knowing loss.
The taking, the surviving
Needed in old age. Forgetting.
We are all the same, we are one.
We are all good, we are all bad.

The time I pass
Alone is hard.
We are a miracle.
A blessing.
Old age is experience
Something to compare
No longer curious
About the world.
We
Listen
With our brain.
Experience.
Compare
Time and passing moments.

I did my duty.
I did my best.
When I could
I survived.
Survived.
So we live
So we die.
When we achieve,
Our time, when it comes
Will be beautiful.
Beautiful.

Jimmie Margaret Gilliam

(1935-2015) was a poet, professor emerita, workshop leader, editor and mentor. Born and raised in the North Carolina mountains near Asheville, she made her home in Western New York since her graduation from Houghton College and SUNY/Buffalo. Her teaching career spanned five decades, twenty three years as a Professor of English at ECC/City Campus from its opening in 1971 to 1995. Her workshop for Just Buffalo Literary Center - The Translation of Silence - was the origin of the writers' group, the Women of The Crooked Circle, who have met weekly since 1991. Her workshop, The Pearls, met monthly at her home (2005 to 2015).

Of her work, Jimmie said: "As a poet, I want to find language that begins with the senses - flesh made word, a connecting of body and mind. I want to bridge the landscape of the unconscious with conscious ground. I want my poems to generate an arc of connection with the reader. The poem will lift from silence incredible personal energy, which may inspire all kinds of makings. The poem becomes a repository for psychic power which may release in the reader or in the hearer her or his own imagination until whole communities will choose art over chaos, beauty over destruction, life over death. Choice based on creative will."

"So many of the lives of women are buried by silence, a silence carefully hidden by layers of fear, anger and shame, often within a self-imposed repression. I know beneath all those thick walls lies a passionate voice wanting to connect to live. If my poems can evoke the desire to open that expression, I will have fulfilled my own hope for my work in the world."

Her publications included: *The Rhyme and Roar of Revolution,* Jimmie Canfield, with Bob Dickens (Friends of Maletesta Press, Buffalo, NY, 1975); *Ain't No Bears Out Tonight,* Jimmie Gilliam Canfield (White Pine Press, 1983, 1984); and *Pieces of Bread,* Jimmie Gilliam Canfield, with artist, Priscilla Bowen (White Pine Press, Serendipity Arts and Dream Seasons, Buffalo, NY, 1987). *Torn From the Ear of Night,* is forthcoming from White Pine Press. Jimmie was the recipient of the prestigious Literary Legacy Award by the Just Buffalo Literary Center in December, 2006.

On September 24, 2015, Jimmie lost her long battle with cancer. She was greatly honored by both the literary community and the community as a whole, and will be greatly missed by all.

What The Mountains Say

Cartwheel your childself
With sensory oblivion and live —
Not to tell the tale only but
To listen for the silent story

Before we were born
We were not mountains —
Not the Blue Ridge, The Great Smokies,
The Appalachians
We were invisible below Earth's crust,
Molten and without voice

Three inland seas are shallow
Vast above our unimaginable peaks
Soft rains fall continuously
Silt and small stones and eroding ridges
Through millions of years build pressure
The seas' floor drops six miles
Crashes the Earth's rim
Cataclysm

We rise up twenty five thousand feet
When the sound settles, hazyblue and golden,
We are two hundred mountains —
Loam of your silence,
Home of your longing

burning flowers

when is changes to was
the real pain comes
sharp
in the image of flowers burning

mourning is active
the whole body lifted
full trigger
the movement of grief

sadness the sweet supple
blanket comes after

there are women
who burn
unnamed by any revolution
women who simply turn
in the image of bodies burning
in love
unclaimed
except by air

Love Poem

your mouth teaches me
the double entendre of lips
which tongue is mine?
your body unfolds me

you call me from the ocean's edge —
nothing keeps me from your mouth's door
we make love -
the fortunate play
the shared limbs
the afterspooning

how more possible the world seems

you make visible the long love —
our anxieties, hopes and fatigues
surrender the partnership of flesh

your sure wave breaks over me
emotion's skies open
we arrive shaken inside our doorway
in the place we've made home
lovers' hollows and curves fill —
one body drapes the nightdream's edge

Four Years Old At The A & P
                    for Alexis De Veaux

My mother shops at the A & P
for the things we can't raise
on our small farm—
bananas, fig newtons
light bread, mayonnaise

I slip away when she isn't looking
fill my pinafore pocket with bright berries

Turned loose by my mother's
frugal concentration
(She must account to my father for every penny)
I go up an aisle alone
the innocent thief

Skipping toward me
is a girl my size
eyes black as her shining face
her hair and *her* dress   *jazzy*   and red-ribboned
She's the cutest child I've ever seen
I want her to come home with me/be my sister
Eyes cling to eyes
I offer her my stolen fruit

When I hug her
all activity in the store stops
North of here
The Mason Dixon line snaps like a whip
Water streams in opposite directions
at The Continental Divide
My mother pulls me back from my delight

To this day I rue the loss
                    within that round moment
at the A & P when we were
no less and no more than
two little girls
holding hands full of cranberries
not yet bruised by color

Graveside

I go to your grave, Mother
The car makes the hillside curve
At Pisgah View
Stops at the Magnolia tree
I am alone
Your bones nudge the scab of my hidden tears
I weep within the rain
I walk up to your place   sideways
As I once approached the Pacific Ocean
At Cape Disappointment, Oregon

I am your daughter on the way to the store
To buy cornmeal   to fry okra
From Rhobena's garden

I have much to say to you, Mother
But now there is only time to arrange the silk flowers
Limp in the rain
I entwine two of them
One red, one pale purple
I do not tell you
Daddy has mowed down your lilacs
The rosebud bush

Your death still takes my legs away, Mother
But I walk on the air/my will
Away from the mirror you hold for me
Deep in the earth

I am your poet, Mother
Though my words do not grace your ears
I am bone of your bone
You stand in my frame
Bone catches in the throat
Of this grief

Ann Goldsmith holds degrees from Smith College and the University of Denver and a doctorate from the University at Buffalo, where she taught English for 10 years. She has also served on the faculties of Trocaire and D'Youville Colleges in Buffalo and for 12 years was the WNY Coordinator for ALPS, a statewide poetry-in-the-schools organization. She has been a visiting poet for Just Buffalo Literary Center and the Canadian Authors' Association, served for two years as poet-in-residence at the Chautauqua Institution's summer writing program and taught writing for 12 years at Buffalo's Trinity Center, which granted her an Excellence in Teaching Award in 1994.

She won the Quarterly Review of Literature Poetry Prize for her first book, *No One Is the Same Again* (1999). Her second book, *The Spaces Between Us,* was published by Outriders Poetry Project in 2010, and she has recently completed a third book of poems, *More Than the Story Tells.* Her poems have appeared in numerous journals and anthologies. Her poem, "If You Don't Mind My Asking," was a winner in the 2002 St. Louis, Missouri Poetry Center's Best Poem contest. She was a runner-up in Canada's 1996 Orillia International Poetry Festival and twice a finalist in the "Discovery"/*The Nation* national poetry competition. She served as a judge on the poetry panel in 1985-86 for the New York Foundation for the Arts. She was honored to be included in the Burchfield Penney Writers and Poets Series in 2010, as well as winning a number of Western New York awards. She has often taught poetry workshops at Buffalo's C.G. Jung Center. Recently, she coedited Norma Kassirer's collected works, *Minnows Small As Sixteenth Notes* (BlazeVOX, 2015)

Emy's Breath

What's the worst thing? I heard in the air
between the osprey and the cliffs,
the lake rumpling and smoothing itself
by my feet, elsewhere shining and still.
Perhaps a bone spoke or the wolf
spider caught in my shirt. *Not counting
cruelty, what scares you blind?
Poverty? Loneliness? Old age?*

A rough basketry of pine and wild grape
had let me through to the beach
but the other night it was pizza, beer
and her voice, singing us far and small:

I lay down golden
and woke up vanishing

Now, as I walked, head down, by a half-buried
oarlock the red balloon appeared,
wilted pod on a string rooted in sand,
with a sodden bit of card bearing a message
from a school two states away:

> *Please send me a fact.*
> Love, Emy.

I seemed to hold her flushed face in my hands,
child still golden, far east
of where I stood with sand in my shoes.

Back through the woods I took the balloon
and laid it like a plover's egg inside my car,
its shell softened to aged skin
still wrinkled around a child named Emy's breath.
Through fields of mist toward night and home
I tried to think of facts for her:
that people used to write on bark;
that alligators fall asleep
when rolled on their backs; that the gut
strings of a cat can be stroked into music . . .

But that was years ago, and friends
have died since then, my husband
missing, parents skimmed off, thin air
rinsing the stone step, the window panes.

> *I lay down golden,* the singer crooned,
> *and woke up gone*

Emy, this is what scares me: that
every breath rides its fading
farther out to sea, deeper into the mountains,
away, away.

But see how the stars bathe us,
how far you have exhaled your question.
This worn red sac still hoards
its dwindling mana
but you have passed over lakes and cities
and now the galaxies open like fans.

Alpine Honeymoon

Just playing, you say, on your heels
in the creek, building a dam.
Nine thousand feet above where I'm from,
coffee roils over fire already fallen
to coals, as curls of new pink light
melt in the water's eyes
and last night's sleeves and stockings
slide down the trees to the forest floor.

Just playing, you grin, the twin
scoops of your hands moving rock,
shoveling sand. The sun still
lurks behind Arapahoe Peak, but already
you are changing the course of things.
The raveling creek slips like skin
in your palms. Last night

I shaped myself to your entire length,
praise rising in me like a hooked rainbow.
This morning I am stupid
and fall silent as I bring you coffee, black.
I want to help, but do not know how
to play this game. The tongues
that transformed me
belong to the language of lilies, salamanders.

Stumbling, putting my boots on the wrong feet,
I am a tree of gold tassels,
a trout dancing, a creek in love.

How then imagine the far November dawn
when I will awaken early in my bed
by a lowland lake, dreaming someone
has spoken, thinking perhaps
it is you, returned from timberline,
holding back the heavy, swaying curtain,
turning my name over
and over in your dissolving hands?

Leaves

How one thing makes way for another.
All winter the cabin in the woods
Holds still for trysts and photo shoots,
Its secret life set out to hang on the wall
With moose heads and naked coat hooks.
The sky rests its forehead on hills
And shores we never wholly believed in
When the leaves filled this space with their tents.
Old swing-set bones, swathes of yellow grass,
One more high-ribbed deer rubbing its haunches
On dry tree slats: no mystery here.
No hidden quartz quarry or hermitage;
No secret cove where oars feather still water
Under a shielded moon. Now the town dump
Shoves forward its bald tires and stained mattresses,
Its amputee chairs and twisted chrome.
Down chalked-in back roads, junked cars
Brazen it out with collapsing porches, Pepsi
Cans, spent shells, headless dolls.
The equalizing light, coming from so far away,
Burnishes a bent spoon, the edge of a cloud.

Maisie's First Blood

Last night when I glanced up
lazily from my book to watch Maisie
playing with one of her toy mice,
it was a moment before I noticed
the faint twitch of the haunch,
the curving red thread across its back.

The toy was a mouse!
Between its delicate cabbage-leaf ears
and the rubber band tail,
a ribbon of gut gleamed
like a slash of paint.

Scooping her up
in a wad of tissues,
I carried her -- Maisie's first trophy --
to the back door.
She seemed near enough to death,

lying torpid in my palm,

so I sat holding her
on the low concrete step
and she was warm in my hand,
her ribs and the twist of gut
flexing with quick breaths.

The night was still and clear,
a few leaves moved gently,
farther downtown a siren wailed.
A late bird spoke from a branch
off to the left and the sky came down
and took us quietly in its mouth.

Half a dozen times she roused,
arching up, her tiny, long-fingered
front paws scrabbling
to move the strangely
inert hindquarters, sprawled
in a slow seepage of blood.

Each time the effort was more intense
before the exhausted slump
and it began to seem wrong
not to watch with her the rest of the way.

So I stayed and stroked the soft fur
of her head and talked to her
until the breath left her belly
and she shriveled into a snail curl
lighter than a leaf
and I put her in the grass in the sky.

Facts and Figures

Old walls have no truck with figures.
They know themselves built from the ground
Up, that what comes down from the sky
Lacks history. What's real is here
Where foundations state their dense facts,
Let clouds and leaves embroider what they will.

Leaves and clouds weave subplots as they will,
Won't be harried into stone figures
No matter what Medusa stare of fact
Quick-freezes every point. Walls are ground-
ing for the quick-tongued embroidery of here
And now, the madrigals enlacing sky

And wall at once, as if it took some sky
To lick and quicken a wall's will,
Ripening moments as on a tapestry, here
The burdened cherry tree and here, the ritual figures:
Hunters, maiden, unicorn, rising from the ground
Of unembroidered, hard, enduring facts.

All walls, of course, stand on simple fact:
A unicorn, for all its hooves and horn, is sky-
Born, pure embroidery, no ground
In common sense. We all know who will
Offer him her lap, and how those figures
With their longbows and their horns have heard

The snapping trap, in sunlight here
Where a virgin cradles death in her lap, a fact
She may not yet have figured
Out, for look how tenderly the sky
Embroiders shadows on her small white hands, that soon will
Seed the garden's brightly woven ground

With dragons' teeth. Already on the castle grounds
The falling fruit splatters ancient walls, while here
Among embroidered fields, truth will
Bury its teeth again in trust, bloody fact
In the heart's wild fictions, nothing under the sky
Exempt, not walls, not one of these figures

Embroidered on the latticed ground as fatal fact,
Though each recurring form blooms here against the same old sky,
Springing back fresh, in season, willful and young, transfigured.

Annunciation

where the burning touch
meets the pale flower

in the quick between
fingertip and shudder

sword and throat—
when the wingèd

messenger
utters a new word

and glory
gives birth to itself

in earth skins—
how then the soul

to harbor splendor
embraces its terror

Gene Grabiner's poetry has appeared in: *Naugatuck River Review, Counterpunch, Rosebud, New York Dreaming, Blue Collar Review, J Journal, Jewish Currents, Earth's Daughters, HazMat Review, The Buffalo News*, and other journals and anthologies.

He received an honorable mention in the 2013 Naugatuck River Review competition and was also a semifinalist in the 2002 "Discovery"/*The Nation* national poetry competition, Unterberg Poetry Center, New York City. His poem, "Recess," was a runner-up for the 2012 William Stafford Award For Poetry from Rosebud Magazine. He has read at the Jackson Heights Poetry Festival in New York City and at the International Festival of Poetry of Resistance in Toronto (IFPOR).

Gene Grabiner is a SUNY Distinguished Service Professor Emeritus, and lives in Buffalo, New York.

Recess

And
again, that spring, they whirled him on the
concrete yard at recess; again, each
yanking on his shirtsleeves to add spin.
A cordon of strong
9th grade bodies, adding force to their
human top. With sausage fingers he tried to break this
gauntlet so many years ago,
but the Yonkers junior high gang spun, and spun
him into the red brick school wall, where it all
stopped: and like petals
opened on some carnivorous plant,
they peeled away. He turned
back to the warming sun,
glasses
shattered, blood
streaming from the eyes.

Spare A Dime?

i.

Vast urban anacondas of the unemployed
ripple muscular down sidewalks, around corners, under neon,
past decorative awnings, window displays;
black-shirted cops
at the ready.

ii.

Relinquishing
of keys,
last click of that office door, final
clang of a locker
at the plant after the
layoffs.

iii.

Blue
abandonment of that woman
who worked
on the line since her teens: where she met her boyfriend, married,
kept house with him, raised three children,
pledged
the flag, was a church regular. She is left
with a stack of address labels for
mail that now will never again
leave that neat, small suburban house,
deftly taken by the bank.

Fingered

When the slim disease
came to Sing-Sing,
the hacks would shove in dinner
on metal trays
with brooms like a
quarantine shuffleboard.

He had blotches on his face,
or his teeth rotted or maybe
he was queer, with a strange cancer—
worked in the kitchen. So when other cons
burned his cell,
he got administrative segregation,
was sent to the hospital—
out of the narrow alleys
of their lives.

One time, this lifer met with the counselor,
filled out a form,
handed back the pen.
She just sat there,
pen untouched on the table.

When the slim disease
came to Clinton, hacks in the yard
were all from Mars. Goggles, gas masks;
what was coming?

In that beginning,
AIDS fingered eight thousand when it came inside.

Uncontacted Tribes

> *...it is better to know where to go and not know how,*
> *than it is to know how to go and not know where.*
> — *Jose Dolores*

Is it better to have mapped the world
down to your street, which, after all, did you know,
was done first to manage empire? Better
perhaps for you now, so you may be
rescued while surrounded by tongues
of fire in vast, seasonal blazes or petrol truck
explosions down the block. Better, now, for
you when the Murray, the Mississippi unceasingly lap at
all your western doors. Is
it better for them whose shelters, huts,
manioc and banana gardens, annatto trees
have been long-embraced by giant forest aunts and uncles? Better
for them whose longhouses are hardly seen when one knows
not where to look? Better for them, when the empire's ranchers and planters
encircle their ancient world? And on that atoll in
the Indian Ocean, for those who saw the seas flee from shore; who, knowing,
headed inland that day. Better now of course for them to be
saved by
us? What
of those many on the dragon island— in the misty highlands, in deep clefts;
better to know where they are on our maps? How much better is it
to know where we are? It's best of course to
know where we are. So much wiser to know
where we are
in latitude, longitude, street level, Google earth.
But, do we really know, and are we really
where— we think we really are?

George Grace is an award-winning artist, arts author, playwright and poet. He is the author of three books of poetry, *American Stonehenge, Night Wanes, Dawn,* and the latest, *Steeling America* (2014). He founded Circleformance, which hosted many local writers and musicians in the eighties, and was revived a few years ago at the Meridian West Gallery on Hertel Avenue in Buffalo. He was the artistic director of the gallery until it closed earlier in 2015. The Circleformance Poetry Series now continues at various locations in Buffalo co-hosted by Lynn Ciesielski. For a living, George remodels homes.

Narcissism Is the Answer

The collective misery of the world
is beyond quantifying. The clock is running.
Today

Another species extinct,
acre of trees clear cut, democracy felled.

Another hundred suspects tortured,
children slain,
homes foreclosed,
dog fights wagered,
workers injured.

Another thousand families bankrupt,
elderly swindled,
deaths to starvation,
land mines planted,
marriages annulled.

I couldn't look any more.
I couldn't ponder the imponderable.
I had to find an answer, to look inward,
to reach deep into my reserves.
And it was there that I found the remedy.

I made the world all about *me*.

You have questions.
You have concerns.

What do we do about lawlessness?
Me. I'm wonderful.

What time is it?
Me. The universe is in my orbit.

What is two plus four?
Me. I'm so good-looking.

Who could make this poem better?
Me. My sexual prowess is legendary.

Dresden

It's not that I don't savor it when it passes my nostrils
cool and holding the right amount of moisture,
sweetening in my lungs,

but like most things I'm supposed to treasure,
I simply don't trust fresh air.

I first tried yoga as a teen, breathed deeply,
and on meditating saw the whole wondrous universe,
but the next day in history class
when I first learned about the firebombing of Dresden—

a grand design, if ever there was one,
to weaken civilian resolve to wage war—

nowhere in the texts, among the casualty lists,

nor in any of the footnotes

did I find any mention
of the thousands of toys found in the ash & rubble
and I stopped doing yoga
when my next meditation led me

to a cemetery beside a schoolyard
where I heard children whispering from their graves:

Do not trust the fresh air.
Bad things rain from it.

Mystified

The daffodils hadn't yet found fissures
in the spring thaw when I pulled my Radio Flyer
down the block to the house with the little girl
with the eye patch. I had some magic to show her,

two tin cans connected by a lifeline that I could run
porch to porch. Invisible in the slot between siblings,
I turned early to giving my feelings to others,
outside my home. And so I told the eye patch girl
that I loved her, more a guess than a certainty.

Well, the treasured child of her parents had no need
whatsoever for the devotion of a boy
who had yet to earn his first dollar, drive his first car,
or even pass the second grade. My prospects
were good on that last item, despite frequent
bouts with the sniffles and swellings
common to all children, days home
spent dreaming of inroads into other hearts.

Perhaps she was holding out for an artist or a poet.
I wouldn't even know for many years what they
were, and had I known, I'd never have guessed why
she'd choose the likes of them,

over a tin can magician
who crooned words of undying love for her.

Jorge Guitart is a Cuban by birth and a Buffalonian by choice. He writes poetry in both his native Spanish and in English, and has been published in print and online in the United States, Latin America and Spain. He is the author of *The Empress of Frozen Custard and Ninety-Nine Other Poems* (Blaze-VOX, 2009), *Film Blanc* (Meow Press, 1996) and *Foreigner's Notebook* (shuffal-off books, 1993). He is represented in the Electronic Poetry Center at the University at Buffalo. Also published have been his translations into Spanish of U.S. poets (e.g. Robert Creeley and John Ashbery) and his translations into English of Latin American poets (e.g. José Kozer and Heberto Padilla). He holds a BA degree in psychology from George Washington University and MS and PhD degrees in linguistics from Georgetown University. He has taught Spanish linguistics at SUNY/ Buffalo since 1973 and is a full professor in the Department of Romance Languages and Literatures there. He is widely published in the field of linguistics. He is also an addict of Scrabble.

**Three Anecdotes on Types of Bones
Missing From Bodies**

1

The great anatomist Andreas Vesalius (1514-1564)
discovered that no executed criminal
had the so called Indestructible Bone in his body.
Since it was doctrine that everyone needed it
to be resurrected on Judgment Day,
the theologians of the time did not like Vesalius's finding.
They were famous for not having a tolerant bone in their bodies.

2

The young radiologist dreamed that his next door neighbor,
the Assistant Professor of French and Critical Theory
(whom he fancied) did not have
a physical bone in her body:
her whole skeleton was socially constructed.
He woke up in a sweat.

3

I am no anatomist or radiologist but I am certain that my beloved
does not have a dumb bone in her body, or a judgmental one,
or a ridiculous one.

Dear All

you are all that we are pleased with
and all that we call hallowed
and the helmets made of pith
and the coins that we have swallowed

you are the garden and the ditch
you are the warden and the snitch
you are what flows and what oozes
you are the wrecks and the cruises

you are the statues that we've kissed
and the chances that we've missed
you are the exquisiteness of bowls
and the tumor in most moles

you are the menace in a cyst
and the promise in the mist
you are the venom in the snake
and the flavor in the shake

you are the triumph of repair
and the syntax of despair
you are the buoyancy in a buoy
and the salt in the chop suey

you are the pro in the ballpark
and the con that fools the mark
you are the lace in what is laced
and the friend that is two-faced

you are the radiance in the moon
and the intentions of the goon
you are the power in a snack
and the beak that goes clack clack

you are the beauty in heliotropes
and of rifles with scopes
you are the glory of matadors
and the bad mood of janitors

you are the yearning and the learning
and the burning and the spurning
you are persuader and fine trader
and crusader and invader

Fragments of Skewed Reports

1
Love of country made him hate
everything else.

2
She became a catalyst in an equation
she could never escape from.

3
He asked his soul to be still
but it was he that became catatonic.

4
Did the heartache compare
to the toothache? No.

5
It took forever to admit into the hospital
the ones that had been caught in rapid fire.

6
Almost nothing could save a dying passion
except miraculous delusion.

7
They read between the lines
only to draw a blank.

8
The exploiters had two strikes against them
and three balls in their favor.

9
There were powerful signs of faith,
pathetic signs of hope,
and practically no signs of charity.

A Page from a Chronicle

In time we ran out of time. Reality was lurking everywhere,
except perhaps on our side of the controversy.
Someone in a distant moment in a distant place
in a forgiving mood that lasted seconds
said that faith and fate made a minimal pair
but only as sounds that reached our ears.
We were like bacteria in the gut—slaves to tradition.
I was trying to help, making some inroads,
but outroads had the upper hand, which was heavy,
like the heavy hand of tradition.
I felt like a specimen, which I was, as part of a long tradition
that kept elongating.
I remember a young figure, weeping, and saying to me,
"I will see you in the past, for I have no future."
I don't remember walking out of things that had been decades
in the making but I was reported doing that.
In those days nights were full of mistakes. At dusk lots of people
invariably started mediocre poems about the failing light.
There was a welter of information in which not a few had drowned.
I was the teacher who no one ever asked why the usual
label for desperados was missing a syllable.
I noticed that many more wonderers
had stopped wondering who had written the book of love.
One day some crazy person shouted at me from a balcony,
"You are in my prayers and you are messing them up!"
And then "My prayers are with you. Please return them!"
I ran away and went into the house. The Puzzle of Life,
the jigsaw puzzle about life on earth
was on the table, with only one piece missing
which would be found eventually under the table.
Later I did remember that the emperor had no clothes,
but he had run all the way to the bank, laughing, not exactly hysterically.

Mac S. Hammond, 1926-1997, was a poet, a professor emeritus of English and the director of the graduate program in creative writing at the State University of New York at Buffalo. He was the author of four volumes of poetry, *The Horse Opera and Other Poems* (1966); *Cold Turkey* (1969); *Six Dutch Hearts* (1978); and *Mappamundi: New and Selected Poems* (1989). In addition, he published several chapbooks and monographs as well as writing for magazines such as *The Paris Review, Poetry* and *Choice*. Three of his poems, "Thanksgiving," "Halloween" and "Once Upon a Time There Was a Man," were included in *Poetry 180*, an anthology of 180 contemporary poems, selected and introduced by Billy Collins. In 1980, Hammond was invited to the White House by President Jimmy Carter for a program honoring 200 American poets.

He became committed to a life of poetry while an undergraduate at the University of South Carolina (1944-1946), where he edited the university's literary magazine. After a stint in the Navy, he transferred to Sewanee because of its literary reputation, graduating in 1948. After a brief, unhappy time as a graduate student at the University of Minnesota ended after six months, he moved to Boston and applied to Harvard where he was accepted. His doctoral dissertation at Harvard, "Sound and Grammar in Wallace Stevens' 'The Man with the Blue Guitar'," was written under the direction of Reuben Brower and the linguist Roman Jakobson. While in Boston he became a member of The Poets' Theatre. His academic career as a teacher took him from Harvard to the University of Virginia, Case Western Reserve University, and finally, SUNY/Buffalo, where he taught for 30 years.

Before and during his retirement, a long-standing interest in the combination of poetry and other media led him to an involvement with a video collective in Buffalo, called Squeaky Wheel, of which he was president in the mid 1990's. Hammond made audio and video recordings, including *The Holidays*, a three-track tape comprising a selection of poems for simultaneous voices, which was recorded in 1968. He combined video art and poetry in videos that were shown in Buffalo, Chicago and San Francisco. He was cofounder of the Nickel City Poetry-Video Association.

Catching a Crab on Wednesday

My father was dying. Only the boat,
The boat we chartered for the annual
Picnic, was calm in smooth water.
Only ripples edged from our ship.
We were the center of the pool, the eye
Of a hurricane, wind that undid
The structures over the years others
Had built. And I was calm.
Only this, this only I can tell.
Only the agile oars, as the saying is,
Were, well-oiled, stuck in the locks.

Disappearing Acts

Dear Karl, I know your Uncle Ludwig
Adopted you, your father dead;
Seven years of litigation erased
Any tenderness he felt for you, nag,
Do this, don't that, everything had to be
Written down the way he wrote down
The Tempest Sonata, The Appassionata,
The Great Fugue dragged around
In his head for years, no time
To play ball or help you study.
Deaf you understood but that
Raving in the musicroom all the time --
No wonder you tried to hang yourself
In the outhouse, your suicide note
Seine Scheisse. I cut you down.
He never knew. Now I am glad
You have joined the hussars,
A corporal yet, and married this month,
Free, at last, from the Great Sounds
Of the Great Man.
                        Why do I write
From this asylum? You are among the boys
Whose fathers have gone mad or disappeared.

The Bride of Frankenstein I

Her seams hardly show where she was
Put together, the worst under her bodice
Where the heart of a little girl of 8
Was sunk into place. It is from there that
The haunting memory of the sourness
Of wild rhubarb, found only in the High Tatras,
Comes, which in her present state of full
Daughterhood she cannot explain, her brain
The brain of a bluestocking found dead
After a musicale at the Baron's castle.
She says, "Rhubarb," her voice like a violin.
She asks, "Father?" her voice like a trumpet.
And the Baron, the maker, tells her
To find in her husband--the monster nearby--
Her father, her brother, her friend.
There was probably some truth in that.

Charlottesville, Virginia

If I fell in the North Rivanna River,
Dropped from a bridge, dying as I fell,
My skin and blood and bones would float
Through Fluvanna County down to the James,
Drift from shore to red-clay shore,
And sweep into Richmond and on by.
Below Richmond I would join the tide
Where hard-shelled crabs click chop-stick claws
And quickly do away with flesh and blood.
Churned in the out-poured turmoil of the James,
My skeleton, joint-free, would scrape a path
Between Old Point Comfort and Willoughby Spit
To be engulfed at last in the large Atlantic flood.
But, before passing on, past Cape Henry, south,
I would take a trip. North at Buckroe Beach
My frame, inched back and forth in the tide,
Would beach and bleach bone-white in the sun.
I could wait for a storm: and, struggling free,
Edge on the mud-packed floor of Chesapeake Bay,
Past the swelling delta of the York,
And stop at the soft expanse of the Potomac.
There, poised between an equal ebb and flow,
My bones would catch in a sunken thicket of trees.
I might lie, tangled in twigs, a year, a century,
Before the tide would wear the trees away
And pull me twenty miles upstream toward the capital.
So close again to vast urbanity, my bones
Might wish to creep on hands and knees
Up to the moonlit, electric city
To perform an ultimate gesture. Absurd idea!
My spindly bones, polished till almost worn away,
Languid in water, with such desire
Would melt, dissolve, diffuse instead
And gush to the deepest mysteries of the sea.

Barbara Holender

is the author of four books of poetry, including *SHIVAH POEMS: Poems of Mourning*; *LADIES OF GENESIS*; *IS THIS THE WAY TO ATHENS?* (QRL 1996 award winner); and *OUR LAST BEST PERFECT DAY*. She has also written a children's book in Hebrew, *ANI CLI-ZE-MER*. Her poetry has appeared in various journals, including *The Literary Review*, *Prairie Schooner*, *Kerem* and *Jewish Women's Literary Annual*, and in numerous anthologies, including *Sarah's Daughters Sing*, *The Helicon Nine Reader*, *Lifecycles I* and *II*, *Which Lilith?* and *80 on the 80's*. Her essays have been printed in *Reform Judaism*, and in the anthology, *JEWISH MOTHERS TELL THEIR STORIES: Acts of Love and Courage*. Some of her poems have also been set to music. She is a native and resident of Buffalo, NY.

Our Last Best Perfect Day

Were you planning on leftovers? you asked
tearing into the devilled eggs, tunafish,
lox and bagels and brownies.
Not a morsel, I said, Eat up.
It's the last lunch we'll have
till your next school break.

You'd come to me with your poetry books
to share a part of you I'd never suspected.
I'd seen the bright turned-off kid,
the jock with the killer dimples.

But I sensed something hidden,
and I wanted to beat on your chest and cry
let me in! Now you'd just casually
opened the door. I had the key, I said,
I just didn't know where the lock was.

You showed me your favorite Ferlinghetti
and I read you that poem by Charles Bukowski—
"There's a bluebird in my heart
that wants to come out
but I'm too tough for him..."
We had all the time in the world.

But the very next day death came for you
riding a high-lift snowplow...
O my bluebird...
and I'm so tough, I'm so damn tough...
It scooped you out of my life
but I hung on.

It's a year now. You're still
hovering, I'm still conversing.
I haven't yet returned
to Ferlinghetti and Bukowski.
Your father isn't ready to share
your poems. So here we are, we two,
you on that side, I on this, with only
the finest thread of separation.
You left before life could do its worst
to you, and I'm here facing it down.
In a way, we're both winners.

Facing the End

Life, the rabbi said, is the shadow
of a bird in flight. The bird flies away,
the bird is gone, the shadow is gone.

Mother, wings spread, you wait,
the greeting grown stale upon your lips.
Death does not oblige.
There's nothing left of me, you wail,
it's all gone, I'm nothing.
No, I say, surprising both of us,
it's all here, in me.

At once your whole life's energy
informs my blood, that woman bond.
How much I bear of you who bore me,
standing in the shadow of your flight,
imprinted with your bright trajectory.

Standing In Front Of the Met Looking Up
On a Night Unseasonably Cold

A crowd   silent   frozen
backs to the murals of Chagall
blazing through the foyer windows
to fountains of crystal chandeliers,
everyone looking up toward
that roof across Broadway.

This is New York, I think,
there's a jumper up there.
But no one shouts Jump!
or Don't jump! Maybe someone just
looked up at nothing and pretty soon
a crowd was looking up too.

I look up at nothing.
A smudge in the sky. What?
Lunar eclipse. Total.
says the stranger next to me.

Through my opera glasses
a dim sphere, smokey lavender,
silver lightly rounding
from the left—an alien ship
hanging over Broadway.
Oh dangerous world.

Maybe the sphere will discharge
hundreds of little men in bowler hats
drifting down on umbrellas.
Maybe someone is right now
working the pockets of all the watchers
waiting for the moon to come round.

Eppur si muove
>   (but still, it moves)
>   *Galileo Galilei*

Forget about the books and charts, drawings, proofs,
telescopes, the multitudinous experiments, letters,
approbations, condemnations

it's worth a trip to Florence
just to see that imperishable relic—
Galileo's right middle finger
enshrined in a gilded crystal cup
atop a marble pedestal
inscribed with reverential verses
in the Museum of the History of Science.

What glory! Galileo Galilei forever
giving the finger to the Pope,
the Inquisition, all of history
for the 350 years it took
to set things right.

His students knew he had the goods,
and the craven dons who pursed their lips
and let him take the rap,
till cowed and broken he caved in.
As one translator has it,
"He was reduced to Hush."
Yet legend says that, sotto voce,
he held his ground
and dreamed of vindication.

Thus inspired, I dream that dream.
Perched on his rolling sphere
I dream I am that butterfly
whose wingbeat sets off a typhoon
halfway around the world.

Speeding starward on a phrase
I dream I hoist a gorgeously
bejeweled enameled claw
to every editor who ever rejected me—
you know who you are—

Relic that I am, I dream I end
upstuck in a gilded crystal inkwell
pedestalled upon a marble book,
the poet's essence, defiantly
reductio ad digitum.

Anne Huiner is a writer and sometimes actor, whose poetry draws from a variety of work and volunteer experience. For two years she taught the Writing and Well Being workshop at the Erie County Mental Health Association. She also designed and oversaw "Across the Lines: Poets Respond to Discrimination," the first event in the nation to combine National Poetry Month with National Fair Housing Month. She was a member of Ice 9, a poetry performance group, and she wrote and acted in the poetry/ performance pieces, "Grace in a Mutilated World" (2010) and "Poetic Justice" (with ModDance Company, 2015 Infringement Festival). She is a member of a women's writing group that has been going strong for over 30 years despite its lack of a name. She also hosts The Spiritual Café at St. John's Grace Episcopal Church.

Rousseau's Tiger

Outside the rain is steady and strong.
The flowers do not raise their heads, but bow them, beaten.
Still, the rain soaks their thirsty roots and they continue. Shining.
What color is the rain? It is no color really
yet through the window, the no color changes
with the light
grey to pearl to silver
to purple-y blue-black as a bruise
landing.

This rain will be here all day. This rain

Is a magic rain, a cleansing rain
a streak down the windows rain
a recalling how green
green can be rain
or yellow or red and how strong
the strands of a web can be, straining
under the weight of rain. Everything shines
and you know
when you walk across that lawn
you shine too.

Can you paint the rain?
Rousseau did. A tropical rain, a grey scrim

behind which a tiger is crouching, fierce and bright
as orange jewels in a deep of green. As if
behind the rain, the essence of fire. Would you call
to this tiger would you
walk through the rain to the other side
or would you stay
safe on this side of the canvas
aching in a place you cannot name.

Aliens

The house of God is locked for the night.
On the stone steps
a congregation of the homeless sleeps
in a kingdom of cardboard boxes

Pieta

After a photo by W. Eugene Smith

Sometimes I give birth to poems
so bloody and strange
it's hard to believe they came from me.

Yet they emerge   naked and twisted
truthful as that photograph of the Japanese mother
bathing her poisoned daughter.

She hadn't known when she bore down at last
and felt the crowning of her perfect child
this child was already marked

to be a witness.   And golden
as her skin is
there will never be enough to stretch across

the bones of her face
the sockets of her sightless eyes
her useless limbs, the ribs

protecting her insistent heart. How perfectly the light
directs our attention to the mother's face.
We see over time

how this life transformed her. The tender way
she shields her daughter's back
from the hard edge

of the washtub while with the other hand
she lifts the water to bathe her child's face.
We cannot know

nor do we ever see
the months of darkroom labor
the photographer spent

to get this just right
to lead us to wonder
what we can do to recognize grace
in this our mutilated world.

Carrying over

Sometimes   when we speak
to each other   it's like that book
of poems   and translations
laid out   on two pages
one side   my language
                     on the other
the original thought in the original tongue

What dialogue   I wonder
is possible   between one
and another   What carries over
and what is left   behind

S. M. Hutton has been published in [*the advancing idiom*], *Artvoice*, *The Buffalo News* – Spotlight: Poetry, *Brigid's Fire* and *NO-MAD-Art+Word from the Buffalo Herd*. She was the winner of the 2006 Arthur Axlerod Memorial Award for poetry. She received her BA from SUNY at Buffalo, NY in Media Study. Until 1995, she studied and worked as an independent video and film production artist. In 2011, she worked as a co-organizer of the inaugural annual global movement, 100,000 Poets for Change, and the event in Buffalo, NY. She lives in Williamsville, NY.

The Post-Modern Shaman

conjures.
(A ride to the give and take creak of saddle leather.)
Hooves step carefully over a place
in an eerie primordial mud where a very
strange anemic plant branches
under the thick thatch of last season's grasses.
A hoof sucks at the same mud the odd plant roots in.

This is no crossword puzzle,
there's no way to make it come out neatly.

Grasping at spring gnats,
there are two suns in the plant's heaven.

On a Photograph by Mimi

Purchased on the eve of
disease in black and white

geometry: a dry Central Park
drinking fountain

viewed from overhead
as in the guise of bird or

God.

Face thrust into a beam
(skewed from the internal shadow)

which illuminates across
the frame and

reveals motes rushing
flickering bright,

normal,

out—

scintilla novas known
like the dark side of

the moon, there
though unseen.

At first glance
none yet has guessed
the concrete subject.

Positions

At five years old I thought
I could never do that.

The corps de ballet dancer
fell, and scrambled
to dance again. What can be said of
an arabesque?

One heel pressed firm
to the boards. The other extended
back
from a flexed hip, straightened knee.
Attitude of the body describes
forty-five or ninety degrees.

A missile or a rafter.

Arms grace
oppositional
before and behind. Head high
the mass of the self flows.

Another means of displacing air
with aplomb.

Louisiana Suite: Crude
(20 April 2010, Gulf of Mexico)

I. Sweet

  Tell me
About the rain
lilacs in Ankara
and no way to get there
but with boundless desire:
A pomegranate nestled
among sour and rotting
garlic, onions and potatoes.

I'm remembering the thought
and not the thing itself
amid the crazy chaotic struggles
with dangerous gifts.

II. Crude

  No sound
from the seabird beached
in a delicious, dripping chocolate shroud.
The seabed hemorrhages black,
and rust with the stain
of ancient bloods, corpses
of millennia long dead
flora and fauna: extinction's poison.

Corporate creatures perform serial deceptive
speech acts as the sky deposits a systematic
distribution of Corexit-laden
condensation on thirsty lands.

III. There is order in a graveyard.

Olga Karman teacher, poet and memoirist—is the author of two books of poetry, *Adios* and *Border Crossings*. Her poems have appeared in *The Nation*, *The New Republic* and many anthologies. Her verse has been set in tile in Buffalo's subway system. She was a professor of Spanish Language and Literature at D'Youville College for more than two decades and served as the college director of community affairs.

Olga was born in Havana of Cuban and American parents. When Fidel Castro's regime came to power in 1959, she sympathized with the aims of the revolution, but when Castro cancelled elections and established his dictatorship, she left Cuba for the United States to marry her American fiancé. She attended Connecticut College, graduating summa cum laude, and then entered Harvard as a Woodrow Wilson Fellow and earned her PhD in Spanish language and literature. After moving to Buffalo, she taught Spanish at Nichols School before accepting a faculty position at D'Youville.

In 1997, she returned to Cuba after 37 years, and she vividly recalled the experiences of her return, and of her exile and her struggle to make a new life in America, in the much heralded memoir, *Scatter My Ashes Over Havana*, published in 2006. In 2010, she published a book of fiction, *A Woman of Some Years*, which was based on her memories of Cuba and America.

Shadow On Stone

On the granite steps
the shadow of the person sitting there
that morning in Hiroshima.

And on the day I left Cuba
my friends died.
Raúl died in his blue sailboat.
Alvaro died
as he brought his violin to his chin
and began to read the first notes
on the yellowed page.
Elvira died
knocking at the door of a safe house.
Evelio died dancing without me.

Sometimes
after twenty-five years:
a voice on the telephone,
or a letter under the door,
or a tape of Alvaro
playing Brahms.
The applause goes through me
like a gunshot.

In a secret place
in this house, in the dark,
shadow and shadow and shadow,
I gather us together
into the first small seed.

Crossing Harvard Yard

Speck of life
how deep you burrowed all fall.
Well into December
you nudged and fluttered,
you made known the outline
of a tiny fist or foot
while Professor Finley
lectured on the *Iliad*.

Achilles' choice, he said, is ours.
Which one shall it be — long inglorious life
or the brief but luminous hero's path?

Bundled up, I made my way home
a little off balance
weighted down with you and my briefcase
wondering what would become of me now.
Gravida, I said under my breath, *gravida*.
And a delicate push from within
gentle as a shower of petals
in a spring orchard
weakened me with awe.

Is there a different glory
in yielding to another's life,
I wanted to ask, and will I know
when I see you crown
in the doctor's high mirror
when I hear you break into the day
with your first cry for air?

Couscous

Morning song
of mortar and pestle
on strong cumin seed.

(I'm bringing you lunch)

Sweet song of red currant

(Your house will be white)

Cinnamon bark for fragrance

(Your dogs will run to my hands)

Aroma of turmeric from China or India

(Damp fieldstones the path)

Tomatoes: pulp, juice, and seeds

(From the porch
the finches will sing)

The sharpness of scallions

(The house will be dark
It has been a wet fall.
In the rooms,
the spirits of leaves
remembrance of rain.
From your windows,
the sheep
puffs of clouds)

Smell, I will say, the cumin.
Let the grains
slip through your hand.
Prayer beads, bits of sand.

We will taste. We will quicken
the beams in your house.
The floor boards and sills
will come level and plumb.

Come and Be Born

Come and be born.
It is early spring on the island,
and the deer have made a path
to your own back door.
Look up at the spruces
green and silver against cobalt blue.

Come with me at low tide and
visit with the starfish, the hollow crab shells
as thin as paper rolling on the sand.
Call to the fish in the ocean,
bring them to the surface,
count them and name them.

We will walk in the neighbor's garden.
This time of year the big houses are empty.
We can rest on the stone bench
under the statue of Buddha and listen
to the bamboo leaves while we wait
for darkness to cover the smooth pebbles.

I will show you Van Gogh's starry night
--opals, he called them, emeralds,
lapis, rubies, sapphires.

I will sing you
the starry night song.

Norma Kassirer grew up in Hamburg, NY and was educated and experienced as a social worker. She was well known for both her art and her writing. Among her books is *Magic Elizabeth* (The Viking Press, 1966), a children's book now considered a classic, which has been reprinted many times and currently appears worldwide in the Breakfast Serials series. Her other books include a novel for children, *The Doll Snatchers* (The Viking Press, 1969); a story collection, *The Hidden Wife* (shuffaloff books, 1991); a story cycle, *Milly* (Buffalo Ochre Papers, 2008); and her novella, *Katzenjammered* (BlazeVOX, 2010). In 2013, she was selected for the esteemed UB Poetry Collection's Three Poems series. Her poetry and short fiction have been published in *Angle of Repose, Between C&D, Blatant Artifice, MSS, TEXTS, Sow's Ear, Yellow Edenwald Field,* and elsewhere.

Her artwork has been exhibited at Betty's Restaurant and at the Western New York Book Arts Collaborative for the release of *Katzenjammered*. She also made beautiful, unique handmade artist's books, one of which is owned by the Albright-Knox Art Gallery. She often painted at the MollyOlga studio and taught classes there and through the Poets in the Schools program. She and her husband Earle were involved with Hallwalls from its beginnings on Essex St, where she painted murals on the ceiling.

She died on February 17, 2013. Her collected works, *Minnows Small As Sixteenth Notes,* edited by Ann Goldsmith and Edric Mesmer, came out in 2015 from BlazeVOX.

The Moving Architecture of the Japanese Fan

1

A large Victorian birdhouse depicts
in miniature the vanished buildings
of an entire urban waterfront, certain
details of each structure sacrificed
to the necessary compression of so
much bygone busyness.

2

Stationed on a tall post, the birdhouse,
closed on its own dreaming self, leaves
no room for entry to the increasingly
skeptical birds cruising the bright sky of
this first warm day of spring.

Meantime,

3
in a nearby souvenir shop, a one-&-
a-half by two-inch cellophane packet
containing faded blocks of pressed paper
lost in a crack between counters for
seven years, (a fate which made
unrealizable

4
for all that time the simple magic of a
glass of water which might have released
the small conceit's potential for brief
flowering) is on this same sunny morning
discovered & placed outside for the
efficient trash collection.

5
A Japanese girl is seated downshore
on a restaurant porch overlooking the
winkling water containing an antique
ship moored at lake's edge, sails folded.
Thus reduced to a statue of itself, the
ship can only hint a past now playing

6
as billowing cartoon in the head of the
thirteen year old boy seated at ship's
wheel. Harboring in his throat since last
Thursday his vanished father's voice, he
is playing at being a boy happily pretend-
ing to steer a ship he knows to be immov-

7
able. Earlier, this boy observed the
birdhouse, commiserated with the
cruising birds & began to follow the
Japanese girl, whose cashmere sweater
depicting the careers of a number of
rock stars greatly intrigued him, &

8
when the packet landed on the trash heap
he was there to rescue it with the pointed
end of a driftwood stick, for the sake of
the lettering in characters on its label & the

heroic gesture involved in its rescue. Now
he is watching the girl on the porch who is

9
sipping a bright red liquid by straw
from a plastic bottle. A delicate girl,
with slender wrists & expressive hands,
she's managing, between sips, a large
unwieldy sandwich. Her hair is straight
& shiny black & a crow in similar feath-

10
er sits behind her on the porch rail. The
girl's wide silver bracelet sifts a reflective
scrolling & unscrolling of exultant birds
as she coolly appraises the Asian man
who has joined her at the table.
The boy is

11
increasingly certain that she is a movie
star whose name he can't recall. Now
she is removing her sweater which she
allows to slither down her back as she
continues talking. The sweater slips to
the floor beside her chair in the folds of

12
its vanishing narrative. A tall man wearing
a black cape next appears in front of her,
facing the boy as if from a stage. Long
bright feathers in red green & blue pro-
trude from the man's pockets along with
chains of paper origami animals. The

13
man, who may be a magician, is blocking
the boy's view of the Japanese girl.
Shouting children surround the man,
clamoring for the origami, pulling it from
his deep pockets & laughing.
The boy stands up, hoping to keep

14
the girl in sight. He waves the driftwood
stick & shouts, but she's gone, might have
become one of the frolicking children.

The man's now spinning in a self-obliter-
ating whirl, his cape grown wing-like,
& in the moment when the boy, mid-

15
gesture, watches the tiny packet as it falls
into the lake, the man & all the children
disappear, leaving the porch unpeopled.
The boy sits at the stopped wheel again,
feeling greatly at a loss. As paper
flowers begin to open in the lake,

16
bright feathers, ignored by the children,
lift & float away. Birds deftly claim the
feathers for their nests, perhaps to present
at the compressed Victorian birdhouse,
which may unfold to admit a bird or two.
So dreams the intrepid boy,

17
still at the wheel of the stalled ship
that's now tipping in a rising wind.
Grown skeptical as a cruising bird, he
rejects the cheap notion that the very
large crow soaring overhead, followed
by a chain of small birds, signifies

18
anything. & yet he knows it's true
as litmus that deep in the lake
those paper flowers
are encountering
some extremely attractive
seaweeds.

Michael Kelleher is the author of *Human Scale* and *To Be Sung*, both from Blaze-VOX. Another collection, *Visible Instruments*, is forthcoming from Chax Press. Recent poems have appeared in *Sentence: A Journal of Prose Poetics* and the *Colorado Review*. From 1998-2012 he worked as the Associate and Artistic Director of Just Buffalo Literary Center, where he founded the popular literary series, *Babel* and *Big Night*. He currently works as the Program Director of the Windham Campbell Literature Prizes at Yale University.

But Do They Suffer?

I hadn't asked myself the question yet,
But then I read that essay, the one where
The late David Foster Wallace describes
In objective detail his moral qualms
About boiling lobsters, not of eating meat,
Crustaceans, or poultry, per se,
Just the specifics of boiling alive
A living creature that, it has been said,
Feels nothing, and where either sense of "feels"
Can be assumed, that is, it feels no pain,
Either emotional or physical,
Once it's been dropped in the pot, it just boils,
Or rather slowly becomes something else,
A light, fluffy, delicate entree served
With melted butter in a dipping cup,
So delicious, I remember my first
Time eating lobster as a boy, we sat
In a fire hall in a place called Freedom,
New Hampshire, it was summer, our family
Of five plus our cousins from Brooklyn
Escaping city swelter, my uncle
Brought a cassette tape with the soundtrack to
Star Wars, or so he said, but it was fake,
Not the real deal, they used synthesizers,
My father scolded me for saying so,
I remember crying after the slap,
Standing alone at the edge of the woods,

Staring into the darkness, wishing I
Or he were dead, I mean, like, what the fuck,
It wasn't the music we'd heard in the film,
My favorite film, BTW, whose
Release was to that point the most exciting
Event of my short, uneventful life,
I mean, it's Luke Freaking Skywalker, Dad,
Don't you get it, either it's the real thing
Or it's some shabby imitation, like
This synthesized falsehood calling itself
Music, a reminder also that life
Might be itself an imitation of
A perfect order that's forever out
Of reach, like in that quote from Kafka,
Further proof (to me, at least) that his sense
Of the real can be trusted, like the taste
Of lobster, to bring pleasure, but also
A sense there might be something else beneath
The surface of what we're consuming,
As sweet as it tastes, as soft as it feels
As it melts on the tongue going down,
Like that first time in Freedom, I recall
That while we ate we listened to a man
Tell jokes, he looked a bit like Milton Berle,
His jokes were vaguely racist imitations
Of Chinese proverbs, told with fake Chinese
Accent, front teeth Mickey-Rooneyed over
Lower lip, "Confucius say, he who eat
jelly bean fart in living color," or
"He who fart in church sit in his own pew,"
We laughed as we dipped our fresh Maine lobsters
In the butter sauce, God did they taste good,
It was as if I'd been eating the
Synthesizer-equivalent of food
My entire life, the flavor, the texture,
Everything about it, though I've eaten
Lobster many times since then, it hasn't
Ever tasted quite so good, as if I
Can recognize a few scattered fragments
Of the lobster in my memory, but
I can't find a way to bring it to life
In all its fullness (Kafka again), like
When I read as a child that my idea
Of God, which I'd learned about from my mom,
Was actually a memory, carried
Over from a previous life, which left
In its wake an idea of perfection

To which I should aspire, and of course fail,
Leaving in pieces my perfect idea,
Which I've tried to put together, and failed,
Producing at best a cubist image,
As in the "Nude Descending a Staircase,"
Like how once you're told the title you see
The staircase, the descent, perhaps the nude,
But you always wonder whether or not
Duchamp is really just fucking with your head,
Leading you away from the truth, the real,
And you crane your neck around to catch it,
And all you see is the flicker of shadows
Dancing across the walls of your cave,
They're beautiful, don't you think? I could stare
At them forever, forgetting that they,
Too, are imitations thrown up by fire
To distract me, and why the hell not?
This is what struck me about that question
In the title of the poem, which comes from
Richard Dawkins, the famous atheist,
Who posed it not to meat eaters, but to
Those whose philosophical systems
Place homo sapiens at the center
Of creation, thereby relegating
Animals to their second-class status,
Allowing for cruel, senseless practices
Such as branding, castration without
Anaesthetic, and bullfighting which, he says,
We would never inflict on human beings,
Most of us, anyhow, because we know
They would suffer physically, nevertheless
We allow such to occur, assuming
Either that animals do not suffer
Or that their suffering is not like ours, is
Of a lesser kind, cannot be perceived
Outside itself, therefore, for example,
As David Foster Wallace stated, we
Boil the lobster alive because we think
It doesn't feel, but evidence does exist
That seems to prove the contrary true, that
Banging its claws against the pot is not
An involuntary response, but can
And should be read as an expression of
Pain, as in, Ouch, that shit is hot, stop it,
Stop it stop it stop it stop it it hurts,
But if we felt like that we'd all go mad
With guilt over our own barbarity,

We might even follow the path of Foster
Wallace and have done with thinking for good,
Tie a rope to a transom and end it,
Just like that, leaving a pile of finished
Books and unfinished manuscripts behind,
The Pale King, I think it was called, did I
Tell you I met David Foster Wallace?
I drove him around town, took him to lunch,
We talked about Aristotle, he said
He thought I looked like actor Greg Kinnear,
I went home and looked on the Internet
For a photo and when I found one stared
Until I thought I could see a resemblance.

The Librarian

Circling around the island again and
Again. This should be filed under 'Sappho.'
It was one of those places I'm not sure
Existed. I can picture it upstairs
In the bookcase at our last house. Later,
We sat in my car, gossiping. He seemed
To have come out of the womb performing these
Grown-up tasks. I remember everything
Perfectly. My mind drifted as my eyes
Scanned the titles on the theory shelf. This
Went on for several years. A lover (man),
His love interest (woman), her pet sparrow.
Having cut my teeth on the difficult,
I put it in my pocket and walked out.
I stole lines, ideas, images, rhythms,
A voiceless glottal positive. Lifted,
Reshaped. An overwhelming feeling of
Heartbreak. Prose is too noisy a medium.
I want the writer to do something more
Than simply hold the mirror up. I want
Her to go way out. Then he saw and then
I saw and he said something like, Oh lord.
The struggles of the martyrs, yawn, these words
Are secretly dedicated to them.
And here's the famous windmill scene, Dear Heart.
I hope to sleep tonight and then begin
A mythopoetic excavation
In the morning. I want to dig it up.
It befalls us to wonder on this first
Astonishment. I have so many thoughts,

Most of them idle. I have a feeling
This is a gift, but I can't remember
Who might have given it to me. We spoke
Of how we'd often been in the same place
Without ever having met. He had been using
An oxygen tank. I never thought him
A tarot card kind of guy. We painted
And sang and danced and listened to stories.
The rest, as they say, is history, of
Which I can only read so much before
My eyes get bleary. The luxuriant
Beauty of the orange garden bears witness
To antiquity. He felt compelled to
Address it every time. Eventually
I discovered I preferred writing to
Generating text, an on-again-off
-again friendship, never quite requited.
I am standing before a wall of words.
My hair is pulled back in a ponytail
And I am wearing gold. How awed I feel.
I couldn't write another phrase. And then
The feeling of having been sitting through
An apocalypse. Three times begun and thrice
Have I failed. I don't think it is a sign
I'm losing steam, having as it does the feel
Of something very much still in process.
We stopped at a seafood shack by the road.
We played poker and yammered all night long.
I never could concentrate on my work.
I found him in his chair. He listened slowly
And closely. I thought of the woman on
The cover of the book of film theory,
Standing near the expressionistic door.
Someone somewhere shouted out my name.
An endless progression spiraling back
Into the genetic past. The empty
Marketplace, the weeds rising like fireworks
Through the floor, the character of a man
Divined by reading the shape of his hands,
Community gardens, luxury homes,
A former factory complex, the word
'Quonset,' the absence of time, the frantic
Planting of vegetables, the hitting of
The road, the one we always seem to hit,
The memory of old books behind glass doors,
Protected from the dust, or most of it,
The dog, its ears, the faint sound of riffling.

Loren Keller was born in WNY in 1930, and has always lived here. He has published six books of poetry, including *No Songs But Whispers* (1969), *The Skier and the Snow* (1978), *Warm Brooms* (1979), *As I Might Hold a Bird* (1983) and his 550-page *Evening Everything: The Collected Poems of Loren Keller* (Harborage Press, 2005), which includes poems written over a period of 50 years. He was a featured writer in the first edition of *Beyond Bones*, and has collaborated with the artist Robert Freeland on a book called *The Shore You Reach*. He has written a novel, *Four and Twenty Bluebeards* (1999), and ten plays, including *What Dreams May Come* (1986), *Walt Whitman, Oscar Wilde* (1988), *I Am Walt Whitman* (1989), *No Spartan Shield* (1990), *First Snow, Last Snow* (1991), *The Dazzling Traveling Chopin Show* (1992), *Blues For Lloca* (1993), *The Gift Of the Magi (adaptation)* (2001) and *It's a Wonderful Life (adaptation)* (2002). He has also written many literary essays.

To Silence

Once upon a time there seemed
nothing more to say. You had
become our native tongue;
all our teachers dead but you.
We looked for you, but knew
it was best not to find you.
Like a found star, you might
have had to be named. And
namelessness seemed so
important here. Some had
gone to other worlds where
language still was used. But we
stayed here wrapped in your
veil, each one alone, deaf even
to the others' breathing. We
trusted eye, not ear; felt privileged
to study faces, mirrors, sunlight,
rainbows. We developed a vision
of amazing clarity, found something
closer to peace than we'd ever
had before. Where did it go? Where
did it go? Where everything goes
that starts out "once upon a time."

When They Flew Away

Many birds: tiny, and
black from here: rising
suddenly from the same
tree and scattering off
into small bushes all
over the meadow. He has
just begun to notice
birds, to really see
them, after years of
thinking he was looking
at them. Is there a way
to put a world back
together? It isn't like
a puzzle, cut precisely
by a jigsaw, fragmented
in a pattern, the pieces
cut to fit, each to each,
together, back into the
whole. No, when a world
explodes, some pieces are
destroyed forever, or
mutilated beyond recognition.
And some are like those
birds: scattered suddenly
into new places, new
surroundings. And he
doesn't know how they
were arranged in that
first tree. He never
looked closely enough
at them. He only started
to notice them when they
flew away in all directions.
He can wander through the
wreckage, picking up
tiny pieces of his world,
holding them in his hands
as he might hold a bird,
to know it in a way he
never did before: the
warmth and tremble of it,
the needing to be free,
the shivering awareness
of minuteness, fragility,
mortality.

Recurring Dream

The old dream about the class
I never teach because I never
find the classroom. I'm all over
the building in that dream, and it
always seems more like the tired
old school I went to as a kid than one
where I ever was a teacher. It even looks
familiar - very old but well kept-up.
If dreams had smells, I'd tell you in
a second whether this is my old K-6.
Without that oiled-and-varnished
old wood smell, I can't be sure.

My hometown simplified some things:
I went to church on Church Street,
and I went to school on School Street,
in an already-old (then) building
called School Street School. I've had
this dream a hundred times (Does every
teacher have one like it?) I walk through
the dark halls and up and down the worn
old stairs as aimlessly as if I'd never been
in any school before. Where the heck did
they put my classroom? No numbers on the
doors, but that's all right, I don't remember

my room's number anyway. I half expect
the principal's voice to boom out of the walls
"Mr. Keller, report to the front office right
away." But no, the school is absolutely silent.
No voices from the classrooms as I pass. No
bells ringing for a start or end. Sometimes I
find the room but it's locked, and no key.
Sometimes the door's open, but it's an empty
room: not just no students, but no desks, no
chalkboards, no resemblance to a classroom.

On a rare dream night there really is a class
inside. I recognize them all, of course, as
complete strangers! And the kids – they think
that I must be another substitute, and I do not
try to explain.

This Place She Returns To
(Marguerite Duras at Trouville)

This place she returns to, the vast apartment
suspended above the sea, the golden late
afternoon light, falling straight down from
the sun, the sand unfolding as far as her eyes
can see, the sound of the breakers, the high-
pitched cries of the gulls, the memory-piercing
night sending echoes, traces, all the way back
to her sorrow-mad childhood, night helping
the words flow; keeping up her writing's
constant momentum.

Sometimes, through the high windows, you can
make out her silhouette, stocky but fragile,
bundled in old sweaters, pushing aside worn
curtains. She is a legend here, like Piaf in Paris,
people nudge one another; "Duras up there, it's
Duras." Admirers come by, leave letters for her
with the caretaker, some sneak up to the second
floor, leave in front of her door some object,
some book, some picture.

As she drives her little car along the narrow road
that hugs the coast, she almost tastes the light,
must seek out again her not-forgotten casino
ballroom, pure white, door opening onto the beach.
This place she returns to, often alone, sometimes
with a lover, they drink too much, she drinks too
much, but she keeps on writing, working, reworking,
her intelligence penetrates the hidden night, the
close presence of the sea, she writes here to the
very end, writes from a need anchored in her gut,
and in her heart, the tide changing, the going and
coming of the sea, helping her words flow.

Charles Burchfield: Orion in Winter

Midnight midwinter
earth and sky
are stars and frost
Sir you designed
the sky to bring
the constellations close
and real
and set the whole
white universe in motion
made frosted earth
in five days less
than God
and wrote the sky
new winter's tales
the stars your
rhythms crossing creasing
skies of yours   the restless
spirits of the breaking
winter stars cold fires
hard frozen leaps of blue-
white flame   Orion and
Orion and Orion
icy stars are
sticking to our eyes
icicling down our spines
down your raw white
tall rock of earth
beneath your wheeling
world of sky

Ageless

"When I grow too old to dream,
I'll have you to remember..."

I'm feeling ageless
today, one in a series
of sunshiny June mornings.
My mother, who was 87
the month before Mother's
Day, comes slowly to the
breakfast table, using
her walker. "The music is
pretty," she says. I must
have it on loud: she can't
hear well. We both look
out the kitchen windows
as we eat our cereal.
The white perennial roses
are blooming, the ones
my father planted long
before he died ten years
ago at 82. The music is
my oldest classical
record: I bought it over
thirty years ago. "That's
Segovia," I tell my mother,
"playing guitar. He died
yesterday. He was 94."
He's playing a passacagli
and corrente by Frescobaldi,
who'd be four hundred four
years old this year. And
I remember years and years
ago my mother's favorite
song was "When I grow too
old to dream." I wonder
if she dreams now. I wonder
how I'll feel if I should
grow too old to...well, to
hear soft music play; too
old to... remember. But
today I'm feeling ageless

Joyce Kessel is a member of *Earth's Daughters,* and her poems have recently appeared in *spitballmag.com, The Healing Muse, Beyond Bones II,* and Kind of a Hurricane Press' anthology of Barbie poems. Locally, she is included in the WNY Peace Center's anthology, *Waging Words for Peace: Buffalo Poets Against War,* and *Nickel City Nights.* She teaches literature, writing, fine arts, and interdisciplinary courses at Villa Maria College. She has written three books, *Secret Lives, Describing the Dark* (Saddle Road Press, 2013) and *Classroom Ouixote* (The Writer's Den, 2015).

At Abiquiu

I stand where she gazed at the horizon
sacred vibrations just beyond my reach
unsure if this is real in front of me
The familiar hills in the distance red & dusty
the almost unseen remnants of tree and bone
vibrant as her canvasses
more alive there in her eye
than in my own amazement

Intonations

Dad was always a lecturer,
a pontificator at meals
of righteous opinions & insights,
a walking compendium of minutia
like train schedules & routes,
the keeper of funeral logs & other passings.
His newspapers were mined & shredded,
articles & columns catalogued
for redistribution in overstuffed # 10 envelopes
with single-spaced 8-10 carbon-copied missives.

So we learned to eat quickly,
avoiding questions or clarifications,
and pitied the letter carriers who
delivered his epistles,
answered the confused telephone calls
from correspondents who could not decode
or follow his thoughts,
& believed we'd have to nail his coffin shut
to keep him from having the very last word.

Buffalo Icons

It serves me right for falling in love
with men whose names begin with M:
Milton, Manny & Michael,
seduced by their passion and their work.
Each month the bells toll
for these local masters
whose artistry transcends
geography and generations.

Milton, the photographer
of steel mills & Chilean peasants,
Neruda with a camera,
revealing families at toil
in homes and in factories,
preserving dignity in their faces.

Manny, our radical dramatist,
elder theater statesman and rabble-rouser,
labor-organizer whose gentle demeanor
belied his fire and taught us
the power of endurance
and persistence under McCarthy's madness.

And Michael, whose claims to fame
go beyond discoveries & open mics,
our musician of the people,
sharing the stage so generously,
giving us Ani and other poets
whose lyrics and faces outshone his.

Three who passed too soon
regardless of their ages
icons of this Rustbelt City:
Rogovin, Fried & Meldrum
lost in this endless winter.

Gunilla T. Kester is the author of *Mysteries I-XXIII* (2011) and *Time of Sand and Teeth* (2009), which was published by Finishing Line Press as a part of its New Women's Voices Series, and was nominated for both a Pushcart Prize and the Jean Pedrick Chapbook Award. She is coeditor of *The Empty Chair, Love and Loss in the Wake of Flight 3407* (2010) and *The Still Empty Chair, More Writings Inspired by Flight 3407* (2011). Her CD, *Songs of Healing and Hope*, with her dear friend, Cantor Susan Wehle, whom she lost in Flight 3407, was released in 2007.

Her full-length manuscript, *Shiri's Piano*, was a finalist for the May Swenson Poetry Award 2009. *The Mountain: Grieving for Harmony* was a finalist for the Colorado Prize for Poetry in 2005. Her poem, "Shiri's Piano," won an International Publishers Prize from *Atlanta Review* and was published in its International Issue, October, 2008. Her poem, "This Time of Sand and Teeth," won the Gival Press Tri-Language English Poetry Award in 2001, and she has been a finalist in The Glimmer Train Open. She has poems in *Waging Words for Peace: Buffalo Poets Against War*, *Poetic Voices Without Borders* and *Poetic Voices Without Borders 2*, winner of the 2009 National Best Book Award for Fiction & Literature: Anthologies, sponsored by USA Book News.

She is a native of Sweden, and has published many poems in Swedish anthologies and magazines, including *Bonniers Litterära Magasin*, Sweden's most prestigious literary magazine. A Fulbright scholar, she authored a scholarly study entitled *Writing the Subject: Bildung and the African American Text*, and published many articles in academic journals and anthologies. She is also an accomplished guitarist and teaches Classical Guitar at the Amherst School of Music.

Spires and Tunnels

I was born in the shadow of a mighty church
old as the town itself, and as gray.
Two tall spires stretched toward the sky
like the legs of a lovesick woman;
she taught us about longing, about love, being poor
and human, wanting what you can't have.

Now in your modern American city I write
to salute your spirit of surprise, the random core
of poets, the loyal hope of lovers.
Here things lead downward to the heart,
down to the river, down south, down to you,
and down to me too in the subway tunnel.

I stand now between two gods, belong to both
even when they quarrel. Here I will read you
not from front to back like a scholar of serious intent
or from back to front like a daughter of Israel,
but like a poet I invite the irradiant irreverence
of inconsistency and coincidence.

Shiri's Piano

You hold the chords like my grandfather
held spring wheat in his gnarled hand,
a big hand and strong, yet it caressed
the silky kernels so gently that they whispered to him
all their dreams of tallness and sunshine and growth

and you break the chords and scatter
the kernels over the dark earth
like he did and they grow and grow
until they reach our mouths
and we can taste their hard nuttiness
warm between our teeth

and they grow in your field until they reach
our noses and we smell again the fires
that licked the dry sticks and leaves, turned old to new,
covered fields in smoke, hid the mystery
of yet another spring, the hunger of our childhood

and they grow until they tickle our ears
and make us laugh with pure happiness
and hear again my grandfather's song
as he walked through muddy fields
feeding his tired muscles rhythms,
singing his hungry body home.

This Time of Sand and Teeth

At this time of sand and teeth
we sink to our knees, crushed like grapes,
ground like corn, crumbled like strong buildings.

I think of how to forget the tone
of our dreams and songs in the morning,
our prayers and dreams at night.

I wonder how we will remember the pace
and the paths up the warlike mountain,
the tracks and the tales of those who return.

They come back—wild eyes, burnt skin—
voices like so many fires in the dark, not knowing
how to paint the source of the light they have seen.

We know Isaac must have wept
and kept a fear of knives, along with his heart;
the voice of an angel made him shimmer.

Some feel at home on Masada,
others choose to stay in the homeless camps below;
both must learn to love and use the weapons we now hold.

On top of the mountain myths are born, heroes and war cries.
Down below babies are born, and mothers who'll steal for food.
Those who hurt howl in pain.

The world is whole and it is breaking—
their pain, our pain—who can name the difference
when all the pieces are ours to embrace?

How I Wish You'd Traveled by Boat

How I wish you'd traveled by boat up the salt-mixed Hudson
to old Erie Canal, caressed by air curling your hair into knots
we could've unraveled together, slowly, without words,
east-west, north-south, so that stupid journalist would never
have called me your "pal" and because that's the way to go,

with dignity the way ancient Viking ships carried furs,
slaves and amber. We, too, vessels of warmth, the enslaved,
golden beauty. Going slowly under clouds until coast
gives way to dark mountains, rising shadows
pierced by night fires, pearls scattered among ashes.

Traveling a day or two, a night, or two nights and a day.
Taking your time. Smoke from the boat's chimney lingers
in your hair, mingles slowly, like a man and a woman in love.
Not in a hurry. It's the way to return, early, before

dawn, cold and eager, still wrapped in midnight's
velvet when poets stay, look at stars, trace a word
or two in dew on the railing or in notebooks. Your book
is closed. How I wish you had traveled by boat.

Write Me like Ashes

You wait for me, your dandelion,
root that digs through street and stone
to page and word; cuts through time,
holds oil and rain, surprise embrace.

The poet's shadow turns like a dandelion
east west with the sun, ignoring poems,
songs, raking air with brilliant gold.

Alphabet of young green leafy spikes,
feisty, defiant beauty: Pick, pick, pick
me that I may die wild in high pitch,
so deep in silence who can hold it?

I am learning. A house of breath
and vision leans into space and cloud.
Three bitter stems of parsley,
one sweet sprig of jasmine.

All the words, I gently erase them,
so you can sail through my pages empty
of your four languages and all the others
still hoping you will notice them.

Dogs bark in the dark, steady flow
of stream and growth interrupted.
How can that be? Hawk in my garden.
Cold air stings the flowering bush.
Ice on every branch, flower burning.

Flame pulling both ways. Such close
space, word to word, no punctuation,
no comma, no period: love does that,
keeps you awake. Tells you: reach
for speech, scale the wall, surrender
only to rose and white fog in your palm.

Left and bereft like a magnolia
stunned by April hail, this city covered
by clouds. *Write*, you say. *Write*
my pear and my apple. No space
for repair or revenge. Write me like ashes.

Rosemary Kothe taught in the Buffalo public school system for thirty years. Her writings appeared in *The Buffalo News, Artvoice* and numerous small press publications, including *Stepping Out: A Journal of Empowerment* for people with disabilities. She authored three chapbooks: *Let's Put the Sky Upon the Ground,* a collection of poetry written for children; *Journey Without End;* and *In the Memory of a Single Rose;* and a collection of her poetry, *Ashes of Remembrance.* These were all illustrated by her daughter, Zoë Kothe. Her poem, "Purple Poison," was included on a CD, *The Word Underneath,* by the ensemble Lake Affect. Her short story, "Grandpa on a Roll," was published by Slipstream Publications.

She held a baccalaureate from Hunter College and a Masters of Education from the University at Buffalo and was a fellow of the Western New York Writing Project at Canisius College. Rosemary volunteered for Just Buffalo Literary Center and hosted readings at the Screening Room in Amherst, NY and at Impact Artists' Gallery. She coordinated poetry readings for the Parkway Literary Guild in Ontario, Canada, promoting a reciprocal exchange of talent across the border.

I Would Like to be a Tree

I would like to be a tree...
because I become easily bored
with the fashions of the season.
My preferences for colors change
as erratically as predictions
on the Weather Channel.
I *do* like green, but then again
shades of green have more appeal to me
than that bright, verdant
dew-kissed leaf of summer.
In fall, I would wear my orange sweater
with the brown pants and red scarf
all carried by that sturdy trunk I hold,
and when winter falls
I would don my bridal gown
of virginal white
to cover my naked limbs.

I would like to be a tree...

where squirrels build nests after foraging
birds sing sweet summer melodies
and rest in my arms
cats could climb to roofs
and mew at bedroom windows
to awaken owners who cuddle in comfort
under fluffy quilts
while they yearn for Friskies.

I would like to be a tree to provide shade
for the aged couple
who hold hands beneath me,
for family picnics,
for the sturdy branch from which
a swing hangs for children's fun!

I would like to be a tree
and dance with the wind
do rituals:
a raindance to nourish earth
send my seeds to faraway places –
my family tree would be endless.

I would like to be a tree:
my old limbs could be severed
recycled for warmth as firewood
lovers could see visions in my flames
children could name my colors
crickets could hide in the dust
of my ashes
teenagers could toast marshmallows
in my flame
and exchange gooey kisses to my delight.

I would like to be a tree
to provide the perfect wood
for carving chains,
Indians,
crafts galore.

Yes, I would like to be a tree.

Dream Dancer

A clear, breezy mid-October dawn
A park sheltered by trees
wearing gowns of orange, purple,
brown and gold:
Out of season now!
Discards float down,
crowning me with an ambience
of aging Fall
Yet I feel years falling away...

I am, in fact, a child again...
Suddenly a maple leaf
caresses my hand –
It becomes my mother.
She is dancing
to the motion of the wind,
Her black hair flies about
her ivory shoulders in sync,
Her georgette dress
harbors the shades of the leaves.
She takes my tiny hand
and lifts me
through a sea of seasons...
Bleak, then colorful
Climates torrid, then brisk
Smells pleasant, then putrid
Tastes delectable, then nauseating.
All emotions are experienced:
Fear, jealousy, pain, anger,
hate, love and ambivalence.

I awaken...the years creep back:
I'm once again an aging Fall,
a withered leaf of seventy.
Mother, do you dance in Heaven?

Boychild in the Sky With Monsters

Pre-K classroom
Sullen four-year-old boychild
Time-out chair
for popping velcro straps
on too-tight sneakers during storytime
Teacher said, "Sit!"
Keep those fingers busy in "learning",
not "annoying".
Sort these stencils by "kind"
and then paint a picture!

Boychild reflected: are stencils "kind?"
Are there any *mean* ones like Teacher?
Boychild, too sad to find humor
in "Clifford's Tricks" or
Arthur's antics during storytime,
used stencils to console himself.
First he drew billowy white clouds
on dark paper
Then he dipped a "kind" house-stencil
in white paint and pressed it hard,
high up above the clouds.

When the teacher-aide touched
Boychild's shoulder and asked,
"Whatcha doin', Andy?"
Boychild said
"The clouds took the Monster House
up in the night sky.
Mommy and her boyfriend Rob live there.
My brother Jacob, my sister Bess
and my father Jay and
his girlfriend Bernice and I live there, too.
My mommy Brenda cooked spaghetti."

Boychild smiled:
He was his own counselor.

Richard LaClair, Professor Emeritus, teaches composition and literature at Erie Community College. His work has been published in *Beyond Bones II* (a Western NY collection), *Elf Magazine* and *The Buffalo News*. He has a particular interest in writing about his experiences living on Evans Bay on Lake Erie.

Alfred

During the pull of the crawl
   swimming in Lake Erie
   I unexpectedly speak your name
   in ridiculous bubbles;
   then swing up my mouth
   to take in life.

Where is your tow-head,
   like a seal's, a walrus'--
   rising in dripping golden rivulets
   in Eden
   in the tree-shaded
   spring-fed pool?

Where are your greasy shoulders
   cold as the water,
   that would grasp my legs--
   pull me under to the
   bottom- the bottom you so owned
   that I always carefully
   hoarded a breath.

Beneath the blue-green water,
   your straw head would flicker
   under the leaf-shuttered sun.

The water was you.

But, now as I surface dive
   in a new pool, your image is not clear
   in the shards of the broken-glass sun
   that rock upon the pool bottom—
   It is not as clear as
   was the surety of childhood

Where are you now?
Your mother said you did not want visitors
   at your hospital deathbed.

But I know you to be too pig-strong,
   too potbellied to be gone—
   And must be in the air breaths above water
   in the pool spray,
   in the sun-striped flickering depths,
   in the water we still share.

Running Light

A game I still play
on fresh December ice
on Delaware Creek.

Leap away from the bank
to skip the crust
of undecided ice,
and stride swiftly
towards the other bank

Feet depress the
crazing ice,
like water striders
dish the summer water.

There is a kind of thought
that runs light—
won't recognize the chance of falling-
or the effects of speed,
the laws of physics;
trampolines on caution.

At mid-point, the
half-inch frosty sheet
cracks and echoes up the creek,
like a shotgun blast,
followed by a slit
cut by a knife or razor.

In the gap
cold, dark water coats
the sinking incline.
In the winter light
a surge of blood-black syrup.

Race, race to
the other side.
Retaining energy from your first jump
scurry up the rising incline.
Drill your feet into the still soft clay
of the safe bank.

Stolen Stones

On visiting the Elgin Marbles
    In British Museum

The exhausted horses pull Selene's chariot
    at the end of night into blue Okeanos

As the forelegs of the lead horse plunge
    from the heights of heaven and
    from the once towering frieze
    of the sun-bleached Acropolis...
    his gaping jaw, his flaring nostrils
    express his weariness.

So the wheels, wood and flesh
    of the falling moon plunge
    into the bubbling, seething
    lethe...into the memory- washing foam.

The faces of the horses
    are taut, intense, occupied---
    cheekbones scarred,
    driven forward, wild, fatigued....
    What a temptation to try to touch
    these stolen stones.

Once firm upon the East Pediment, now
    leaving the sky, leaving the wind
    pulling the hours into the sea
    driving into the sea, out of the air.

Not confined to a nation, too beautiful
    to hold even in the viewer's eye.

David Lampe is a native Iowan who did his graduate work at University of Nebraska. He taught English (Chaucer and Shakespeare) at Buffalo State for 37 years. He is the editor of *Mortals & Immortals,* a 2014 anthology of participants in the Burchfield Penney Art Center Writers and Poets Series. Happily retired, he lives in Buffalo, where he enjoys travel, his family and the rich cultural resources of the city.

After Cataract Surgery

"They look like trees to me
but they are walking about"
-Mark 8:28

And when I woke early
that April morning
birds sang

and when I stepped into
the backyard and removed
the bandage from my eye

the colors of a cardinal
flared, were crisp as he flew
from our exuberant holly

to a forsythia bush
whose leaves of shimmering
light were a nimbus beheld

through a shudder of tears.
Yellow scales fallen,
the trees walked

Prague Castle

North aisle Saint
George's basilica,
a plundered pieta.

Both heads, arms
even the legs
(already broken

in deposition)
are gone. Yet
a mother's fingers

still support a torso
where wounds
still bleed.

A cluster of crimson
and gold dried flowers
adorns the simple altar.

All-Hallows

After Reformation service
in our rural Iowa church that crisp
autumn Sunday, we went
upstairs to change clothes
in that house that no longer exists.

And there my father taught me
to tie a Windsor knot, the
same knot I use today,
have taught my sons to tie.

Fifty years later I learn that
in Poland All Hallows
is a national holiday –
families visit graves, leave
flowers and lighted candles.

As we return to Krakow
hillsides twinkle and
despite Reformation prejudices
I sense clouds of witness, deeper
ties than I can imagine or explain.

The Rocky Mountaineer : Vancouver - Banff

1

Morning haze glows
illuminated by sunrise
as eagles glide, skimming
the mystic margin.

A tufted mountain jay
hops on empty aspens,
bright eyes focusing on
the graveled trout stream.

2

Heaped railroad cars
flash by, a bright
yellow blur

masking the clear
Thompson river
till like a screaming star

a bald eagle explodes above
the sulphur load, a bleeding
salmon in its talons.

David Landrey spent 38 years teaching literature, 35 of them at Buffalo State College. For three of those years he taught in Ankara, first at Bilkent University (1988-89) and then on a Fulbright Grant at Hacettepe University's Department of American Literature and Culture (1991-93). He studied briefly with Charles Olson at SUNY Buffalo. He is the author of *Intermezzi to Divorce Poems and Dinner Table Scenes*, from Jensen/Daniels. *Divorce Poems and Dinner Table Scenes* continues to develop. *Consciousness Suite* was published by Spuyten Duyvil. He is working on a sequel, tentatively entitled *Dancing in the Dark*.

From: ***Consciousness Suite***

VII

Amber lights through pre-dawn fog
recall Ankara's dusky pungency
as if all senses unite as
       one as
Central New York and Anatolia
gather strands of awareness
and persuade me of mind's coherence
      as if
connections were real, spirit whole
and those I knew and know
were now present, presented
      as if
distinct entities, each to be
always also conscious
      as one
whole spirit of the rest and
of me so that each and every
      one
sustains all
          else there be
    none.

XIV

—*I have never yet met a man who was quite awake. How could I have looked
him in the face?*

——Henry David Thoreau

Never quite awake, not even
those moments
            or so
it seemed
            in class
                        in love
                                    or in
the deep intensity
            of conversation
                        of meditation
                                    or of
the appearance of a poem;

rather: somnolence,
the somatic totality
generating always
            what?
is it proper? an inception?
and what appropriate application
to patch upon or into
our meeting with another
as our eyes glance
            away?

XXIII

Pain strands weaving us
tied to power
the kraft of it leaving us
stranded amid confusion:
how to hold diaphanous threads
shreds of "life as we knew it"
or thought we did or
        did we
think or grasp and
        will we
in the new order
the "world forever changed": or
        can we
and if so what?
What what is there
outside
        inside or
all around our stranded selves?

XXXIII

We turn away
then back and then
again turn   turn   turn
a touch in time
when our orbits meet
so briefly sweet
I almost know you
known so long so many
days together that
        —what?—
we act in concert
sing a melody then
off on swing outward
        upward
                downward
face to face
bemused by images
of selves and souls
fused in memory
and then again
        turn

to ...

... the others
mothers   brothers
fathers   children
          sister spirits
psyche-sent
impinging gently sometimes
          harshly
always briefly and

with what
          if any
residue in our depths
          if any
if some great repository be
that is
          self and soul
that will ...

... insist
          intent
on life and links
to others

                    oh mother
                    where are you
                    who have you
                              been
whose fury in the veins
          remains
manifests itself
muttering of lost lives
present now in mind
or in its absence
filling the void
the passage where the echoes
flit ahead fleeing
or duck behind
back into
          what
was there ever
for your bitter anger
spilling over
seeking its level

perhaps
a place to meet
at last

XLII

To know love's meaning
            may be
the end of consciousness
and   oh   it takes so long
to reach the end and
            maybe
if and when we do we
            what
yearn to start again
to know sooner
            maybe
to realize the end to
bring it to form before
the end of mind
occurs to us and
            maybe
our whole selves
            may be
at last.

From the new collection: **Dancing in the Dark**

Listening to the voices of the shadow who knows
The inmost secrets of our hearts,
Thumping,
Asking for entrance
Into the growing inner darkness.
    "Family Radio" by Stanford J. Searl, Jr.

Mid-Twentieth Century Vermont
flowed into my Buffalo living room
as the winter afternoon shadows
grew the gloom of my own memories
in the context of his.

More than half a lifetime blurred
but inarticulately returned in
a single fleeting moment
wherein his family became mine,
the sound of 1940s radio resonating
in my own inner darkness.

Who was I then?
Who are we now?

Our lifelines flow as does his Black River
fouled by mills, the food of our lives
filling memory: baked beans,
New England suppers present to us
in Buffalo and Culver City,
the games we play and our ceremonies
so etched in synaptic paths
that we build our present in patterns
immemorially prescribed.

* * *

Late afternoon light fades, offers a glow,
an aura 'round simple objects, that fades
in its turn leaving silhouettes in view.

He ponders what's in mind to match each shift
as darkness engulfs him and what is left
when nothing's seen and mind slips out upon—
        —circumference she said—
when consciousness flits about the room and
self and soul suspend in the vortex of
household   heartbeat   memory   love and death.

A footfall resonates—where? whose?—inside
and out, stirs the grand collage, brings the mind
back to the edge of some awareness some
feeling for the presence of all that is.

Celeste Lawson embraced poetry following her life as a dancer and choreographer, experiences that contribute to the texture and tone of her writing. She's a recipient of three individual artist grants that supported her work to recreate dances rooted in the ancient traditions of North Africa and the Middle East. In 1997, Lawson published a poetry collection entitled *I Was Born This Way*, a reflection on the women she encountered in 1995 when she traveled with a delegation to the United Nations/ NGO Fourth World Conference on Women in Beijing, China. Also in 1997, the Urban Libraries Foundation, the American Academy of Poets and the Buffalo & Erie County Public Library recognized Celeste as Erie County's poet of the month in honor of National Poetry Month. She celebrated this honor when she gave a reading at the downtown Buffalo Public Library's "Ring of Knowledge," accompanied by the late, legendary jazz pianist, Al Tinney, and his trio – a highlight of her artistic life. Celeste has been featured in readings at The Gray Hair Reading Series, The Screening Room, the Center for Inquiry, the Juneteenth Festival, Housing Opportunities Made Equal and The Buffalo Book Fair. She has had poems, essays and articles published in *The Buffalo News, Artvoice, Buffalo Beat, Her Magazine, Earth's Daughters* and other regional publications. Currently she is a columnist with *After50 News*. Celeste has been part of the Women of the Crooked Circle poetry group, and had also been part of The Pearls, a small group of poets who were writing under the tutelage of the late poet and professor, Jimmie Margaret Gilliam.

Portrait of Love in Pieces

Picture perfect, you and me
balanced with light, line, and composition.
Blending, but not without texture.

Our landscape formed panoramas
sharp strokes and wide sweeps.
New colors on taut fabrics.

Our geometry was fluid
mixing imagination with pleasure.
But spills muddied the palate.

We splashed turpentine, pulled, and tugged
rubbed furiously until the landscape bled.
The canvas split, stretched beyond the frame.

Passing Through Her
(Reflection III)

It wasn't easy to say goodbye,
leave behind her invincibility,
her era of innocence.
Her uninhibited lust had matured,
ripened, even spoiled in spots.

Fruit still in its skin,
her rind curls at the edges,
withered by years of providence.
She flaunts stoic expressions, used by her daily,
disguises her melancholy.

She watched her youth twist,
peel away from her in shame
for not crying when it hurt, really hurt.
She caught no tears in her eyelashes,
only swallowed the salt.

Soon she turned to sand,
ground herself into glass,
molded herself into the shape of
her lover's favorite cup -
then cracked between his lips.

Taylor Arrives
(For my daughter at the birth of her son)

The eleventh hour is here.
Her face twists in splendid anguish,
wet with woman's toil.
Her hand clenches mine,
eyes searching for answers
that remain hidden.

Crones lend breath, deep and old.
She exhales unspeakable pain
from a pit of sweetness.

A dark chestnut appears
between quaking thighs.
It cracks open --
and the wail
a sharp, swift arrow.

On Parting

Parting is a gift that draws us near
Untouched love
Well-known pain
A swift blow to feelings never expressed
A warm breeze for thoughts of things yet to be

Parting is the sun coming up on a night of tears
Moonlight on fond memories
Shadows on ardent confessions
A shock to spur growth - renders weakness
A tremor of far reaching consequences - immediate impact

Parting is a tightly packed drawer of recollections
Lists of the finest bistros in town
Photographs, ticket stubs
Shop receipts, program books
A new solitude of one at dinner
A familiar comfort of one on the sofa

Parting is a dream from which you cannot awake
Unsung love songs, unwritten postcards
Well thought out speeches that remain unspoken
Far apart, feelings ever so close
The path that brings us together

Grocery Store Parking Lot

Blue smoke snarled from the tailpipe
of a beaten down, pick-up truck,
so old it looked generic

Slowly it moved forward
rusted camper top, creaking and rocking,
sides covered with handyman tools of every denomination

Nails were hooked on and pounded into the metal body
rags tied on with frayed rope,
ladders stacked atop the hood steadied with bungee cords

The hands I saw on the wheel were as old and knotted
as the ropes looped around the hanging paint cans,
plastic pails, brooms, brushes, and the bicycle

I wondered who was waiting for this heap to chug home
who was waiting to see this rickety body unfold,
emerge from the worn-out leather seats

His eyes held a mile of resolve and acres of sadness
he maneuvered his wobbling cargo into the street,
I thought, he must be angry, but I didn't see it in his face

To and fro I watched the ghostly heap
bump its way into traffic
swinging an old man's dreams in empty buckets

Seaside

Salt air settles in the back of my throat
My sound similar to the cat stretched across the doorway

Three steps forward, my feet feel cool stone steps
Jerry-rigged by friends during a late night bar-b-que

Three steps down I feel the grit of sand
Toes curl under

Crickets click a monotonous lullaby
In sync with the rumbled whisper of ebbing tide

Receding waves leave debris of seashells
We are brief moments, hopefully cherished by someone

Sitting on the steps, I wait for night to wash me
Two crickets land on adjacent stones – steady, fearless next to me

They know, we are eye-to-eye with the sea
Equally small

Encounters with Nature (1)

Softly at first, then louder
a subtle click, click, then click again
starts with a bubble in the well of my stomach
forces my lips to curve upward - and just stay!

Sounds ever so smooth make their way into my throat
hum to the syncopated blink of stars
hum to the sexy sway of willows not weeping – but dancing!
my veins pump a rhythm that spans from my hair follicles
to the tip of my red painted toenails

The night is restless
vibrating with the prickle of grass blades moistened by twilight
my soul wants to tango, wants to step out and turn sharply
wants to swivel my hips, kiss my lover, wants to shout sweet nothings
at clouds rolling by, wants to whisper in your ear
wants to sing songs that rhyme with never ending verses

Karen Lee Lewis is an independent Teaching Artist, and a Teacher Consultant for the Western New York Writing Project. She recently participated in a National Seminar for Teaching Artists at the John F. Kennedy Center for the Performing Arts in Washington, DC. Karen also teaches creative writing workshops for nonprofit organizations and art galleries throughout Western New York. Her "Picturing Poetry Project," with Amy Luraschi, was the subject of a documentary film by Jon R. Hand, and was aired on PBS. Karen is a fellow of the Banff Centre's Wired Writing Studio. Her work has appeared in the *Sugar Mule* anthology, *Women Writing Nature*, *Red River Review*, *Nomad*, *Stormy Weather*, *Nature*, *Buffalo Spree*, *Teachers & Writers Magazine*, *The Society*, *Slipstream* and *The Buffalo News*. St. Louis's Architrave Press published a broadside of one her poems and a guest review by Karen of Keetje Kuipers' book of poetry, *Beautiful in the Mouth*. She is also a Pushcart Prize nominee. Editorial work for *Traffic East* magazine is archived at www.trafficeast.com. Karen's photographic work appears on the covers of books from *Binge* Press. Her full-length poetry collection, *What I Would Not Unravel* (The Writer's Den, 2010), is available at Amazon, and her chapbook, *Solitude*, is available at The Burchfield Penney Art Center. Website: www.karenleelewis.com.

Roots (The Pedregal), 1943
self-portrait by Frida Kahlo

She has cut herself again
flesh a slice of ripe cantaloupe
she has cut away her crucifixions
emptied a space so that life can flow
her lungs are dove's wings fully fledged
earth is a rind breaking into faults beneath her

A seed needs something to prop against
Frida's spine grows supported like a vine
exposed to sunlight she blossoms closer to the ground
her bloody roots seek the ocean
on either side of the Pedregal
a barren land that ends
in a desert mountain of stone

Are we not all in between
two great bodies of water

the one we have come from
and the one we leave behind

How many times did she open
her body to a promise
How many hours did she lie alone
held only by the leather fingers of her corsets

Looking at her I am unbraided
Her hair holds all the darkness of the world
I want to brush my fingers through it

Does any artist believe
that making art is voluntary
Isn't it all an act
of reclamation
What we release
What we make room for
What we cover our scars with
In order to feel whole

Parting Gift
(*after Man Ray's 'Cadeau, 1921'*)

Her parting gift—
fourteen tacks
glued to the flat face
of the iron he loved
A sharp crisp seam
straight down the middle
She could have chosen
a golf club, his favorite pitching wedge
but he would find this clothes iron
harder to replace
One tack for each year
she felt nailed to the floor
One tack for each year she was dulled
by the weight of the heat in her hand
She pressed her palms
against her shirt
knowing she would leave this world
and all in its wrinkles
in all its mountainous
freshly hung glory

The First Hands

The first hands to touch you
were not your mother's
someone else held you fast
as you unwrapped yourself
from the wet blanket
of your mother's body

The first finger's print
language left in the white wax
varnish that you shed
cannot protect you any longer
as it is washed away
your body cooling
in a world full of hands
that are not your mothers

She has been busy
relinquishing you
to each new fear
to every risk
known to a woman
inherent in your being
touched

Shiver

Whether the Cooper's Hawk has
secreted himself inside the blueness
of the Spruce. The sun inching
behind the clouds. Within the darkness
the first snowflake. The wind
filling the morning's footprint.
How the yearling fox with mange
can warm her nose against
skin and bone, her blood
condensing like mercury in a
glass bulb, her body lowering
itself. How I want to wrap her
in muskrat fur. Everything rushing
from right to left. The shiver
of the creek rippling like a dried
snakeskin in my hand.

Frail Grace

Her pain cannot be relieved
dehydration reigns   flesh time
balanced by water and salt
everything about her thinning
corpus diminishment

Winged vertebrae
seek soft landing
within ribbed cage
consumption accumulates
her body   weathering
summit of scapula disintegrating
femur, ligament, cartilage, fascia—
an *archaic torso*

It is not heartbreak   that will
thrust her over the threshold
a century of matriarchy
has taught her to withstand
its threadbare ways

She is a frail grace
solemnly shaped
by fusion and loss
the once terse mandible
known for proffering
blistering vesicants
now opens   in solitude
she is on her way
to the door
her pale hand holding
the railing firmly
slippered footfalls
soft as petals
fortified by sun

David Lewitzky is a 74 year old re-
tired Social Worker/Family Therapist living
out his sedentary life in the moribund rust
belt city of Buffalo, New York.

He has recent work in *Nimrod, Red Wheel-
barrow, Tidal Basin Review, Columbia College
Literary Review, Passages North, Roanoke
Review, Future Cycle* and *Poetry Bus,* among
others.

Despite suffering from the debilitating dis-
eases of hemorrhoids, psoriasis and gout, he
soldiers on with his poetry. What a guy, that
Lewitzky!

SUN DANCE

I have taken upon myself the task of explaining the Sun Dance
Of the Cheyenne and Sioux, the people of the plains
The most sacred and severe of rituals

It is liturgy involving self-torture of an extreme kind
The skewering of the breast and back
The ripping away of flesh

If you are spiritual for true
Revere the buffalo that feeds you, the eagle that inspirits you
And you know that creation dwells in you and must be brought to breath

If you are displaced, invisible, judged unreal
Pushed to the edge of the world which is the center of creation
And you are tasked with remaking the world

Resurrecting your troubled self
Hideous pain may perhaps be seemly and needful
To bring about the Earth's birth, to gain grace

But I can't explain the Sun Dance
I'm neither Cheyenne nor Sioux
I'm a marginalized Jew forever wandering in mind

The tasks I've been given

To repair the world, to heal myself
Involve fasting and atonement

I fail these tasks for I am soiled
And when I fashion poems in the service of creation
And a search for purity

It is harrowing and terrible for me
In my blasphemy
In my civility

WALTZ NOTES

1

From the German 'waltzen'
Meaning 'to turn' (to roll, to glide and slide)
The turning dance

"Turn now and rise"

Think of revolution
Meditate on feelings, on resolve
On the directions of desire, on self

"Wrest the matter
Into your own hands"

2

Started in the foothills of the Alps
A folk dance, rude in unrecorded time
Boys and girls in shorts and birkenstocks
Happy campers, quaint

Danced upon the tongues and teeth of towns
Quickly captivated Berlin, Vienna, Bucharest
Fascinated Old World Europe – 1750, 60, sometime thereabouts

Took on the New World   Waltzed into its mouth
Dancing revolution   Voracious, universal wave

The next big thing

3

Glide and turn: Face on face, flesh on flesh, and smooth

Across the floors of public spaces
Reception halls in churches, civic centers, cabarets, bandstands in the parks

Heating up the burgomeisters' daughters, the hip young herren
Trysts, as ever, in the cellars, in the shadows
'Let's meet in the square beneath the big clock'

4

And so it is a dance of change, herald of a revolution
The fixed and classic figures retrograde, passé, and out
Desire displacing process   Old rules danced away

Avid dancers resembling angels, swift, intense and spotless
Demanding purity, satisfaction

Ruthless perhaps

5

Inspired by buzzwords: 'Nation', 'sacrifice' and 'liberty'
The young and disaffected, hot to trot
Impatient, waiting in the doorways, by the open windows

Like leggy crested spiders dancing on the kegs and barrels
Waltzing on the skin of time

The smitten dancers crave the bloody birth of beauty
The ecstasy of lightning, the slap across the face, the music of the blade

6

And one day waltz becomes the poetry of flight, of reaching for the sun

And one day all men created equal

And one day bombs and unmanned missiles - Machines that equalize
And random faceless suicides one day (All things being equal)

And one day someone said "If I can't dance I don't want your revolution"

And one day we're waltzing beside an enormous bitter ditch

And one day a hail of glass, a sobbing wind
Chamber music: Laments and dirges

And bells chime one day like shattered crystal

Days of Awe

7

I'm an old man with stories to tell and I am a violent man
And Julie's my forever dancing partner violent at her core
And Terpsichore's the whirlwind of conception
Generator of creation, revolution

And revolution's when all the ghosts that ever were come out and howl

And waltz, like revolution, and like me, has seen its better days

****

Notes: Quotations in Part 1 comprise the poem/fragment: "Turn Now And Rise" by Charles Olson.
Quotation in part 6 attributed to Emma Goldman

Alexis Machelor O'Donnell

"I like to write out there, in the world as I am going about my day or gathered with friends or hiking round a mountaintop...It all starts with a line. I begin to hear verses in my head, and then I must get them out. I write them in my little notebooks or on receipts or napkins (whatever I can find at the time), and later when it comes time to transfer them to the typewriter or computer, I write them across and down the page exactly as they appeared in the notebook--for me this is how I like to express these poems, these 'songs of life'. I have the utmost respect for the learned poet, and the careful editors, but for me my poems are immediate expressions of my soul's true feelings and the music I hear from the words in my head. I want the reader to feel and hear what I did when I wrote it down and thought it out. When they look at my pages I want their eye to go down the page the way it is supposed to sound. So I guess I'd call my poetry natural, playful, exuberant, soulful, and jazzy...visual music. I hope you do too..."

Out of the Blue

Out   of   the   Air
    then   drenched
                with   tears

      and fuzzy hallucination,

       A shrouded veil
        Upon my
         face,

   I   saw you
        standing there

      Sun upon
      Your face
I saw yellowgoldamber
            olive   ochre

<u>Blaze</u>

through   the

Haze ----

I knew you
before

So long ago
I don't
remember

when

And here

we are

I
taste the
morning air

on land that gives me calm –

the bluebirds
protecting their
young

and you
protecting
them --

There's a lift
to my soul ---

as I sit
here   and

think   of
all   we've
done, and where
we've been
Days of green
and leaf

mist on face
and dust on feet –
Nights of
endless stars
and cold
aching
draft –
and tended fires ---
I know there's
still much
more to **see**
this ain't the
end of
you and
me

I feel a sense of
Peace because
the   Lord
led us this
way
From that
Moment
I   Fell
into your eyes –

All's Well
and I
realized

I'd never before known   **eyes**
like   Mine

(--A.M.S., 04/17/08, 7:00ish p.m.)

Mountains I've
        climbed --

    And those   not
        tried ---

    the   gravel
        sharp   jagged
            rocks
    lept on like a
        Mountain goat –

Leaping   from
        edge to edge –
    the air   that fills
        your   lungs –

It   may   burst
        but   man it feels Sweet –
The dry   soup
    the wool   socks you dry
    on the line
     and reuse
    on Calloused feet

    I Keep   these   images
        in My   mind
Places   I   have not
        been
places   I   long to return

use   them   when
        I   sit
    listening   to   my
            boss
    takin   exams

    drivin'   on   the   290
    when some   asshole

cuts   me   off

Someday I Will
    be free

Someday   I will
Write My journey

I'll   draw
   I'll   write a
        tree
    a   bird
a   little douglas squirrell
  who runs in front of me
Someday I will   not
      need   to drive
       to strive
No bills no tax
  no Mindless store lines

   I'll take my
    pack
   and Wander
     off
   with my best
    guy   by my
   side

   and

  a   mat
    a pen
    a pot My hands –
    and My

Unhurried
   Mountain Mind

Sam Magavern is a public interest lawyer, currently codirecting the Partnership for the Public Good and teaching at the SUNY Buffalo Law School. His poems have been published in many places, including *Poetry, Antioch Review, New York Quarterly* and *Paris Review.* A book of his poems, *Noah's Ark,* was published by BlazeVOX in 2014. His non-fiction book, *Primo Levi's Universe,* was published in 2009 by Palgrave MacMillan, and he has also written the screenplay for an independent film, *The Last Word.* Web site: www.sammagavern.com.

Magavern grew up in Buffalo, except for two years in the Philippines. During high school he sang in a punk rock band called Brutus and the Senators. He attended college at Harvard and law school at UCLA, and he spent 14 years in Minneapolis, working for the Legal Aid Society, before returning to Buffalo in 2004. He is married to the artist Monica Angle, whose beautiful paintings are included in *Noah's Ark,* and they have two daughters.

Balinese Ritual

Your body mesmerized me:
With your eyes deep as lakes,
With your shoulders like mansions,
With your blackberry lips,
With legs tall as trees,
With the shake of your head
Like the wind on a mountain

   – all worn so casually,
Like the gown of the great golden
Goddess that they throw into the sea.

The Plough Horse's Morning

Before they strapped on the yoke,
I had a few good moments.
I was nuzzling in my feed bag –
The oats were not so bad –

When a butterfly flitted in,
Unannounced, bearing no burden.
I got to imagining myself
A little thing – flighty,
Inconsequential, golden, all wings.
Then the farmer cried, "Heigh-ho,"
And I plodded off to work.

The Discovery of Atlantis

Will you ever get out of the bathtub,
        William Henry Bumberson, his
Mother used to enquire. In
A moment, sainted Mama, in just one
        Millisecond, I'll be out. Only
I'm just exploring
                    an underwater empire
Of vast proportions, with
                    a civilization
So advanced, complex, and ultimately
Benevolent, that it makes
The extra-tubbial world look barbaric.

The Acropolis Diner

I.   Over at the Acropolis Diner
          I thought about you
          Losing your mind to time. Your
          Self has gone into hiding,

          And we, the local police, only
          See you when
          You taunt us with a clue.

II.   And the pain wanders through
          Like a disorganized
          Procession of mourners. They're unsure
          Just who is in the casket,

          But the dust, the blunt road
          Has told them that they are lost.

The Eleusian Mysteries

Blessed is the man who walks down
Into the moldering darkness with
No coins in his pockets and no long
Resume designed to impress Pluto

His mind swept utterly bare except
For the memory of these three things

A waterfall behind which he once hid
A warbler call he once truly heard
The harbor of your warm calm arms

Manhattan Sidewalk

Love is not all honeyed lavings
And wafting fragrance. Let me
Tell you about the ache and
Bristle. Let me tell you about
The entire Manhattan sidewalk
Bustling inside of me whenever
I see your face. Some are eating
Hot dogs with spicy mustard.
Some hurl imprecations into their
Cell phones in English, Urdu,
Amharic. Look, the man in
The black suit just tripped and fell.
But they are not trampling him.
A small circle opens: an oasis.
And the woman carrying the bird
Cage with the fluttering parrot
Sets it down ever so gently to free
Her left hand so that she can help
The flustered stranger to arise.

Dennis Maloney is the editor and publisher of the widely respected White Pine Press in Buffalo, NY, which celebrated its 40th year in 2013. He is also a poet and translator. His works of translation include: *The Stones of Chile* by Pablo Neruda; *The Landscape of Castile* by Antonio Machado; *Dusk Lingers: Haiku of Issa*; *Between the Floating Mist: Poems of Ryokan*; and *The Poet and the Sea* by Juan Ramon Jimenez.

A number of volumes of his own poetry have been published, including *Sitting in Circles*, published in Japan in a bilingual edition; *The Pine Hut Poems*; *The Map Is Not the Territory: Poems & Translations*; and *Just Enough*. His book of Yosano Akiko translations, *Tangled Hair*, was published in 2012 by Palisades Press.

Since the birth of White Pine Press in 1973, Dennis has published a wide range of international voices in English, from Latin American women writers and Korean Zen poets to literary works from Slovenia, Bosnia and Herzegovina, and Albania. White Pine Press' publications also include Nobel Prize Laureates William Golding, Juan Ramon Jimenez, Gabriela Mistral and Pablo Neruda.

Crossing the Yangtze

We cross the Yangtze
on the new concrete bridge
into tomorrow
last year we would
have taken a ferry across

The river, wider
and more immense
than my imagination allowed.

The river of countless poems
of poets going in or out of exile,
or sailing off to a new post.

But today hulking grey barges
carry the iron ore and steel
from the belching factories
of the new China
out to sea and the world,
The sky a dirty hazy grey.

We cross the Yangtze
on the new concrete bridge
into the future where the
road you are told to follow
is smooth and the only thing
worse than having choices
is being unable to choose.

Children's Drawings

The drawings are rough and crude
like those my son
or your daughter
brought home from school
full of awkward lines
and smudged colors.

Blue, green, red, yellow...
but unlike those drawings
of houses with oversized doors and windows,
with colorful rainbows & stick figures,
a bright yellow sun dominating the sky,
with children at play
in tree forts four stories high,
these are different.

These are drawings
of children caught in war
images of planes
and helicopters dropping bombs
on huts which burst
into orange-red flames
and soldiers in green
with machine guns and machetes
to kill the fleeing capesinos,
slicing the heads of women
and written in shaky captions
'shut up you whores,
you guerilla wives, we sharpen
our machetes for your heads.'

Sometimes in Winter

1

I move inward
with the first snow
falling on the city
that gathers
like dust
in the dark places

2

Day and night
snow falls
without stop
creating a
stalled magnificence

Walking and
the storm plays
a harsh music
leaving its icy score
frozen on my beard

I trudge toward home
like a german soldier
headed for the russian front

3

There is silence
in falling snow
ice forming on
a slow moving stream
a clean whiteness
filling old tracks,
nestling in the forks
of an old cottonwood,
filling grassy fields
until only the heads
are above suffocation

4

The enormous wind
howls over the lake
and up the frozen streets
hurling walls of white
past the office window

People are thrown against buildings,
the nativity scene shudders
as the four walls explode
and dance down main street

Abandoned cars strewn about,
drifts high as houses,
for five days the city
is almost still
as people learn
to walk again

That same wind
less intense later
carves the snow
with delicate feminine curves
soft as a sculpture
of Jean Arp

5

Everything empties
into white

Susan Marie is a human being, an endless stream of conscious thought, a never ending river of keys and leaves that fall, autumnal, and oh, how they sigh towards winter's fierce breath of those who came before us courageous enough to speak, love, live and die, so words such as these are able to be published right now, one human right, in solidarity for all people writing words upon dusty chalkboards or trunks of trees, where dark black ink stains like a tattoo upon the cerebral cortex, coursing their ways onto radio waves, spiraling sentences to the sky, where they take flight and dance, forming paragraphs that turn into clouds.

Shahada

my spirit knows your own, brother
who is my friend
and my love
yet you are my brother
here and now

Jibril placed a solitary feather
of majestic angel's wing
upon both of our foreheads
gifted us with sight
to show what could be
and cannot

my brother, do you realize
how I know you,
as I do not even know myself
as you know me,
as you do not know yourself

look, look into a mirror
there i am
in your eyes
deep concentric pools of truth
lie beauty

we have been gifted with understanding

a treasure princes and kings
have fought and perished for
centuries past
connected as such
now

i am oceans away
my brother
who is my friend
yet my love

my spirit knows your own,

brother

aerials

a celestial war raged
as stars barricaded themselves
in symmetrical militant procession
opposing the purpling morningtide

the sky spit forth the clouds
and with it, the moon
leaving itself barren, desolate

my eyes, now wet with brine
held and caught your glare
illuminating this now velvet backdrop

yet no solace was evident
in the firmament this morn'
but two sharks teeth, your eyes
void and emotionless

and i stood apprehensive
in complete darkness
as your hand reached down
from behind the trembling stars

with skeletal grip
impeding breath
you held my thorax
until my throat burst
thunder and lightning

and i vomited thrushes
hidden deep within my belly

simultaneous, they took flight
your spirit, juxtaposed

a disconsolate sketch

of atriums and ventricles

ascending
Heaven.

such perfect death

the tulip raised
her bloodied lilting head
to rest in the outstretched palm
of the hero, now fallen as martyr
lying wasted
in fields of sweet grass

armor as warrior
                heart of lover

and she, eye of God, heaven's palette
a solitary tulip
closed her own eyes in solace

peaceful as the slain lover
masked as warrior

and wept for them both
as her lover wept in suffering
for his beloved

both to sleep
an eternal rest
of princes and kings
not as two
but a most perfect union
below skies of cerulean

and with last breath
her diaphragm ceased

her head, comforted in the crook
of the fleshy part
of the palm of her lover
she spent her last moment
on Earth
smiling

in peace

such perfect death.

Alive in a Time of Dying

The days meld into nights into days of unrest to rest, my voice. I'm guessing
the full moon rising, she may speak on my behalf.

SisterMoonChild shall bat her eyelashes spiderlike to each constellation as
they sparkle and dim upon the backdrop of this grand stage.

This place we call Earth, it is a Hell birthing breathing dragons of denial and
greed and in between, beauty. The blooming of new life.

The irony that existence is dependent upon black vs. white, good vs. evil,
night vs. day, man vs. woman, sun vs. moon, and you vs. me.

Where are the ones standing and speaking for us all, we're outnumbered.
Where is the golden chalice, my cup of poison, the holy altar?

I shall gladly drink my share to elevate me from a state of betrayal. Hand me
a crudely chiseled cup made only by the hand of man.

Bring it to my lips, love. Heaven's kiss. My eyes shall close, breathing cease,
yet my spirit shall soar as pure divine energy.

Oh, what silly creatures to dream a dream upon dreams that may or may not
exist according to each of our own waking states.

I shall attempt to reach a state of being and non being, of living while dying
alive, of pure esoteric flight, of thinking without thought.

How grand it is to be alive in a time of dying. The fresh buds shall bloom
when the frost sleeps during Springtime's coming of age.

And Summer shall welcome Fall, prepare her for Winter.
Drink, friends, this cup of mine is yours. It is sweet, oh, yet it is bitter.

John Marvin earned a PhD in English after retirement and began work as a poet and independent scholar. He participates in the rich Buffalo, NY poetry scene, and has been a featured poet at many readings. His poetry has appeared in scores of journals and 'zines', including *The William and Mary Review, River Oak Review* and *The Comstock Review*. He has literary criticism in recent issues of *James Joyce Quarterly, Hypermedia Joyce Studies, The Worcester Review* and *Pennsylvania English*, as well as a chapter in the book, *Hypermedia Joyce*. John's poetic stance reflects an experimental approach to breaking free of the Romantic lyric that has dominated poetry for more than two centuries. His favorite venues at the moment are *Indefinite Space, Slipstream, Hotel Amerika, Tribeca Poetry Review, Plainsongs* and *The Literary Review*.

What's So Spatial About Time?

> Woe Es war, soll Ich warden.
> Sigmund Fraud

And I could be bounded in a nutshell.
And I could count myself a king of space.
And I could have bad dreams.
And what a peace of quirk is a man.
And thinking makes it so.

And there surges a torrent between
    "Putting allspace in a Notshall"
        and
    The Universe in a Nutshell.

And to think a man trapped in a shell
    could radiate random quanta
    across infinite time wraps
    around lost horizons.

And and.

We seem to be a seam

Now, fascination [...] is a nihilistic passion par excellence, it is the passion proper to the mode of disappearance. We are fascinated by all forms of disappearance, of our disappearance. Melancholic and fascinated, such is our general situation in an era of involuntary transparency.

Jean Baudrillard

we shiver

a westerly
from across a frozen lake
chills a path through
wraps and layers

yet though grey on grey
a line appears
formed by sewing together
perhaps it is a dream
pieces of cloth or leather

within a membrane
reflective and absorptive
electrons lulled
by imminent phase change
gradually come to rest
in a basin of potential

a basin without shells
without resistance
to waves of intensity
where nothing can disturb
an emptiness

a hollow place
in a void
in a world of seems
any way you spell it

differ defer nature

my tribe and your tribe
can wail to be born
across the waters of a canal
dividing uncertainty
from ignorance

an eerie channel
wisps of fog
in mourning
or is it gnats twirling
like little water spouts

from this distance
always from this distance
as a collar tightening chill
penetrates layers
of shorn wool

modified plants
and chemicals
yet still still no ripples
on a surface
reflecting willows

and goldenrod
taking issue with the wish
you whisper
under breathing
too soft to hear

but breath
none the less
as a word put off
slips into a past
between the banks

Écriture from the Black Lagoon

Mission Update from the Starship Fakawe:

Of that blue world I sing this one last time
Whose modulated broadcasts reached our clime
Then ceased abruptly prompting us to send
My probe to learn what caused their sudden end.
Piercing space on cosmic waves my notes
Should beat me home by six or seven rotes.
My down is fluffed and in the cryonest I perch
To sleep perchance to dream.

Now as I sang before, the world I probed
Was once the roost of cultured animals,
Intelligent though surface dwelling beasts,
That named themselves "Persona sapiens"
As we learned from their oddly amelodic, unrhythmic transmissions.
I sang how each P. sapiens lived life
Alone among the chirps of their machines
Which could communicate and entertain,
Or run in a productive mode although
I don't know what it was that they produced.

Each sapiens lies nested in a cell
Of a roost that spans the whole south polar land
Of their blue world.
In most remaining lands rest those robots
Who once saw to the needs of P. sapiens.
The central portion of one continent
Is covered with a lake of dark liquid
Contained within enormous earthen dykes
That stretch from shining sea to shining sea.
Every machine is in working order,
But no Persona breathes. There are no signs
Of violence; only those miles of cells
Containing emaciated corpses.
As my song closed the only question was,
"How did they die?"

Coda: Well now I think I know.
Deep in the brain of their master server,
Called "Ultanet," a planet-wide system
Of data storage and distribution,
Was where I found the answer to my quest.
Its rhizomes intertwined through every nest.
The first message that I decoded was

The last entered. The death of the author
Had just occurred. Even as the writer
Tried to reach out to other P. sapiens
They were always already dead. So yes,
This is the final message of the last P. s.

TO: anyone@anyhowtown.com
SUBJECT: anything

    I'm sorry for the breech of etiquette, but I have to communicate with someone before my signals lose their referents. Someone respond to my transmissions, or as our ancestors used to say, "Open the pod bay doors please, Hal."
    I like to remember how, during the last century, we achieved total privatization. Everyone now is able to live a perfect simulation of everything that anyone can imagine. The recent discovery of a new use for dirt has finally provided a source of virtually unlimited wealth. Of course, dirt is now too valuable to waste on agriculture. Unfortunately, the government program to make food from all that useless petroleum stored in what was once called the United States (an old metaphor with no vehicle) lost its financing due to the balanced budget amendment. Still, I know something will work out, it always has. Unfortunately my modem is under sanction, I can't seem to find anyone who will break penal protocol, and something is wrong with my feeding tube so I'm rather hungry. Nevertheless, my portfolio is full of top soil futures hedged with options on gold so I'll be fine. I'm just going to rest for a moment. Do you read me?

Signing off 'til someone responds,
Agemo D.N.A. Ahpla

Janet McNally's poems and stories are published or forthcoming in publications such as *Best New Poets 2012, Gettysburg Review, Mid-American Review, Hayden's Ferry Review, Alaska Quarterly Review, Ecotone, New Ohio Review, Crab Orchard Review, Crazyhorse* and others. She is a graduate of the MFA program in fiction at the University of Notre Dame, and in 2008, she was awarded a fellowship by the New York Foundation for the Arts. She won The White Pine Press Poetry Prize in 2014 for her manuscript, *Some Girls.* She teaches creative writing at Canisius College in Buffalo, New York.

About her poetry, she says: "I'm drawn to poems with strong imagery and lyrical language. I'm a fiction writer, too, and I look at poetry as an alternate way to tell stories. I've always loved myths and fairy tales, which loom so large in our cultural consciousness without giving the characters true voices of their own. I want to remedy that, to give my readers another way to navigate the stories, a fresh lens through which they can see those myths."

Lilith, Happily

1.
The second time they started from scratch,
rolling the clay with their own hands. God sighed
as he did it, knees sinking into the loose dirt
beneath his favorite tree. He held one rib, curved
and tender, for its magic.

As for Adam, he was slow to start the potter's wheel
spinning, afraid she'd turn out like the last one:
long-limbed, furious, full of laughter.
But he wanted her willing, so he got dirty,
plunged his fingers into the earth.

When they finished, they stood back,
happy, and watched the second one's
first steps. She was a doll.

2.
Later, Lilith would laugh when she heard
about her replacement, the lolling eyelids
and too-wide mouth. By then she was sending

postcards with no return address, stopping
at mailboxes in dusty Midwestern towns.
She would lean out the window of her blue
Chevrolet pickup just to feel the sun
on her shoulders.

When she heard the girl had eaten the fruit,
Lilith shook her head though no one
was watching. Hadn't the woman ever
read Snow White? Even if you forget
the glass casket and pig's heart
in a box, apples from strangers
are never a good idea.

For the first time she considered calling.
She stood in the phone booth, held the receiver
in her hand. But would she ask to speak
with Adam or the girl?

3.
Now she lives near the Pacific with a stuntman
from the movies, making jewelry out of copper and jade.
Adam moved, she heard; left no forwarding address.
Strange, she thinks, that it's him she remembers
as she watches the manufactured accidents,
each imaginary explosion as unsurprising
as the death of a minor star.

O—

It's a lot to ask the hips to separate,

to make room, the secret bones
unhinging. The pelvis a bowl, a cave,

a door to get from there to here. Perhaps
you ran your fingertips across

ivory walls as you passed through,
searching for a window, a light

switch. Maybe you tucked your chin
and closed your eyes, tried to dream a little

before you reached the outside. When your lips
touched the air you opened them, made an O

like you'd practiced. With your eyes on the ceiling,
the lights, a bloom of air filled your lungs.

In my arms you willed your eyes to focus, and I
looked at you, remembering the ways

my bones fit together when I was eleven
and practicing *pliés* on the barre

in our basement. The solace of gravity,
the consolation of bone. We repeat things

because we don't know how to start again.
This is only an echo of everything.

Maggie As Sleeping Beauty

When she woke from her coma, one pupil
       had grown larger, as if it had bloomed

           while she slept. Her hair kinked in pillow
       waves for weeks and sleep creases mapped

hurricane trails across her cheeks. How could we
       tell if she was the girl we knew before? We couldn't

           ask her to show us where it hurt, because
       her bones had all knit themselves back together.

We had to trust that she would remember
       what we remember, though we had extra

           days and weeks spooled like old film
       in canisters. You missed those days,

we said. You slept, stretched under a hyacinth
       sheet, and when you woke you tested the ground

           with your toes as if you didn't believe it,
       as if it were glass or smoke or some kind

of water and you were hanging above it in the air,
       just waiting to let go.

Kristianne Meal perpetuates Rust Belt Books in Buffalo, NY, where she coordinates many wonderful theatrical and musical events, art exhibits and readings. Her chapbooks include *Twenty-Two, first pallet* (Little Scratch Pad, 2007) and *TwentyTwo, here, now now* (purple loosestrife productions, 2010), which is "Lovingly Dedicated to the 'Higgs Boson' Particle, otherwise known as The Missing Mother of Matter," and in which the last five poems of this segment of Kristianne's are included.

voice of the mustcracker
has no tines to continual
        choral elations
and dirges of all that is past
ancient lost and beautiful
bloodied or bodied,
the vast expanse of
        particular mirrors
and lapses and on

rather, the entitlement of being
not til you can will and be
by the divide invention of your
own hand the second one

sphery sea words
soakened trenchcoat
one person's lumping along
            the shoreline
what a thing is   then forward
                then forward

words on beaches blowing
    into sand
blame pearls   tight tears
wet sleeves
          poking points

not knowing one's grasp
to pull surface from a line

not knowing knowing

ever etching permanencies in sand
circles
          triangles
                squares

smoke truths from your
    watery eyes
fathoms waggle off
          to delicate jellies

on the shore of the wake
she lakens

*   *   *

when were we last tangible
to one another?
o yes, i was a rock
      sun baking by the sea
and you, the guano of a tern

how we mixed and exchanged-
vapor oils vibrations
saturated permanency
      brought on
by wind and sun

us scorched to one
til the tide covered and
   swirled your ash away
the moon's liquid beams
and i beneath
sparkling back at ol' white eye
     the information   of sunlight
of us consummated
        zinging
along the canopy
      a monkey

* * *

here   is
the dark of day
the hidden night
black sun time array

no vinegar will be given

something is going to fall in the darkness
its weight unbalanced   is shifting

an object   plastic bag   gravity
the thing moves intermittently
before its slide

      off the table

* * *

I cannot translate you
if I am to possess you

possess me that I cannot be translated

I am possessed therefore illimitable for translation

flash the light to no transparent setting
     to parallels between us
       milky hallways

we both had to go out n learn
some new skills right here
in these same coordinates
and we arc'd real far
then began to loop back
as gravity would have it this wasn't
a question of possibility but a
function of nature as one
delves the sweet duration
of color
      not dark pupils

insofarashenceforthheretowithinasmuchas

    is   is   is

        *   *   *

in raccoon circles
in circle in circle in circle in
circle in circle in circle in circle
in circle in circle in circle in
circle in circle in circle
in circle in circle in circle in circle in
circle in circle in circle in circle
in circlewheeeeeeeeeeeeehaaawwwwwwww
c'mon little digger goin' git goin' git n take
n turn you in goin' turn you...
        blastema stump

oooo mummy i go crazy
for you i
deem you for
sake of me
mummy i
squeeze and squeeze
bitty drops
to see you see me
squeeze mummy

You lie curled
under a blanket
hands tucked tween
your knees your head
and feet are missing

mummy my veins
they patter gainst sky
                leaves before rain

is that you there
all curled up under
those blankets
last night?

oooo mummy you tantric me
            yes I said
                    mine

Marge Merrill works in the long-term care field, learning from a variety of experiences spread over 30 plus years. Her work has appeared in *Beyond Bones I*, *Hanging Moss Journal*, *New Verse News* and *On Barcelona*. Marge finds inspiration in the well-crafted line, the local poetry community, her garden and the blunt force words of Charles Bukowski.

Hand in Hand

Between rheumy coughs
rainbows of recollection
phantom smiles
barked laughs

a spoonful of ice chips

tired bones
green apple drowsy
in a tangerine haze

go gently.

Walk the Floor Blues

Listen hard
to softening air

old jazz men
vibraphone
bass
piano

deep night
cricket counterpoint

whiskey fingers
sleeping arguments

blues words walk the floor.

Back of the Classroom View

Last desk
last row by the windows
bored with the rules
taught by pickled spinsters.

Tell me
why
writers picked up pens—

a season of reasons
if you can, Miss,

never danced
on your back
by moonlight.

Best Friends

We welded ourselves
against street floods
diapers
retainers
and sailed hormonal seas

through bake sales
miscarriages
dragged-out divorces.

Now,
one of us
wrapped around all of us

girls,
we deserve
new shoes.

(Untitled)

I am more
than linen semaphores
in crisp apple light.

I exceed beer habits
horses
and Friday nights.

Your mountain
will not snuff
my light.

I am not yours.

In Response to a Bewildering Poem

Sea salt
butter drawn and quartered
succulent metaphors
from Wolfgang Puck

hold the oysters

and the tofu
stuffed with fermented cabbage
on a stick.

I'm goin'
down the street
to Maurice

he grinds fresh
sears sirloin
with Bermuda
fries in skin

and I don't wonder.

Standing Before Unblinking Gods

Pleasant dressed
knife blind
he sells corn-brooms
at the public market.

Amid the symphony of muscled senses
grandpa
shrill granddaughter
a bartender says *stop in*
a soft voice smells of a warm bed
footsteps pass him by.

Hungry for touch
in hard lonely boots
standing before unblinking gods.

Edric Mesmer lives in Buffalo and collates an international journal of anglophone poetry and commentary, *Yellow Field,* the earlier incarnation of which was named for Sally Hoskins Potenza's painting in the Burchfield Penney Art Center, *Yellow Edenwald Field.* He is the author of *Intaking Water* (The Orkneys: Seapressed/ meta, 2011); *Yrtemmys* (Buffalo: PressBoardPress, 2013); *Faun for a Noon* (Red Glass Books, 2014); and 2014 "Outriders Selection" competition winner, *of monodies and homophony* (Outriders Poetry Project, 2015). He also coedited *Minnows Small As Sixteenth Notes* by Norma Kassirer (BlazeVOX, 2015). Currently, he serves as cataloger to the Poetry Collection of the University Libraries of the University at Buffalo.

Flagging legends

From my bathroom win-
        dow a mosaic fount mud-sunk...

But from my bedroom   the nightshade
    of a stop sign flung over the fire hydrant

                Sinews of arrest bequeath

       the fixed shade of diurnal rapture
         In yards concretized

    pools that fall from a trampoline's surface

         in the locution of fortune
    quincunx

The Doubting Optimist
        in a window for modernity

     daringly faces away
        as the Pleiad turned   ever after Troy

Even she counters countenance never so much as by archetype

                                Rested thereon
        "something represented or indicated in a work of art"

                    However she hopes she is wrong

The Alstons surround their reflexions

drenched in all save their tunics

            a plum rolls through the bank of myrtle
made blue by spheroids sodden

this oblivion, one beyond transversal

chooses capitulation—ar-
dent Aesopian

            (here is a bar that rends the
jar thither)

our coordinates the dif-
ference of cobalt from sea salt

or of water...pusil-
lanimous,
            the kept brine
poolside

barred drapery in
expulsion

A khimera

In his dream
the vocabulary may begin:

[Cyrillic **D**]
O{
91

Though she is muted
he is reading her face;

though he cannot listen
she is thoroughly cursory.

You can take: take Stravinsky.

Lapped
as the conch

is the French
horn's bell;

tonight
empyrean

symbols
what you will:

analysis

in excess

horny toad.

Of a sudden
there is orchestra—

weren't allover these chambers
alchemic?
4'33" rhyming
meaning melodious.

[A saint's]

apostrophe{

the <u>date</u>?

Tablature
scant tableaux,

the eye on
its nightstand ev-

anesces; nor
composure or

carbon makes them one: rosette.

Defiling phylum
in whose image

your arm foregrounds
mine "and thou art borne."

Perry S. Nicholas is an Assistant English professor at Erie Community College North in Buffalo, NY, where he was awarded the 2008 SUNY Chancellor's Award for Scholarship and Creative Activities and the 2011 President's Award for Classroom Instruction. He received the SGA's Outstanding Teacher Award on two occasions. He has been a guest lecturer at Daemen College, Villa Maria College, Niagara County Community College, and most recently, at Empire State College in Athens, Greece.

Perry has been nominated four times for the Pushcart Prize, in 2006, 2007, 2008, and 2010. His poems have appeared in *Common Ground Review, Literary House Review, Caesura, Word Worth, Not Just Air, Slant, Feile-Festa, Louisiana Literature, Chautauqua Literary Journal, Chest, The Healing Muse* and *New York Quarterly*. His poems have appeared on fifteen occasions in *The Buffalo News* and he has published over 100 poems, in print and online. He has also published four full length books, *The River of You* (FootHills Publishing, 2009), *What the World Sees* (Saddle Road Press, 2011), *Small Crafts* (The Writer's Den, 2012) and *Beginnings* (2012). In 2013, he published *The Company We Keep*, co-written with his wife, Maria Sebastian-Nicholas, and in 2014, a chapbook, *Ancient History*.

Perry Nicholas was, until early 2014, the co-host of the Center for Inquiry/Just Buffalo Literary Café, and he has also co-hosted the Lewiston Arts Café with Maria, who is a singer/songwriter. He was a coeditor of *Beyond Bones*, a WNY literary journal. Recently, he judged the Just Buffalo Annual Poetry Contest, and has judged the *Word Worth* journal's poetry and essay contests.

It's Been Years Since I Was Read *Goodnight Moon*

Listen, moon, it's not your fault.
I'm just crazy tired of you
giving it away to just anyone who
happens to glance around, then up.

You ask why I distance myself,
so abruptly, so mercilessly
from the unstable, why I can't learn
to forgive them or myself.

We blame everything on our parents,
so here I go again. I never knew
what to expect, which phase,
which page they would turn for me.

So goodnight noise, goodnight air.
Combing the house, nobody there.
Goodnight boys and whaddya think?
Every day ends with goodnight drink.

But when a cow jumps over my fence,
I want nothing to do with him, sacred
or not. Moon, you promised things would be
different, judging by your constancy.

I don't have room for ups and downs.
I need to hold some tiny faith.
To be able to wander outside,
look up, and *know* who's showing.

On the Porch With My Daughter, Now a Woman

It takes an effort to ignore the tug
of my office, urging me inside to record
some of this. Poetry perched beside me,

long legs drawn up to her chest, shoulders
defying sunburn, we achieve a rhythm in our talk,
volleying familiar phrases: the persistent robin,

a chimney-like neighbor, the tired song
of the same-old ice cream truck.
We anticipate responses before they land,

comfortably serve them up without thinking.
She listens more closely today, especially
to the pauses, as if focused on the odd music

pillowed in my chest. Her ear used to rest there
while we napped, always the silent scanner.
She hasn't lost that ability, and she counts down

my rant about how people who Facebook
are not friends and texting is not writing,
at least not by any definition I was ever taught.

I am her friend. She is my friend, I lecture.
She's content to share this concrete step as equals,
as I join her in a father's perfect awkward crouch.

A Momentary Gift

One of the sweetest, most dangerous things
a woman can do is cut her hair for you.
Among the earliest odes we know.

Listen closely to all the lyrics;
they haven't changed much over the years.
You fall short of yearning, along with

an unsurprising broken heart,
misnomer of forgiving magnitude.
The truth is it always grows back.

There should have been a song
to capture the moment a woman
frees the tight curls after a shower

and shakes her hair down with an infectious
smile, almost apologetic sigh, studying
your eyes for a rare, unscripted reaction.

Don't question why she did it.
Don't leave her raw, open, and wet.
Think of it as biblical or wonder

at the purity of it, maybe.
Accept the gift, tuck it away,
use it to repair any fissures

in your chest, or just desire her
until the next cut you dare acknowledge,
or the next time you catch her humming.

On the Light Side of 2 A.M.

you pulled into the drive
as I waited to *babble*,
as you sometimes call it.

I could see the tired lines
around your mouth, no smile,
no hug tonight, and I waited again
for you to shower, slide into bed.

I brushed your ruffled hair back,
as I always do, but you mumbled
Don't talk, let me sleep.
So, somewhat surprised, I waited, watched.

You waded through reams of sleep,
flutters of eyelids, softening of lines,
face transformed like an actress
removing her stage makeup.

You won't remember saying it;
I don't care if sometimes love goes silent.
Hearing your heavy breathing is better
than any poorly unwrapped words.

Hotel Filoxenia

The hotelkeeper, Marika,
does everything she can to make
this place what its name suggests:
friend to strangers.

I'm an odd Odysseus
dragging a suitcase up
a hundred stairs, huffing,
embarrassed I'm still searching at my age.

I'd just as soon hole up in my cabin
than fight my way along cobblestone paths
with half the heart I had
when I played soccer here as a boy.

I hesitate to hold onto Marika's arm
since men don't touch married women in Greece,
but she senses I am struggling,
takes my elbow anyway, stares straight ahead.

We don't need to say anything—for this final leg,
she's a silent figurehead guiding her sailor home.

Joe Nickell was a sixties poet and anti-war activist (a federal fugitive from 1968 until pardoned by President Carter). He has worked professionally as a carnival pitchman, stage magician, private detective, blackjack dealer, riverboat manager and university teacher. He is currently investigator for a science organization. He is the author or editor of some 40 books (shown at www.joenickell.com).

Nickell's commissioned autobiography appears in *Contemporary Authors* (vol. 269), and he has been profiled by the *Today* show and *The New Yorker*. "A person's life," he observes, "is his most creative possibility. I am disappointed by the increasing technological trend toward virtual living." As a poet admittedly influenced by the Imagist movement, Nickell states, "I wish for poetry to be the art of language." He writes in a style he calls "improvisational rhyming."

The Gift, Among the Wildflowers

**(In memory of my mother,
Ella Turner Nickell)**

In spring,
during
the awakening

of the earth,
death

came in the night for her.
A last breath.

Then
        at the hillside
        graveyard
the wind
carried her name

among the wildflowers.

I do not listen
        for her voice

or imagine
    I glimpse
    her face

haunting the shadows.

Instead, I recall
(through a child's

eyes)
her eyes

watching
the child

searching
in the field,

reaching
among the wild–

flowers.

The Fortune Teller

(for <u>Diana</u>)

As if she
were you, she

held my hand
 in hers,
   gypsy

palmist,
caressed
  the skin,
traced
  the lines

that led nowhere.

She guessed,
pressed
  on,
  saw in
  my eyes then
the lost

look,
 she
looking
  at me
looking

for you.

The Discovered Daughter

(for Cherette)

1
I would've searched
for you, reached

    back in time
    in some
    temple or tomb

and clutched

the Golden Princess
    with sapphire
    eyes, treasure
of lost love.

2
But ours was a secret
like a parchment

locked
in an old clock,
that ticked
and mocked
and took

its cruel time.

3
And the scryers
not seeing ever,
the tarot readers
turning over

The Lovers,
        The Fool,
others,
but never
      the real
card that would've

trumped them all.

4
It was a picture
        of you, your eyes
        those
of my ancestors

staring back
from antique

frames.
            And I woke

to find us waking
        in each other's dream,
to hear us speaking,
        at last,
        each other's name.

The Wait

This is the weight then:
the cen-
        ter of the thumb's whorl,
the final
       zero
       I go
in search of the worth of - -

the blank
clock
    that tells me when.

Let me say then
when

I will speak such worth

of myself,
or else
      end
with what I know,

and let my life go,

my hands
be twisted

roots in the roots' hands.

Millie Niss (1973-2009) earned an Honors Baccalaureate in Physics and Math in Compiegne, France and her BA magna cum laude in mathematics from Columbia University. She undertook graduate mathematics studies at Brown University, followed by an MFA program at Emerson College, before Behcet's Disease caused her to abandon her formal education. Her earliest publications consisted of innovative mathematical proofs and research sponsored by the National Science Foundation.

Best known as a widely published web artist, she created http://sporkworld.org in 2000 and her Sporkworld blog, http://sporkworld.tumblr.com/ in 2007 with her mother, Martha Deed. Millie's graphics, videos and web installations have been exhibited in galleries, including SCOPE 2006, huffingtonpost, Dvblog, Iowa on the Web and in many other venues. Her poetry has appeared in dozens of print and online publications, including *Beehive, Big Bridge, The Buffalo News, Museum of the Essential and Beyond That, New Verse News* and *Unlikelystories.org*.

Millie died of hospital-acquired infections following a bout of Swine Flu in November, 2009. On February 19th, 2011, a special Big Night in her honor was held at the Western New York Book Arts Center. Her book, *City Bird: Selected Poems (1991–2009)*, edited by Martha Deed, was published by BlazeVOX in 2010.

Slightly Fictionalized Version Of Bush's Speech
At the Site of the Minneapolis Bridge Disaster

Whaddya know? This bridge is broken. This bridge was necessary for crossing the river. You can't cross the river now on this bridge. You can't get to the other side! That is because this bridge has fallen in the water. This is not good. As your president, I am very proud of our highway infrastructure, and it is a sad day when I see exit ramps and traffic cones crushed into rubble. But don't worry. My good friend Mary will fix this bridge. That's Mary Peters, my Secretary of Transportation. She has a good heart. She is joining me in praying for the bridges of America, to ask God to protect them from any future harm.

People need bridges to get to work. People need to go to work to feed their children and to promote the national economy. If this bridge does not get rebuilt, China might some day beat us economically and become a dangerous military superpower. The Chinese do not share our values. They have no respect for the American way of life. They imprison Christian pastors who dare to put God above their godless state. But do not worry. This broken bridge has been a wake-up call for America. We can no longer ignore the yellowy red menace lurking in the East.

I am proposing a new piece of legislation, the Minneapolis Bridge Disaster Relief Act of 2007, which will provide twelve billion dollars in new military and Homeland Security spending to protect us against China and Chinese-influenced sleeper cells in American cities. This bill will provide American-made weapons to Taiwan and India, put surveillance cameras in Chinese restaurants, and add everyone with the last name of Lee or Wong to the national no-fly list.

Once this bill is enacted, and I am counting on my friends in the Democrat Party to join me in getting this essential national security measure passed before Congress adjourns for its summer recess tomorrow afternoon, America will be even safer from Red Chinese terror attacks than it was before the bridge broke. You can count on me, as your commander-in-chief, to keep you and your loved ones safe from the crafty Chinese. So why don't you pick up the phone and give your Senator or Representative a call asking him to support my bill. You can tell him the President told you to call. Or you could use that Internet thing my friend Al invented.

I just want to remind you before I get back in my helicopter: Our safety as a nation is not a political issue, it is a national issue. In the fight against global terror, there should be no party politics, no business-as-usual in Washington. I have a message to the Congress: "The people of Minneapolis are counting on you. Do not put special interests above the needs of the bridges of our Heartland."

God Bless America and God Bless the City of Minneapolis!

A Cross-Cultural Linguistic Mistake

Tanya the Tyrannosaurus tries even Rudolph's resolve:
he – a stolid gentleman of medium height and intellect
– simply does not have room for dinosaurs
(outside of Spielberg, et al.)
in his world.
and when one comes bounding in through the garden door
(mind you, Tanya is a very small Tyrannosaurus)
Rudolph says merely "shoo!"
as if she were the neighbor's cat
– alas –

Tyrannosauri do not have the same nervous system as cats
and they are not domesticated
and "shoo!" sounds like a war cry
or worse – a mating call
Rudolph seems a very disappointing male Tyrannosaurus
but Tanya has never seen a male Tyrannosaurus
She ate all her litter mates as a wee babe
and has been living the bachelorette life ever since
minus, distinctly minus, dating
because it's hard to find a date when you are a Tyrannosaurus
in a world of men
And no one has yet said "shoo!" to you
since they have usually fled in terror instead
for you are not THAT small a Tyrannosaurus
but you appear in proportion to a person's capability to deal with you
and Rudolph could only manage a cat-sized Tyrannosaurus
which is fortunate considering that he is about to mate with it
I'd like to write the rest of this story
it went down in medical history
but it is distinctly x-rated
know only
that it ended in an emergency room
in Southampton, NY
and yielded no offspring

The Carmelites

      sell souvenirs
      near the entrance
      of Auschwitz slowly
      or faster if they choose

      an apple tree
      creates a shadow
      and the crosses
      are like lenses
      focusing the light
      conveying immanence

      losing consciousness
      between sleep and waking
      keeping silence
      cinematically
      not as in a Chinese garden

random apples
pose hard questions
about the light
long since dissolved
into space

the trees are a ceiling
holding silence
and the blossoms
hide memories
of distant cries

It's a Whitman Morning!

The homeless woman on the corner calls out in a language she alone speaks.
Her words bounce off the curb, fall into the Hudson, and penetrate the
oceanic depths.
Their saltiness is my saltiness... the words that come ashore on the jagged
rocks of Marazion
       have the salt of my sweat in them.
You, too, are a part of the anthem – Do you recognize your voice?

Whimsical, awkward, arrogant, coy... America tests its newly deepened voice:
The clack-boink of basketballs in the courtyard of my building is a part of it.
The tinkling of an ice-cream truck pulling the desires of youth through
the city streets like an unmatching
       thread used to mend the pocket of a beloved coat
The crash of a florist's iron curtain sealing off dahlias and daylilies from the
lustful night
The salsa music flowing from the foot of Samuel Tilden's statue
The creak of windows exhaling essence of bacon fat and coffee into the
morning air
The boom of a door slamming on a former lover;
He will never shave here again.
The whine of an ambulance carrying an expectant mother of twins
The braying of the Staten Island Ferry as it disgorges its load of commuters
on a hot August evening

All these are a part of the song but they are not the song.
No scholars' glosses, no learned lexicons can amplify this melody.
I bathe in it and embrace the limpid swell.
I draw it close to me and with a lover's soothing words appease the waves.

Marjorie Norris is a Buffalo-born poet who has been published in journals, collections and activist papers nationwide, including *Juggler's World*, *Room of Our Own*, *Common Ground*, *Arizona Mandala Quarterly*, *Santa Rosa Review*, *The Other Herald*, *Persimmon Tree*, *Beyond Bones*, *Brigid's Fire*, *Rain and Thunder*, *Poets Against Apartheid*, *Artvoice* and *The Buffalo News*. She won the Greensboro, NC Triad award for her poetry and was a Just Buffalo Writer in Residence. She has taught creative writing at SUNY at Buffalo, Chautauqua Institution, Feminist Writers in Ithaca and Womonwrites in Atlanta. Her books include *Chautauqua Breathing* (2004); *Two Suns, Two Moons* (2005); an anthology, *Trees of Surprise* (2007); *Resilience* (2007); *Woodland Heart* (The Writer's Den, 2011); *Slanted Windows* (No Frills, Buffalo, 2013); and *Matisse: A Life in Metaphor* (Saddle Road Press, 2014).

Kitchen by the Sea

I am already lucent, poured like falling rain*
Yes, I'm hungry for morning, poems feeding
From the mouths of swallows, distance in my palm
Yet my fingers still curl around my steaming cup
And sea churns toward me, a repetitive mantra
Brimming with shells and salt and some lost
Memory ancient and true

Each day I search for one hidden fable filled
With water's vastness, its cold and bottomless
Depths, light hail coating my window. In this
Morning kitchen I sit by the stove, rooted
Among plants and pots, fallen butternut
And colored gourds. Looking out to sea,
I think of Orpheus, whose music made
Even the stones cry.* This is the future,
I say to the plants and shells around me.
I am one of you

*Rilke, "Orpheus, Eurydice, Hermes", a poem

278

Soyez Sage

"the light of truth's high noon is not for tender leaves"—
Gautama Buddha

Be careful of the light
(wear sunglasses)
its wisdom
not for the uninitiated
(wear shades)
(darken the pigment of your eyes)
(pull out your visor)
(wear a cap)
then look below
into the pool, Narcissus
let the sunbeams filter
over the deep
see the dappling effect
throw in the small stone
of your soul
let it ripple
as light plays
like fairies on dark water
now take in the sunned fluid
quench your thirst
one warm sip after another
to penetrate,
take in the light
incorporate
(now take off your visor
and your blinders)
let the light shine out
from your body, your eyes
then face the truth
sizzling in the skies

History

In the hidden places are the moments
Of truth: when I gave birth
To my daughter's truth she mirrored
In bright lights with hair the color
Of tomato, when I opened the book
And saw her name, when I found
My own and knew I was a woman,
When love stole surprisingly in
The night and opened her story
On the moon-strewn sheets,
Whenever light breaks into the
Dubious crevices of this living
Breathing space, when real
Cracks through, this is the angel
Of history

She says Don't Look Back,
It is a widow's muse when you
Look back, it is dark veil
Over the oilcloth, it is
The candle's drip, it is
The place where the scent
Of incense walks into a room,
When you absorb it, the scent
All about you is a garden,
Solomon's seal, African
Impatiens, Japanese iris
And bulbs will burst forth
From everyone's garden
And everyone is who you love

Does the angel of history
Come to touch you in the night?
Come to weave the disparate
Pieces in the garden, come
To soak you in a fine green mist,
The dark tropic of who you were
Once: a mere girl attached
To a string, attached to a bright
Kite in a golden field? Was the
Field dry then, without water,
Was the field full of poppies
Or the promise of summer rain,
And when you held yourself
Ever so minutely aloof, did

The voice comes to you like
A cool well, did it whisper
"Here now, you are in this
Garden, grow now, be your
Own sister, write your own poem"

How Grief Travels: Poems about 9/11

After: Airborne Pieces in NYC

Before you know what happiness really is, you
Must enter a deep garden where white butterflies
Live, soaring between kale and carrots and cabbages,
Testing the bright cutting essence of vegetable,
The taste of earth and acrid sky.

And, as you enter, you must notice every blade of grass
And how they lean lime and yellow at the base
Of hemlocks, thinning out on their trail to the trunk,
Encircling the tree in the mud.

When winter comes, the roads will look sweeter for
The snow that covers gravel and scattered branches.
And the trail then to anywhere will be white, calling
To you, telling you where to place your feet.

I have learned that a white butterfly can lead you
When you don't know where to find a path. Those
Resonating butterflies, all origami, cheered the
Children of Nagasaki, a real one will push you
To enter the core.

This must happen before you enter kindness, before
You can know just what is happy, how friendly
The earth is.

Squaw Island

Today the sun gives me
Late September glow, the grasses gold
Upon the little island surrounded
By the mighty river

Birders walk by, arm in arm,
Binoculars ornamenting their
Chests. Think of the cormorants!
I tell them, awestruck, and they
Nod, then pointing to the herons,
Etched on the sky like the soul's
Calligraphy: joyous and unbounded,
Determined in their pointed faces,
Saying yes, and there, and yes

You show me the morph heron,
The white one with a lace of black,
While all the while, I've only
Known the green, those herons
Called common, so named for
Their numbers and their
Middle size

Suddenly, as if on a strain
Of Bach, up mystical
From the Niagara plumes
A blue one, giant of nature
Captured in majestic flight

We all watch, the four of us,
The bird couple, and you and I,
My dear, clear-eyed in the river's
Wind, the arching trees. We all
Then see it: blue, without binoculars

Redwing

In the grassy flats between my house and yours
The red-winged blackbird has found a nest
Carrying our songs between the harvest of
Years, the moments of eternity

Do you love me? Only marshy grasses
Can answer, only the nest of the redwing
And the bird moving, solitary and swaying
On that brown cattail waving, can tell
Of a heart as profound as autumn,
As close and sensible as a star

Foretelling

Could I have made it different,
The first dew on the grass
My muddy childhood
That held the buds of its own
Foretelling? I carry my shoulders
Differently now, relaxed in sun
Yet still apostrophes in hail,
Up against the wind, up against
Myself

How time has sweetened that burden,
These days as toothsome as the friendship
Shared with stones, a crooked circle,
A slow ripening Bosc among the faster
Berries, a holy sage pulls me to the river,
Where we are blessed again and again
By its silver waters, its cormorants
And ducks, its caterpillar crawl
Then our own swooping lift
On a heron's wings
Up, over the great River

Susan Dworski Nusbaum

received her BA from Smith College and her law degree from the University of Buffalo Law School. She is a retired criminal prosecutor living in Buffalo. She has been a frequent participant in the Chautauqua Institution Writers' Festival and poetry workshops, and served on the Board of the Chautauqua Literary Arts Friends. Her poems have won First Prizes in the Chautauqua Poetry Contest, Just Buffalo poetry competition and the Hauser poetry competition at the Chautauqua Writers' Center. She has read her poetry in the Writers and Poets Series at the Burchfield Penney Art Center, at the Center for Inquiry and in the Gray Hair Reading Series sponsored by Earth's Daughters and Just Buffalo. Her work has appeared in *Connecticut Review, Nimrod, Chautauqua Literary Journal, Harpur Palate, Wisconsin Review, Sow's Ear, Earth's Daughters, Artvoice, The Buffalo News, Poetry East* and other publications. Her poetry collection, *What We Take With Us,* was published by Coffeetown Press in June, 2014.

Shore, Mountain

We hear the sound before we see its source,
a low moan emanating from a hollow interior,
barely audible under gulls' cries, the throb of surf,
an iron barrel-buoy bobbing on its anchor
three long miles off-shore, *basso ostinato*
against the anchor chain, spreading to the water's edge,
where we stand listening, as years ago we listened
to the chanting of monks at Swayambhu,
single Sanskrit syllables from perfect silence
resounding mountain to mountain, tritones resolved
in thin air, long-horns held to soundless mouths,
sacred breath pressed through lengths and breadths
of burnished brass, spilling into the red soil.

Star Music

On a summer night by the lake,
you can hear the stars singing,
like crickets humming
or waves pulsing under water,
with a little buzz of electricity
arcing between them and your ears,
making you gasp,
so surrounded are you by the sound
as you stare into the foam of the Milky Way,
peaceful, without inflection,
but pitched clear as air after rain,
the luminous turned audible.

Listen. Their voices follow you
even into the January dusk,
when stars begin to fall, settle
on window-lamps and porch lanterns,
chased by headlights down driveways,
over branches laced with radiance
like forgotten Christmas decorations.
Pianissimo, they murmur beneath
dopplering sirens, pedestrian signals
that chirp away the diminishing seconds,
their music constant
through the wind-blown harmonics
of the long lake-effect night.

Departures

A woman is dying
in the C-corridor at LAX
just outside the restrooms.

A stream of travelers detours
around the clot of EMTs
hunched over her body,

diverting their carry-ons
to each side of the island,
rolling and bumping

in the headlong rush.
Some turn from the pantomime—
the silent chest-pounding,

the somber arrival
of the oxygen tank—startled
by a sudden turbulence overhead.

Two bare yellow arms, weightless,
palms up, seem to float from the edges
of a bright blue plastic shroud,

the medics standing back now,
hovering in a circle
as if to give her breathing space.

*

My plane rises,
its trajectory parting the air currents
like a *Noren* curtain.

From the serenity of clouds
I imagine the terminal scene
transformed into a Zen garden,

Ryoan-ji,

blue sky, shimmering rock, void
held in place by furrows of sand
neatly raked, all flowing toward home.

Vanishing Point

There once was a time I climbed
on a snow-bank in a vast backyard,
looking up at a white sky edged
with bare branches, deep as vanilla pudding
and broad as the row of garage peaks
zigzagging the horizon.

There once was a time I careened
in a garden under an endless night sky
sizzling with signals from light-years away
to a world I thought I'd inhabit forever,
the air pricked by fireflies and abuzz
with the mystery of alien planets.

Now that wide world exists behind me
in a swath crowded with wrong turns
and dead ends, and moments of such beauty,
such bliss, I turn back time and again
for one last look, one last heart-full.

Along the vee of my shrinking path,
the curbs grow high with obstacles,
the bodies of the dead.
Yet I scan the trail ahead, lest I miss
what might be moving toward me—
an errant breath of white sky, perhaps,
or a spark from an undiscovered galaxy.

Marc Pietrzykowski: "The world is filled with impossible stories. Robert Ripley roamed the world collecting them for his comic strip, *Believe It or Not!*, and I read small paperback collections of the strip voraciously as a child, wishing I could have a job that cool when I was a big person. And now I'm big, and I have a similar job, cobbling together my own impossible stories out of the many I've collected, sometimes in the form of poems, sometimes as songs, sometimes as novels or essays or jokes told in airports. The world is made of stories, but it's the impossible ones that help remind us how our dull, cankered lives might fit some greater pattern--or at least make us believe, for a moment, that a pattern could exist. As part of that job, I have been lucky enough to publish some books (details available: www.marcpski.com) and even found the time to start a publishing company (www.pskisporch.com). It seems my wish came true, I have a job as cool as Ripley's: I compile impossible stories and offer them for others to read. Maybe someday I can have a museum in Niagara Falls, too."

The Insult

The telephone rings, or it rang, once upon a time,
Now it beeps or whistles, the doorbell, the alarm clock
    also are digitized
And at the church they press a button instead
Of pulling on a rope—so it rings and a plane passes by
Overhead, making the cheap ceramic bells painted
With a scene from somewhere in Germany
Rattle in my mother's china cabinet.
It is how she must have imagined heaven:

A small cottage on a hillside and impossibly blue frocks.
Still the phone continues to bleat, yet another
Human being bent on proving their sympathy
    and worth, or it could be
They want to tell her how she finally won
The lottery, some rocket fuel to blast her clear
    of that narrow pocket
Wedged between poverty and oblivion—it's too late now,

You tapeworms, she's already won the gift of a lifetime:

Watching the birds from the banks of the Rhine,

The sun fixed in the sky, shining a buttery yellow.

The Grinding Wears the Stone Down, Too

These were the days of the week: 6 am: rise, evacuate, preen,
mumble at the pigeons on the ledge.
Morning light hissing up from the underworld
as I made toast. Butter for you, jelly for me,
7 am: kiss-and-part, ache, endure,
then home again and, perhaps, the weight of you.

And thus I became a cretin,
fat
and grateful
for every little jelly stain
and buttery lip. Home by 6 most days of the week,
weekends a fog of crumpled sheets
and tree-lined strolls; these were the scenes that dug
a hole in my skull, trepanned me
and let all the wrong of this world leak out.
Specific details are nothing, they make you a fool,
a town idiot fumbling with beads and string—
they will make you a believer,
and that should be warning enough.

Use my example, tack my photo
to kindergarten walls: this is what happens when you believe
that details add up to something more
than another detail, this is what happens
when 5 pm comes, when the train shudders into the station,
your hands stained, your ears full of chatter, your dank stairs,
your oven lit, your glass of vodka, the stupid way you sit
and wait. Wait to hear a key
squeak the lock. To feel a hand
upon your neck. For all details

to fade into mush, for the truck
to come and haul away her clothes,
for the lake to swallow her ashes
and turn them into fish. This is what belief
gets you, children: half a man,
surrounded by details,
waiting to be rid of them and all that they insinuate.

In the Train Station Watching Footage of a Plane Striking a Building

O mankind! We created you from a single pair of man and woman,
and made you into nations and tribes, that ye may know each other...
—al-Qur'an 49:13

And so it is that certain tragedies
seem to float across the sky
at arbitrary points in our field of vision:
the smoking shells of buildings, colorless
streams of gas hissing from overturned tractor-trailers,
rail cars crinkled amidst clumps of oak and pine;
our own small horrors trail off them like tow ropes,
wind-whipped cords braided from pink slips,
falls from trees, a split lip beneath the jungle gym,
this or that parent embalmed and sleeping...
in the great spaces between each lies cancer, idolatry
and the instinct for joy that struggles to float free
from the mind and the eyes that fail to see.
Such tragedies are crumbs left on the trail
and the crows, the crows are everywhere...

I stand and watch commuters huddle
along the platform, watch
them board their trains, uncertain, afraid
of becoming part of an unwanted history,
a story of Empires: seep
and contract, cleave asunder
and coalesce: I watch as we gather
like rainwater pooling on a ledge.
How do we persist, with so much

to despise, so much to withhold, such a constant
baring of teeth, it is remarkable
we have not devoured ourselves completely...

And instead, on the day a far off speck
grew immense and black in the sky,
on a day when our magistrate slunk fearfully
from trench to trench, a day that saw an island smoke,
when the dead in their numbers crowded the turnstiles
and the next world shuddered from the weight of them
and the shudder was felt here, in our teeth, we turned
to one another and with a glance, apologized
for every wrong we had done, and all those
we'd imagined done to us. What we found, on such a day,
reminds us we are human,
and it leers at us from the blind heart of the forest,
and it waits with the patience of a seed,
and it thrives on tears as well as rainwater.

Peter Ramos' poems
have appeared in *Colorado
Review, Puerto del Sol, Painted
Bride Quarterly, Verse, Indiana
Review, Mississippi Review*
(online), and other journals.
Thrice nominated for a Push-
cart Prize, Peter is the author
of two books of poetry: *TELE-
VISION SNOW* (Back Pages
Books, 2014) and *Please Do
Not Feed the Ghost* (Blaze-
VOX, 2008), and two chap-
books: *Watching Late-Night
Hitchcock & Other Poems*
(handwritten press, 2004) and
Short Waves (White Eagle Coffee Store Press, 2003). He has criticism in *College Liter-
ature, The Faulkner Journal, The CEA Critic, Mandorla, Pleiades and MELUS.* He has
been invited as a poetry fellow to the CoLab Residency at St. Mary's College of Mary-
land, the Virginia Center for the Creative Arts (VCCA) and the Constance Saltonstall
Artist Residency. He holds graduate degrees from George Mason University and
SUNY/Buffalo. An associate professor of English at Buffalo State College, Peter teaches
courses in nineteenth and twentieth century American literature.

Birthday

A little after midnight—the skies clear
over Washington D.C., below freezing
at Dulles International Airport,

the sloping lines of its buildings
disappear into the snow, the plowed snow
spilling over the walkways thick

and powdery as cake-mix. Lit by floodlights,
baggage handlers push the stacked luggage
between sliding glass, follow the well-dressed

as jet engines whine. West of the continent,
eight thousand miles across the Pacific,
a small jungle village explodes—

This is your home. This frosty distance
under the moon. In secret locations, the astronauts—
declassified—slip into their bright suits.

The Nineteenth Century

There was nothing left on earth
to discover, so we finally took sick.

Low doses of mercury prescribed
by the physicians kept us in bed

long afternoons, the curtains blowing
through open windows and at night

we dreamt of children—their milky limbs
and torsos androgynous. Convalescing,

we spoke of our lives, gatherings
at Harper's Ferry, speculations out West,

the words we left in our boot-prints: *Turkey Foot,
Indian Grass, Rattlesnake Master.*

History groaned, the millennium approached—
we knew this but succumbed in the end

to fits of nostalgia, to bourbon and verses
of Jimmy Crack Corn until dawn.

And yet—to have gone out
the other way—beside the river—

bright-eyed and shirtless, exsanguinating,
our teeth exposed in the dim daguerreotypes...

Watching Late-Night Hitchcock

And before we know it, the sexy lead is
—Mother of God!—rubbed out.

It turns out we don't know exactly
what we want. Rilke wrote that beauty is nothing

but the beginning of terror. That's fine
for Germany, Prague or wherever. Not here.

We like things clean: the boat flag
snapping in the breeze,

the platinum bee hive
sipping gin from a bird bath.

Our Lady of Porn

                Rumpled and slashed
with mud you were—low,
        as any detective story but quicker, say, and charged,
                        fraught with more nerve.

Your awkward entrance and trembling
                before belts and buttons, lace, nylon
or eye-hooks torn asunder, the slowly-opened thighs,

        your palette of grease and saliva,

berries and cream or toughened flesh-rubber, la mode
        your endless latex and stiletto fetish.

Swelling, panting, and breaking again, lithe
        and never quite funny—O flickering

queen of the money shot, scorned, furtively kept
        and always bursting

your sweaty trousseau: forever and ever, your million children
        drown in television snow.

Still Life

Old humanism!—crackling black and white,
split-leaf philodendron on Eastern horizontals,
spiny palm plant and fan, old primitive
modern twentieth century ghost—I do
miss you. *I* still believe. Come back.
I'll greet you straight, Humanism, lonely
as a Giacometti, a bold and sexy Brancusi.
We'll stay up watching Hollywood-adapted
Tennessee Williams and cry. *Night of the Iguana, Sweet Bird of Youth,*
doomed and beautiful in Technicolor, our conviction
for the utterly New. Old Humanism!
dozing on a cheap motel sofa, dangling
your lit cigarette over the waste paper basket. Bogart,
Doris Day, Picasso, even the Flintstones—all your cards
and killers, your pinups and private dicks and savage
architecture, pagan, luminescent, the living room drapes
and windows open, a bluish TV screen glowing
in every rancher, stars and a laugh track
over the crickets.

Stay up with me, Humanism.
I'll make us Betty Crocker, break out
the Crisco, the margarine, marzipan
and baking bowls, the old ones, white glass
with blue daisies from Corning, even my avocado-green
electric mixer. Anything, Humanism. Stay:
I'll let you lick the beaters.

Sara Ries was born in Buffalo, New York, where her parents have owned a diner since she was two years old. She holds an MFA from Chatham University in Pittsburgh, where she received the Best Thesis in Poetry Award. Her first book, *Come In, We're Open*, won the Stevens Poetry Manuscript Competition and was published in June 2010 by the NFSPS Press. Her poem, "Fish Fry Daughter," was selected by Ted Kooser for his *American Life in Poetry* column. Her poems have appeared in *Earth's Daughters*, *Artvoice*, *Blast Furnace* and *The Buffalo News*. She currently hosts the Poetry & Dinner Night Reading Series at the Woodlawn Diner and teaches at Erie Community College and at Villa de Leyva in Columbia, S. America.

Christmas is Three Days Away and it's Raining

You are stage-curtain-tall, hunched at your desk,
flipping through photos to gift. *Next year,* I say,
I think I'll write poems, place them in boxes and wrap them.
You like that idea, so I sculpt these words for you.

Yesterday I burnt the grilled cheeses.
You smiled and said: *That's the oldest trick in the book,*
burn dinner so you don't have to make it again.
You were quiet, and I was hungry for words fierce and fresh.

We're in Buffalo, picturing ourselves in Buenos Aires,
but this is our life right now:
Your trumpet is by the door for band practice
and you, musical you, are whistling as you stir the pasta.
My first semester of teaching just ended,
so our table is a scatter of graded essays
and your dirty socks are boats on the kitchen floor.

Remember you said: *I feel like we're mostly in your country*
but you don't always come to mine?—
I'd like to be in your country more
but my words are waterfalls
and yours are hors d'oeuvres.

I store your words like fine china in the cabinets of my mind.
These are years old: *When I see you, all my worries melt away*
like ice cream on a metal mountain.

Christmas is three days away.
I return, drop my bags and umbrella on the couch.
You are hanging a glittery trumpet on the tree.
The whole time shopping, your favorite song was stuck in my head
and now it's playing. *I bought this for my mother*, I say,
and hold up a scarf. I decided on the green one even though
the purple scarf was stunning, and I couldn't stop staring at it.
My mother would like the green scarf.
You point under the tree, the one we gave a second life to
after it was discarded by the real estate party, and say, *Open it.*

It's the same purple scarf from earlier
and you bought it not knowing my want for it.
That's how it is with you.
Even wordless in different countries, we meet.

Sometimes,
before I say goodbye
I dish you some ice cream.

And sometimes,
before you have to leave
you light me a candle.

Prayer at Johnson's Corner

I order an omelette from a truck stop diner
in Loveland, Colorado
two hours before a plane will take me
away from the Rockies.

I wipe lipstick off my mug.
I imagine a lady sits here every morning
and eats poached eggs. After another cup of decaf,
she paints her lips, says: *I know I'm old,*
but I'm nowhere near ready to leave.

The waitress refills my coffee; it splashes
outside my mug. She shakes her hair more grey
through whiffs of bacon, says, *I'm not with it.*

I do that too, I say. *I'm a waitress.*
She looks out the window and pauses
as if the mountains just whispered:
Coffee spills are tiny decorations.

I come from a diner in Buffalo
and any exit will take me back. Back home,
when I look out the window when I spill coffee,
the only mountain I see is a closed steel plant.
It took thirty years for that plant to lose all breath.
Now our diner has more coffee stains
than customers. But sometimes,
behind the barbed wire, geese lower
their beaks to grass.

I check the time, button my jacket.
A man at a booth scribbles something
on his paper placemat. He wears
black boots, leather vest, jagged beard.
The waitress serves him steak.
He takes off his hat, bows his head
folds his hands, closes his eyes

and everything:
the mountains, steel plants, flesh, everything—
become soft and they flow into
each other and then
he opens his eyes.

Becoming Waves

We drove for hours
along the California coast
as the ocean stretched by.

Sherri lit a cigarette,
turned up another song
I didn't know.

I kept my eyes shut, sick to see
so much borderless blue
and not go in.

When Sherri finally parked,
I ran to the ocean in my bright red bathing suit.
Just me, the sand, and all those shades of blue.
As I reached the shore, Sherri snapped this picture.

Look at me, a blood stain on a blue blouse,
arms outstretched, about to be swallowed,
wanting more than anything to be swallowed.

If you look long enough,
the waves will turn me into them,
love me that much.

Sherry Robbins is a poet and teaching artist. She has conducted creative writing workshops throughout New York State and abroad since 1977 and was given the Just Buffalo Literary Center's 2012 Literary Legacy award. She is currently an arts-in-education consultant for the University of Coimbra in Portugal and for Portugal's Belgais Center for the Study of Arts. As the owner of Orchard Press and co-owner of Weird Sisters Press, Sherry printed letterpress works of poetry for her own and for other small presses. Sherry has two chapbooks of poetry, *Snapshots of Paradise* and *or, The Whale*, as well as the complete edition of *or, The Whale* published by Blaze-VOX, and dozens of poems published in literary journals and anthologies here and in Spain and Portugal, including *Salmagundi*, *Denver Quarterly*, *Poets at Work* and *Earth's Daughters*.

Another Silent Night

Some things come back
and some stretch out
in one direction
till they're gone.
This year in a new house
we light the candles
but omit the words
that urge on and welcome
back the sun.
Let light speak to light
this time and let
the houses that brought us
to this house line up
to the vanishing point
without fuss. Old
unraveled words can
vanish with them
and in their void
something will be born
with no language
but its own immediacy
to fix the dark forever
to the finite sun.

The Castaway

Down into the Dead Lakes
down to their Queen
and her hoard of pearls
down, a pip, a point
of self dissolving
in her arms
down to where strange
shapes of the unwarped primal
world glide by, down and
drowned and up again,
indifferent as my god,
am I now to make sense
when sense is a lost oar
bobbing on her vast blank body?
Stick to the boat
is good advice.
Leap from the boat is mine.

The Quarter-Deck

That inscrutable thing is chiefly
what I hate.

A dead whale or a stove boat.
These are the choices?
Keep your gold doubloon
nailed to the mast.
That inscrutable thing
is chiefly what I love;
the awful rowing
toward it,
unarmed
and dangerous.
It
will not
swallow me.
It does not want
so much as a leg.
It wants
inside.
There's the rub.

And what tune is it
ye pull to, women?
Row Row Row

The Grand Armada

Darling girl,
seconds away from rowing out
to the expanding rings of madness
where you will chase and be chased
by every imaginable distraction,
buckle your power belt,
sharpen your knife,
your eyes already hunger
for the storm.

Darling girl,
you made this mute calm here
that first night you drew
mortal nourishment from me
while your old eyes feasted
on unearthly reminiscence.
Ponderous planets of unwaning woe
revolved around us, yet, deep down,
deep inland, you fed me joy,
a joy that's now my permanent home.
So leave me in this underwater nursery,
battle is our birthright, too.
Grip your oars, clutch your soul.
Who knows to what strange waters
contraction may some day impel you?

The Symphony

When I first
split into womanhood
(forty – forty – forty years ago!)
the world split in two
like an apple.
Men were frightening,
women more so,
and some days
I hardly knew
which half to bite down on.
It was hot then
and maybe the sky
was a woman,
the river a man.
You couldn't learn
these things in school.
It was hot
and hard to think.
Alligators, snakes, mosquitoes
bit. The air was
fat with flowers,
the slow, slow accents
of heat-colored birds.
I didn't know
if I moved my legs
and arms or something
moved them for me.
Everything was alive.
That much I knew.
And I was alive too,
but alone. Is that why
I moved north
where gray sky,
frozen lake make everything
feel dead and people
crowd together
in heated rooms
to say real things
to each other as if
they had a life in common?
I like it here, like
getting older here.
Some gray hairs grew
the old-fashioned way

but some grew out of joy.
I used to think this place
could save a soul cleaved.
Lately, though, as I fall
out of womanhood,
I don't think much at all
in halves or opposites.
If there is a time
and a place for everything,
maybe it's here now,
when everything swims
through as if here
and now were porous
and everything is singing
Just You Wait.

Gary Earl Ross is a writing professor recently retired from the University at Buffalo Educational Opportunity Center. The award-winning author of more than 200 published short stories, poems, articles, scholarly papers and public radio essays, he is the author of the short story collections, *The Wheel of Desire* and *Shimmerville: Tales Macabre and Curious*; the children's tale, *Dots*; the novel, *Blackbird Rising*; and the staged plays, *Sleepwalker: The Cabinet of Dr. Caligari, Matter of Intent, Picture Perfect, The Best Woman, Murder Squared* and *The Scavenger's Daughter*. Playwright-in-residence at Buffalo's esteemed Ujima Theatre Company, Ross is a member of the Just Buffalo Literary Center, the Dramatists Guild of America and the Mystery Writers of America, which awarded him the 2005 Edgar Award for *Matter of Intent*.

Evil—An Abridged Autobiography

in the beginning was the worm

and the worm was without form

newborn and hungry and writhing

in the fledgling human heart—

i was the worm and you fed me

the wet purple strings of your own soul

hunger taught you to kill for your belly

but i taught you to kill for a belly laugh,

to wade through viscera with a smile—

jack-booted and wrapped in many flags,

gloating behind the many masks of god,

i have walked all the battlefields of time

i have watched you fall by the millions
beneath the studded wheels of imperialism,
manifest destiny, racial supremacy, caste systems, class systems,
ethnic cleansing, collectivization and other blind ideologies
—and laughed while whipping my bat-winged horses forward

i lashed backs that built pyramids and
grew fat inhaling bloody dust in the roman colosseum—
i dined with vlad the impaler in a forest of death and
slipped into witchfinder dreams at salem—
i piloted the amistad and gave the sick to the sea
and held down the slave women i told you to take

i introduced poverty to women in whitechapel
and offered them a deliverance from hell named jack—
i taught rasputin to preach and lenin to write
and little joey stalin to rise above his stature—
i turned on the gas at auschwitz and treblinka
and later licked the cyanide from adolph's lips--

from lynchings in america to suttee in india,
from plowing ruined flesh into cambodian soil
to sacrificing ogoni lives for nigerian oil,
from the extinction of indigenous peoples
to the honor killing of veiled rape victims,
i have been everywhere, caused everything

i shred hungry children and child warriors
with concertina wire boots—israeli, palestinian,
american, european, chinese, indian, african—
child appetizers in the endless feast of souls,

where i peel skin from history's sacrificial lambs
before tearing into them with yellow fangs

as i once walked slave quarters by night
i stalk the floors of far-flung factories
whipping awake those who sleep beneath
their sewing machines, forcing the fearful
to immerse their arms in toxic sneaker glue,
parting reluctantly with every penny i pay

later i shoot out another mosque window and
pour smack into another vein, poison into another
sky, and anthrax into another envelope
before sharpening another box cutter and
boarding *all* the planes—whom should i bomb today?
nuclear perhaps? i stop to think, why not?

i am a shadow parasite as old as time
a blood suckling as young as this instant—
i gorge myself on your fear and your hatred
i am pain-fed to ungainly size, swollen to
ungodly proportions but always small enough
to find another way into your heart

which i consume,
slowly,
from the inside out

Jane Sadowsky has had poetry published in *Beyond Bones I*, *The Empty Chair: Love and Loss in the Wake of Flight 3407*, *Voices from the Herd*, *The Still Empty Chair*, *Earth's Daughters* and *The Buffalo News*. Her poem, "Harvest Reflection," was nominated for the Pushcart Prize by the editors of *Beyond Bones*. "Toward the Light," was chosen by composer James Piorkowski as the lyric for his composition, "Toward the Light (Flight 3407)," which has been performed in concert by the trio ANA. Her poetry collection, *Journey*, which is illustrated by her own beautiful nature photography, was published in 2008.

Jane has been been a featured reader at the Screening Room, the Center for Inquiry/ Just Buffalo Literary Café, ECC South, Wordflight and the Stop, Look and Listen series at Impact Gallery. She is proud to have performed with Loren Keller and Verneice Turner as "Not Just Plain Jane" at the Buffalo Infringement Festival in 2009 & 2010.

Jane works at a school for emotionally handicapped children. She has a love for birds, and the outdoors, and a strong interest in Native American spirituality.

Two Worlds

The River once talked to my Ancestors,
as did the trees, Standing Ones,
and the Winds, too,
telling them where to move and when,
where to find the Four-Leggeds,
who would lay down their robes,
that we might live.
Wisdom in the Four Directions,
in the stones at our feet,
bringing together Fire and Water, Earth and Air,
in the womb of our Grandmother.
Grandfather talked to us in the sunrise,
sent the Winged Ones as messengers,
sang us rainbows,
and all the world breathed as one.
The Spirit Road bridged the night sky,
path to the Old Ones.
We were one with our Relations.
Complete.

then the strangers came,
talked to us as children,
brought us to their ways,
and walled us in.
boxes.
the only star they knew to look upon,
post and transverse,
marked their sacred spaces.
confined,
outside for them was nothing,
void.
with their ways,
they took away the sky.
they stole away our tongues, and taught us theirs,
so the only beings in the universe our offspring could speak to
were their offspring,
deaf, dumb and blind themselves
to the blessings of Creation.
they chopped down the Standing Ones,
and hunted our brothers.
they left us this sterile wasteland that cries out to us,
but we can no longer hear.
our hearts no longer trust.
we can no longer speak.

~~~~~~~~~~~~~~~~~~~~

Come back,
we come back,
as the grasses return after fire,
as the cones release the seed
after burning . . .

~~~~~~~~~~~~~~~~~~~~

Stone Bear dances healing
between the Worlds,
Healing
for the People.
Heartbeat of the Mother
moves the dancers' feet.
Drum-rhythm,
echoes in Stone Bear's chest,
moves his paws in time,
Dancing.

The dancers spin,
beads and elks teeth talking together,
feet finding the old prayers,
feathers nod, yes, this is the way,
and the Worlds turn, Sun-wise,
in Stone Bear's chest.

Old One, born of the Mother,
your Heart Songs move the mountains,
stir the winds to life.
The walled-in boxes crumble,
just shadows now,
empty.
We bring the others with us,
outside,
those who seek,
who'll listen --
hand in hand we dance.
The Wild holds us to heart again,
Free.

Early April Woods

The leaves are not greening yet,
new growth lies hidden beneath caps of bark.

Nests are still unwoven, winter-downed twigs a mat beneath our feet.
The summer flyers not yet returned,
their songs not yet unpacked.
Broken branches skreel together, shaken by the wind.

Snow's pure, soft-rounded beauty has aged into soot and wrinkles.
She lurks still in rooted shadows.
Snowmelt reveals the refuse blown to wood's edge,
the baggage once kept hidden beneath her skirts.
Plastic bottles, take-out cups, a broken thermostat.
Grocery bags wound and tangled into thorny hair shake and rattle
menacingly.
A slug makes its silvery trek along the underside of a floppy disk.
Marauding crows shout their war cries overhead.

Last spring, I saw the myrtle warbler alight on an overhead branch,
the magnolia warbler flash and preen its yellow feathers.
The catbird sang like Lady Day from between the vines,
while the orioles worked together on their hanging cradle,
weaving outside-in and inside-out to the sapling's soporific sway.

The jags and prickles of our hidden fears,
laid bare,
will soften, too, with new love's greening.
Already, the subtle hues shine in our eyes,
the fine deep red of heart's new branches rises
from the dusty blue-violet of the old.
On wings of goldfinch song, we touch the sun.

Amrutansh (Amol Salunkhe) studied Mechanical Engineering in Pune, India and came to the US for Graduate Studies in Industrial Engineering. He currently works in a Software Startup in Buffalo, NY and enjoys designing and developing software. Years of training in analytics and logic do not pollute his sense for aesthetics and pathos that guides his poetry. Amrutansh has been a regular on the Western New York Poetry scene, and his work has been published in *Beyond Bones I*. Amrutansh has cherished reading poetry in Marathi, Hindi, Urdu and English and some in translation. Tukaram, Kusumagraj, Gulzar, Rumi, Neruda, Rilke, Emerson, Thoreau, Frost and Merwin are some of his favorite poets.

The Headmaster and the Planted Tree

A small sleepy town; a prominent central statue
A narrow main street, few government buildings and few businesses
Post office a postman, a police office and guards and a small bank
Farm-equipment agency, a tobacco dealership and a jaggery wholesaler
A barber, a tailor, a sweetmeat shop and a butcher
A grocery store, a cloth store and a bangle shop
Green and red and yellow bangles and smiling shying maidens
Scene by Scene simplicity and life

A small sleepy town; a prominent central statue
Scattered new dwelling—stone houses and asbestos shingles
Tarmac roads and mended potholes and emerging cracks and covered drainages
Packed old neighborhoods—earthen huts and straw-hatched roofs
Dirt roads and cobbled pathways and narrow alleys and clogged gutters
Scene by Scene continuum and life

A small sleepy town; a prominent central statue
Mornings and roosters and crow calls and alarms
Newspaper delivery, cow-milking, egg collecting, water-hauling and other morning chores
Heavy breakfasts and lunch-tiffins and leaving working men and gazing waving women
Young and Old Farmers and bullock carts and tractors

Black alluvial soil, vegetable and vines and wheat fields and sugarcane stalks
Factory workers—bony lads and men—and bicycles and buses
Boilers and dryers and chimneys and soot
Generation and generation bequeathed vocation and life
Generation and generation cerebral-manacling and life

A small sleepy town; two neighboring knolls
Small village temple, deities and priests
Worshipers and oil lamps and garlands and flowers
Two storied hilltop high school and winding dirt pathway
Handful students and threadbare khakis and whites
And oiled-heads and patched-canvas book-bags and torn books
Scene by Scene hope and life
Scene by Scene new-horizons and life

A small sleepy town; high school compound
Treeless campus, large barren land and scarce water and loose earth
A broken iron-gate and door-less classrooms and un-plastered walls
Cracked stone floors and fractured chalkboards
Flat row houses and leaking roofs and disgruntled teachers
Math, science, history, geography, civics, language and art
Scene by Scene modesty and life

A first row-house; a passionate Headmaster
An amicable housewife and a gentle daughter
A gentleman and a loving mate and a caring parent
Or a son of the soil and social reformer and strict principal
Or a dreamer and an altruist and a philanthropist
Providing education and equal opportunity and ridding poverty and
empowerment
Scene by Scene toil and life

A first row-house; a passionate Headmaster
A kitchen garden and half grown herbs and spices and flowerless marigolds
and mums
Fallow land and dying plants and frustration and dogged determination
And new seeds and cow dung and effort and water and attention
And a vision—full grown trees and painted buildings and plastered walls
And new chalkboards and happy smiling teachers
And honest discourses and polished students
Graduating leaders and innovators and scientists and philosophers
Scene by Scene dream and life
Scene by Scene enlightenment and life
Scene by Scene redemption and life

The painter next door

A strange new city; my past sorrows
Unknown faces and towering skyscrapers and unexplored boulevards
Hurried commuters and worried pedestrians and stop signs and stop-lights
Crawling-honking motors and pedaling cyclists and dangling traffic lights
Packed roads and flooded side-walks and awed tourists and bewildering sights
Moment and moment; chaos and life

A strange new city; my past sorrows
Affluent neighborhoods and posh cars and scandalous penthouse
Graffiti dwellings and petty larcenies and boisterous fights
Dress suits and leather sandals and worn-out jeans and sneakers
Expensive apartments and cheap rooms and four course meals and street food
Moment and moment; disparity and life

A two bedroom rental apartment; three flights of stairs
Buzzing households and loud televisions and louder radios
English and Chinese and Arabic and Spanish and French
Old men and old maids and young men and maidens
Families and couples and singles and couples
On-looking neighbors and dispassionate smiles and warm hellos
Returned greetings and clouded thoughts and daily schedules
Moment and moment; recurring scenes and life

A two bedroom rental apartment; three flights of stairs
Workdays and gorged lunches and half cooked dinners
Weekends and activity groups and acquaintances and wine
Concealed sorrow and drowned emotions and keepsake routines
Emptiness and unhappiness and repression and memories
Moment and moment; tribulations and life

A drab art studio; three flights of stairs
A worn out widow and dark hair and white strands
Sunken watery blue eyes and wrinkled forehead and smiling cheeks
Bed-room and kitchen and kids-room and studio and books
Picture frames and black & white pictures and colored pictures and dust
Recent wakes and commiseration cards and funeral bills
Moment and moment; agony and life

A drab art studio; three flights of stairs
A canvas and color palettes and brushes and strokes
A lost widow and dark hair and gouache strands
Deep blue eyes and focused sight and upright frame
Colors and static scene and paint-stained hands

Moment and moment; passion and life

A worn out building; third floor
Open doors and crossed paths and vicarious moments
Isolated-man and emptiness and furtive glances
Isolation and Repression and Emptiness and Sorrow
Passion-drunk-widow and content and reassurance
Art and Expression and Unity and Joy
Moment and moment; expression and life
Moment and moment; unity and life

The Goodbye

Mother's love for a child is so natural—the child is her natural extension
Her image; her blood; her flesh
Father's love is more subtle—it develops over time
But if you saw him you would disagree
He could clearly hear her pulse in his wife's womb
He could hear the melody in the single syllables
And the two syllables "PaPa" sounded the sweetest of all
But he knew her also through the silences; the muted words and gazes
And in the eyes behind those gazes he saw the curiosity
He knew every dream and amazement in a stare
The bright tint in her hazel eyes
When he brought her a balloon or a cone of ice-cream
But he saw the dark red hued eyes sunk deep into her face
And the wide pearly white smile on that face
He knew every smile she wore and the emotion in it
The blush and purity in her smile
When he draped her dolls and fixed her dollhouse
But he saw her stolidity and drooped shoulders
And extending from the shoulder he felt the warmth of her hug
He knew every vibration rising from the marrow to her bones
The jumpy excitement of the tight hug
When he brought presents and glittered the holiday-walls
But he sensed the wanting reassurance and consoling
He felt her pain when he nursed her through nights
He knew her hurt her anger her suppressed smile
When a boy in her class pulled her pony tails
But in these moments he taught her lessons of life
As he had taught during riding a bike
His gentle words made her dust off dirt and rise
He spoke with eyes assuring her

He spoke with smiles when she dressed and saw herself in the mirror of his
eyes
Through the seasons they spoke in these private languages
And developed several dialects of love and affection
And of resentment and frustration and anger and anxiety
And never did this dialogue stop

Until now when words are amiss
Senses are senseless and eyes are watery
And touch cold with apprehension and worry

A grown woman parting on her wedding day
She hugs him tightly, tears running through her eyes
Words barely rolling out she says
"It'll be alright!"

Peter Siedlecki is a professor of literature and creative writing at Daemen College. His poetry has been widely published in such journals as *Stone Country*, *The Nantucket Review*, *Beyond Bones III* and *Intentional Walk*. Two collections of his poetry have been published, *Voyeur: Poems From 1980 to 2000* (2006) and *Going with the Flow* (BlazeVOX, 2014). He is director of the series, Readings at the RIC.

While serving as a Chair and Dean of Arts and Sciences at Daemen College, he says he had no time for what he really loved, poetry and woodworking. "Both take time," he says and "the flow should be natural, from the heart, but that flow has to be directed and even impeded by the head... I strive in my work to use personal experience, but to avoid the personal, the confessional 'I' like the plague. I aim for the more proprioceptive 'I,' the one that experiences and conveys the personal more universally."

Two Field Mice

Two field mice dead,
Decayed and dried
into each other,
making withered oneness
of the two of them
in the dark corner
of this plastic depth.

Imagine the hunger
that brought them here,
the gnawing longing
that led to grittily penetrating
the cover of this heavy-duty,
Roughneck garbage tote,
then descending
into its bowels
to find nothing,
not even an escape,
nothing to put one's teeth into.

Going With The Flow

I share my life and spread it out now
between the Niagara and the Hudson,
and I am—in a way—like a river,
eager to flow away and toward,
away and toward, testing the test
of Heraclitus
and acknowledging the persistence of change,
the persistence of movement,
the persistence of decay.

Is this the condemnation
of which Sartre spoke—that I am condemned
to be a river connecting two rivers?
That I am condemned to this relentless change
and to embrace the beauty
Of the sad death of summer
which occurs in blazes of color
that make my eyes laugh
and my heart cry?

Bruce Defines Eternity

As Shetland Sheepdog,
it is Bruce's anointed duty
to define
and defend
the flock.

Assuming dictatorial privilege,
he admits and excludes
its members.

Squirrels are to be excluded
in all instances
if only for their
inability to ground themselves

Demonstrating
rank and tenure,
on a scale between
God and theologian,
Bruce determines
that the squirrel he saw
through the kitchen window,
in the branches of the maple,
is there forever

to be barked at
whenever Bruce looks out the window
and long after the squirrel
has become invisible
to the eyes
of any members of the flock.

Pain

The surgeon,
Looking at the x-ray
And shaking his head.
Said he didn't know how
I was able to stand the pain.
That was ten years
Before I asked him finally
To replace my knee.
But I knew nothing of his pain
Or of what he was able to stand.
Or of what anyone is able to stand,
I merely stand
As long as I am able to stand.

Where the water
wears away the soil,
stones collect
to make a little wall
through which the water
makes a slower way.
Or, if no stones volunteer,
the water loosens tree roots
into a slow descent
and prostrate hulks
become impediments or bridges
or mere hulks awaiting decay.

Pain belongs to each of us
separately.
It takes from us
what we are able to give.
It telephones us with stories
of little children burning and dying
and dealing with deformity.

It demands a ransom
That will make its stories stop
We pay, or hang up
carrying images from the stories
in our memories
letting them fade or intensify,
standing as much as we are able to stand.

Irene Sipos is a native Buffalonian who completed her graduate work in American Literature at the State University of New York at Buffalo under Robert Creeley and Leslie Fiedler. Her work has appeared numerous times in the *Buffalo News* and in publications including *Artvoice, Lilith Magazine, The Comstock Review, Waging Words for Peace: Buffalo Poets Against War* and *Earth's Daughters*. Irene's poem, "Thank You, Mr. Burchfield," appeared in the 2009 Burchfield Penney Art Center Newsletter commemorating the opening of the new gallery. She won first place in the 2011 Buffalo Boom Days Poetry Contest. Also in 2011, Irene served on the Planning Committee for the Buffalo State site of 100,000 Poets for Change, a global poetry event. In 2012, she and colleague Lisa Forrest, in recognition of Buffalo State's *Year of the City*, organized a series of onsite workshops called "The Olmsted Parks Poetry Project: Exploring the Poetic Nature of Public Spaces." Irene is retired from the College Writing Program at Buffalo State, where she has also taught Introduction to Poetry and led poetry workshops through the Rooftop Poetry Club.

Freelance

You wanna know why the sky
is white on an August day. You
wanna know why the wood
fits the way it does, why
there ain't no balance in
this world, no matter how
many times you measure.
Test again with that level
but still it's topplin', all the rich
ones over there, all the hungry
ones over here, the talkers
and the not talkers, the barkin'
dogs and the quiet ones, the men
and the women who want stuff and
don't want stuff and who got too
much time and don't got any.
It's crooked, won't lie down
right. You wanna know where to go
with it, what to do with it, how

do you try, can you transmogrify
with words, with paint, with nails.
The sky is wide open, it's hot, it's white.
The porch is broken, it's unsteady.
The mantelpiece is detaching.
You wanna know why,
why this guy, why.

Everyone Says I Love You

We recognize variety, 150 species
of roses, 140,000 kinds of rice,
52 shades of blue. Some say
the Inuit have over 100 words
for snow. Everyone says I love you
but not a day goes by that I don't
wonder how we fail to differentiate
kinds when it comes to love. I love
garlic, I love mail in the mailbox, I
love leopard shoes, and I would love
more words in our language to distinguish
creatures from objects, to demonstrate degrees,
subtleties, distinctions. Poor 4-letter word,
too many job descriptions, both verb and
noun, we have so much expectation of you
to express affection for technology, junk food,
commodities, and the preposterous phenomenon
of life. I *loof* Woody Allen when he tells
Annie Hall how much he *lurves* her. I *luff*
Yo Yo Ma, but not the way I *lurf* a good night's
sleep or the way I *leaf* an autumn day,
or *loaf* a crusty fresh baguette and not,
my darling, the way I *lovitiate* you.

We Run We Run

How many Jewish women
in America sleep
in safe beds, plummet
into dreams like mine
last night? Decades younger,
brazen, I am lying to a uniformed
woman. These children, I say,
work in this house, they set the table,
cook the dinners, clean the kitchen.
Their presence is sanctioned by
the authorities. Her mouth taut, she
nods, turns her back. We run we run;
we run through rooms, hide in closets,
behind furniture, bolt through a side
door into sunlight. We run we run;
we run into a man, tall, a rifle blockading,
interrogating. With more words I
obfuscate. We run we run;
we run, a chain of small hands,
I beseech hurry hurry hurry,
no way will I let danger penetrate,
no way will I relinquish defense of
hammering ribcages in these small
bodies. Who am I? Not a brave woman, not
a survivor, not a child of a survivor, not
a grandchild of a survivor, not a traditional
woman of a wholly Jewish universe, just a
Jewish woman like so many, imprinted with
indelible memory of what I do not remember,
of what I never saw, of what no one close
ever told me, but what rocks my being in
the depth of night.

Poetry

don't do it because you
want to get something off your chest
it's not about your chest

it's about what wants
to sound itself out, to skip and slide
into shapes of spaces and swooshes
spoken or broken
in lines
on the page

don't do it to shove in a drawer
you have enough stuff in your drawer
don't save it, spend it, send it
donate it to a pocket,
leave it on a subway seat
scrawl it on a rock, chalk it on a wall
don't lock it, don't block it

place two poems
in closed fists and offer
this hand
or that

Judith Slater's poetry has appeared in a number of journals, including *Prairie Schooner, AGNI, MARGIE, Chautauqua Literary Journal, Sow's Ear, Minnesota Review, Connecticut Review* and *5 AM*. Ted Kooser selected three of her poems for his website, "American Life in Poetry," one of which was reprinted in Reader's Digest. Her first book, *The Wind Turning Pages,* was published in 2011 by Outriders Poetry Project.

She holds doctorates from Ohio State (literature) and SUNY/Buffalo (clinical psychology). Her interest in the way story reveals character led her from the teaching of literature to writing and the study of psychology. Carl Dennis and Irving Feldman have been poetry mentors, as well as numerous writers who taught in Chautauqua Literary Arts workshops. She has a private practice in Williamsville, where she lives with her husband of many years in close proximity to children and grandchildren.

Star Nursery

--for a grandchild

Somewhere in a galaxy
brilliant newborns nestle in whirling gases,
sparks whose light will arrive at our planet
tens of thousands of years from now.

Of all the small, already dying sparks
falling through the smoky golden swirl
we call the universe, I picture you—
drifting down through spacelessness

to settle briefly, curled and cradled
in salt waters, sailing through pre-history,
losing gills and tail, mitten hands meeting,
head nodding like a ghostly flower,

until, guided by the signal of your mother's
heartbeat, you approach our harbor,
arriving with your own question,
here, at our particular address.

Birth Mother

The wind is harsh in this cemetery.
Only a small group has gathered
for the burial of her ashes.

Sixty years ago, she handed me over
without remembering my sex
or the color of my hair.
A red-haired boy, she told the man she wed.

But I looked and found her in later years
and was pleased to notice
her nose and brow were like mine,
as was her quickness to cry.

When she lay in a nursing home, her brain
unraveling, I'm told that she grasped the arm
of a stranger and pulled him to her, whispering,
"I've been a good girl."

I think of an April day when she, nineteen,
alone in a boarding house,
knew it was time and walked to a hospital.

Each of us places a rose on the grave.
Now when it's too late, I long to offer her
a child's fistful of dandelions,
sleep in the curve of her body.

Christmas Afternoon

--for Jerry

The same time as always,
we walk out with the black dog.
She's all that is visible in the storm.
Caps pulled down to eyeglasses,
we trudge as she leaps and leaps,
blooms of snow riding her sleek back.

We talk of other years,
of the red dog and the yellow dog,
of our children in fluorescent snowsuits,
the mothers who muffled us in scarves.
Crows are screaming. We can just
make them out, wheeling over evergreens.

We are arctic, strange
shapes in a dissolving landscape.
I shiver and lean into you, feel
your arm tighten around me. The crows
settle. The young dog bounds forward.

Home with a Cold, Reading

Set me this day on a privileged path,
a wicker tray with toast and marzipans
and sugared tea in blue rose china cups.

Grant me long gazing out at flights of birds
and planes with purposeful trajectories
while the world goes on without me.

Let *Life stand still* as Mrs. Ramsey wraps
her shawl around Death's head. Draw down
the window shades with crocheted pulls

and bring me dreams of summer seas.
And treetops, let me fly.
Grant me slow waking to my place again.

Josh Smith is an internationally recognized poet whose work has been published by sundry outlets, including *The Buffalo News* and *Ploughshares*. He has been invited to read in cities across North America, and is pursuing an undergraduate degree at Harvard. Josh splits his time between Buffalo; where he won the 2012 Best of Buffalo award for Best Poet; and Toronto, where he has been one of the hosts of the Art Bar Poetry Series, Canada's longest-running poetry only series.

You Might Be A Poet
(With credit where it is due, to Jeff Foxworthy)

If you're more worried about your kids going through your old letters than your old photographs....you might be a poet.

If you actually know what the dot on top of the lowercase "I" is called....you might be a poet.

If you haven't bought a pen in three years, because you've accidentally stolen one from all of your friends in times of need....you might be a poet.

If you've ever said the phrase, "I can't leave the house tonight, there's a PBS special I really want to see"....you might be a poet.

If your other activities include origami, ornithology, and not getting laid....you might be a poet.

If you think Maserati is somehow related to the sonnet....you might be a poet.

If your spouse has ever said, "If you don't put that pen down and come to bed, I'm going to go make love to the neighbor"....you might be a poet.

If somebody asks for your favorite quarterback, and you say, "Quasimodo"....you might be a poet.

If you drink half-caf, light whip, caramel toffee macchiatoes at 9am on a Tuesday....you might be an asshole. I mean really, who drinks that shit?

And if you've ever read the letters in a Penthouse magazine, and said, "I could do a better job than that"....you might be a poet.

Stalling

2:18AM EST,
I should have called an hour ago to check on you.

But I'm not ready to have this conversation,
At least not until I've written my wedding vows;
Not until I've prepared my Letter of Recommendation for my niece.

I'm supposed to have finalized my thesis paper by now for chrissake!
I'm not ready to have this conversation,
It can't be time already.

Could a rain check be possible?
This conversation is not advisable for anyone with less than a 3.9 GPA.
I don't even meet the legal age requirements for this sort of thing,
You need to be fifty years-old, at least, right?

I am not ready to tell you how this will all be okay,
I am not adequately prepared to put a positive spin on this.

Your son is never coming home.

If there are six more devastating words in the English language,
I don't want to know of their existence.

It is now 3:06AM EST,

Your son is never coming home.
Your friend, is never making this call.

Tienes

Mi cabeza nadando alrededor tu cuerpo,

Mi cuerpo alrededor tu dedo,

Mi corazón debajo de tus pies.

Carole Southwood has lived all her life in Niagara Falls, New York, except for when she attended the University of Iowa writing program. She is the author of the novel, *Call Me Shady*, writes poetry and fiction, and has studied with Marvin Bell, Ted Berrigan, Irving Feldman, Carl Dennis, Mac Hammond and Raymond Federman. She teaches at SUNY Empire State College.

Shuffling Off to Buffalo

Beautiful flowers fill the fields
where I play at night.
Dark inside me where the fields are
I am alive in beams.
The people in my dreams don't look anything like me
except sometimes, as I've been told,
that is who they are.
One of them who could not possibly have been
was wearing a red and blue bandana
and sang about hell.
The fields of flowers are always like heaven
with a grand light in it where it is, albeit, dark
and the people are more often those who are not like myself,
yet if indeed they were, so then might be the light,
the flowers, the fields, beams, all of it
and the many of them
for I am plenty.

I Get a Kick Out of You.

Interesting that you can't see inside
anything sealed
even if it does have eyes. For all we know
there could be Abraham Lincoln disguised
as a German Shepherd, though there is a certain familiarity
with humanity one has which precludes
in one's mind the likelihood.
Contrary, perhaps, to popular belief,
the easiest thing for one to look at most knowledgeably
would be God, but this of course is just conjecture.
People do seem to know so much about him
and his intentions, the assumption, if not ludicrous,
seems appropriate.
Looking at a person who never speaks
is puzzling,
though it can at times be puzzling to look at anyone,
even a talker.
The meeting of eyes puzzles me the least,
but they move, you know, they move
yet even so, it can be better at times than looking at nothing
like a wall, or into an empty cage.
If you move in a circle slowly
around a light you're looking at
which has no apparent source
there is nothing else to wonder about.

Each person looking at the same landscape is different,
and there is no way of knowing anything about those people
without more to go by, but I can tell you this:
last autumn
as I was looking at the most astonishingly beautiful landscape I'd ever seen,
it occurred to me that even the seemingly ugliest people I've ever known
most likely know the names of all the primary colors.

Portulacas

It's like a war
to pick a flower
and like a war
to pick a word
or two, or three
and twist and turn them into victory.

I've had a headful
and I've had an empty vase,
living near gardens
that belong to other people
or to nobody so not to me.

I know the feeling
of war on blooms
the verbal explosion
after the doom. I know the feeling of my head
as a pistol, yet
as a womb, though, yes
more so, a pistil.

How would it be
to open
as the tulips to the sun,
as a word to one
with a projecting eye?
Or to close,
simply to close around the coming
of the piercing stars
like the submissive
portulacas?

Meredith on the Verge of Her
                        -- For M. Brown

If one can smile—no—
can break into a smile so suddenly,
how far away can she be
from the star of Divine Spontaneity,
the kind which we have thus far only imagined
to be nothing less than constructive
if one wished upon it
not to mention progressive
and possibly even infinite
with possibility?

She can't be very far away
at least From the Star
of this-is-even-better-than-the-way-it's-supposed-to-be-for-now!

Just before her smile breaks beamingly,
her eyes show that something from seemingly out of nowhere
is about to glow,
to change, if not her
or even just her face, then the likes of me and mine
for sure, and such contagion being the case,
how far away can this be
from the Isle of Smile,
from the big This or the big That
or, better still, if anybody will,
from the big Thee?

Trudy Stern, artist, poet and tea mistress, with her partner and husband Michael Morgulis, illustrated and published folios of broadsides, including Tea-Leaves Poetry (2009) and the inaugural broadsides for the then fledgling Just Buffalo in early 1978. (In those days, she was known as "Trudy Dreamer.") Her first chapbook, *Ghost Dreams*, was published by Local Color Editions in 2013. "April Fool," "Untitled (High Wire)" and "Pneumonia" were published in slightly different forms in her latest chapbook, *Taurus in Lake Erie* (Saddle Road Press, 2013).

April Fool

The winter's duel
Of light and dark is done.
The air is warm,
the sun has won.
Rake in hand I stand.
Time has come, I feel
to dig and plant. But
cruel April's ground is soaked.

Pools mark the spots
where mounds of snow have gone
and rivers run along the garden ruts.
Soon leaves of peas will peek above this muck.

For now cool air buoys
sweet robin songs
in the pear tree,
brush my ears and touch my cheek.

Rules for these days of early spring are few;
  1-Wait for May to go to work.
  And 2-
  It's time today to dance and be an April fool.

Pneumonia

Pneumonia play me.
fremitus.

Whispered pectoriloquy.
Ah, egophony.
Ancient echoes of my sounds,
Sounds in me and
in my fevered lungs.
Rattling cliffs and valleys of
my battered frame.

Deep, Dark, Tortured wind.

Years clang, hours chime.
Minutes twitter and persist.
Shadows flee
Across the grounds

Dark lakes
hum and drone.

Pipe my music
play my lungs
Each moment an attempt to breathe.

Oh symphony of adventitious sound.

Effort
Comfort
Fever
Wheeze

Still alive I know
Because I breathe.

Summer Heat

Now the days are getting long.

Summer heat begins.

Lettuce shoots to seed and

Kale can't stop its burst of yellow flowers.

July, the month of Caesar - soon

Sultry, sexy, simmering.

Last night I sat at dusk

Sweat ran down my sides,

eyes stung with salt.

No breeze, no air, just steam.

Sun slants low and late, shadows grow.

Days too long. Too short nights.

By 5 am too bright to stay between the sheets.

By 6:15, I'm in the weeds.

Untitled

High wire, no net

Life with you is tricks

Acrobatic feats unleashed

Point my feet and dive

In your completely crazy pool.

William Sylvester

graduated cum laude from Columbia University in 1940, and also studied at the Sorbonne in Paris and the University of Cologne in Germany. During the war years from 1941 to 1945, he was a navigator flying supply planes for the navy. After the war he got a masters in English from the University of Chicago and a doctorate from the University of Minnesota. He taught at Kansas State College and Case Institute of Technology in Cleveland, before coming to teach English, comparative literature and creative writing at SUNY at Buffalo from 1965 to 1988.

He is the author of many collections of poetry, essays and translations, including *Curses Omens Prayers* (1974), *Honky in the Woodpile* (1982), *Heavy Metal from Pliny* (1992), *Fever Spreading Into Light- Five Lectures on the Sources of Energy in Literature* (1992), *War and Lechery, The Poem* (1995) (all from Ashland Poetry Press) and *Nightmares—They Are Zeros* (The Buffalo Ochre Papers, 2009). He has had poetry and fiction published in *Poetry, The Commonweal, Western Humanities Review, Nimrod, Kansas Quarterly, 80 on the 80's: A Decade's History in Verse, New World Writing #5, Exquisite Corpse, Iowa Review, intent., House Organ, Swift Kick, Buffalo Spree, The Buffalo News* and many others. He has also had articles, reviews and translations in dozens of scholarly journals. His translation of Aeschylus' *Agamemnon* was published in *An Anthology of Greek Tragedy*, ed. Albert Cook and Edwin Dolin (Bobbs-Merrill, 1972). He has given talks and lectures in universities and colleges all over the world. Recently, he was the founder-editor of a small press called Buffalo Vortex, which published work by Kenneth Warren, Michael Basinski and Sheila Murphy.

He lives near his children and grandchildren in Bloomington, Indiana.

Suppose a Dream Swept King

shocked awake by some bright fragrance
wide eyed wanting to hold a vision of
night mares trampling armies to dust

slips on a sensuously
sweet thin tunic
booms his dream into one
man after another
dream words invade men proud
of their beautiful hair forcing
resonances out of random
moments raging a unanimity of war

They can no longer be men
except at the moment of killing
they explode into an infinity of zeros
zeros creating zeros

This is the Poem of Our Great Grief

How we went to war
How we stayed at war

Where is the hidden poem of righteousness?
The sexuality of it
Phallocentric uptight righteousness?
How male and female sexuality went to war
Tantum religio potuit suadere malorum
The red core at the center of the whirled
Magma matter
Colorless hotter than blue restless
Elemental bits caught in a swerve
In 1953 spending as much on war
In constant dollars as 1944

Where is the closet of our grief
Where is the great hidden poem
Of sentimental Helen at a wall
Beyond her agony hiding her violence?
O sentimental violent Paris
Where is the poem of your agony
There was a Helen before there was a war.
Did Paris remember her?
Did she remember his sea dark hair
Three inches thick dark as his eyes
Purple or blue like the deepening of
storm drive troughs, sea whispers turn shrill
water swells and falls away,
destruction moves outward

When the wind filled out the middle sail
The strange working of a nightmare in daylight
A dark wine smell flowed
The sweet air tasted of real wine
A fragrance grabbed the sailors
Grape vines grew upon the sheets and cables
Dark male clusters bunched with ivy
Luxuriance flowed fierce as any lion
Tipped their minds over into the water
Swimming within the sea, the priest
Cursed for his daughter, he
Remembered her as a pretty girl in sunlight
Before he had to obey a god and kill her

343

He went to the shore of the many sounding sea
Bee d'akeon para thina poluphloisoio thalasses
He raised his hands up to the sun
And chanted, chanted for sunbreeding death
E eid pote roi charient epi neon erepsa
Get even for me and kill kill kill
And the sunlight spread black death

Some sailors felt a moon engendered noise
Moved by memories of peppered goat cheese
Olive trees grapes, smell of charred wood
Dove into the isolating dividing water
Hoping to be transformed into androgynous
Dolphins for naked little boys to ride
But remained human, and began swimming
but 180 degrees off course.

Some say one dolphin survived

When We Are Small
Again In Heart

we muse a bit in the marble vault
little specks on the wall
glinting brass helmets
plumes hang limp needing
wind and air to flatter us
protective plates hide the pegs they hang on
a mess of clothes dumped in the corner
my heart falling into modesty
battle rhythm falling and rising
remembering souls and energy straight out
energy at right angles to its motion
remembering how we waited in silence
fearing the sound of the great heart within
as we wait memory painting our former
world before colors drained away...

"Some animals love humanity"

Some animals love humanity
A god loved a woman
she
in a tower
protected
The god came to her in a
shower of gold
Some animals and gods
move toward love of humanity
toward our hope of piety.
(Terrible when it is absent)
That's what I
Aelian
have tried to say
even if I didn't stick to one animal at a time
I tried to say it simply
just the way I talk
in plain Greek:
philanthropy
moves the whole
cosmetic scheme

Balustrade

a rail upon a parapet
above a row of *balusters*
pillars curving columns
more properly double
curving calyx like a flower
slender swelling below
rises to a bulging blossom
of the wild pomegranate

that's emblematic
the real taste of a real pomegranate
tied Persephone to Hades
through the winter until
Demeter releases her
that way we have our seasons
a lady's cool hand
slides along a balustrade forever
in a poem by Keats

Quick Within Slow Change

sixteen summers had never seen
Caribbean blue in her New England sky
she pressed the small of her back against
gravelly tar paper on her diving board
memory of a chlorine smell
an inside pool for a moment
evoked a sense of sea broth
until a pine forest fragrance
brought her deep breath
transpirations of   blue within blue above her
rolling her into a fall
free fall down into pine
tainted   dream water
dozing like a dolphin
dying so easily amazed
how she floated under
sleeping a little until
a sudden strain brought her up
gasping
she came gasping up
gasping into the light
the blue within blue above her

Patricia Tansey is a lifelong lover of poetry. She graduated from UB in 1977 with a BA in Biology and has worked as a molecular biology technician. She was a board member of Niagara-Erie Writers in the late 80's and catalogued Western New York poets and compiled their writings as her project for that organization. In 1989, she founded and served as board chairman of a literary press called Buffalo Press, which published an anthology and a number of chapbooks. She has been a featured reader at The Screening Room, Wordflight and Center for Inquiry Literary Café, and has been published in the recent anthologies, *The Still Empty Chair* (inspired by Flight 3407), 2011, and *Beyond Bones III* (Fall, 2011). She also enjoys cooking, gardening, art and photography and has travelled all over the world. She often goes to NYC to see her son and his wife and two grandsons.

Honey

If bees could suck the green
out of trees,
I would, if I could,
have a proboscis that could suck
the strangeness out of dreams.
If I were as uncanny a thief,
I would steal the pain out of
the hands of a clock,
which cuts my life.
Like Bonnard, I would steal
the light out of windows and
the gold out of the dawn,
or like Van Gogh, pilfer pinwheels
from a star.
If I were a butterfly,
I would capture music from the wind,
or if I were a flower, I could
run away with rainbows.
Memories distill to dreams,
and honey flows sweet and golden like heaven
long after the flowers have died.

From: **At Kenneglenn**

We wind through the shifted light
cathedral of cleansing waters,
Where the living crop out from the layers of the dead,
Where the roots wind through centuries.
No end to the eye's climb to the nearest sea age.
We find an arthropod fossil in the grey shale,
And traces in sandstone cry softly a muffled identity.
Tiny frogs make microcosmic circles in the shallow water.
A dead heron stares with grey and yellow eyes,
Blue feathers still form a wariness and regal poise
Around his wounded entrails
I see the top shelf of space teetering at the
sun's edge, enclosing a world of teeming death,
A gorgeous crypt of everything once ago,
The high sides leaning on the now up there,
On the path to Hillcrest, where Dave and his family
spent most of the summers of the last century.
Time creeps so fast down the eons of the rocks,
Tree crowned towering ledges of millennia.

The sun smiles beatifically on the wave edge,
and frowns on rocks which make prayer hands in the water.
History falls behind on the rock ledge.
Playbacks flicker in the shifting sunlight.
What we are and were to each other
Slips along the shale.

Faces of Devonian monsters stare, mirrored in the creek-flushed stone.
Time when the fishes first filled the ocean,
Plate skinned placoderms, sharks, and the first amphibian
Wandered in the awakening rocks of the leafless forest.
A circus of coral, yellow fringed cylindrophyl,
Towering cones with flame colored tentacles, the
Green Pleurodictyum, the pink calymene and yellow crinoids.
Just above the creek bed, wafers of the warm
shallow Mississippian sea beds, where fairy gardens of crinoids
danced on their dainty stems.
On land, plants evolved into every living hydrous niche,
And as the seas retreated, great swamps with towering trees, lycopods, and
tree ferns.
Thirty foot dragon flies soared, and the first reptiles
weaned themselves from the sea.
Further up the sides of the creek, Permian visions dance in the sandwiched
stones.
The sail backed carnivore, Dimetrodon, the needle nosed aquatic mesosaurs,

and amphibians with heads like Chinese hats roam among the conifers and
tongue ferns.
In the reefs, strange creatures with the bodies of snails and the heads of
octopuses
crawl the sea floor.
High up in the rocks, the Paleozoic dies with the trilobites, and many of the
bryozoans,
crinoids, horsetail ferns, fish and amphibian.
The Mesozoic flies over us with the first birds, the first mammals,
the first flowering plants, and the first dinosaurs.
Triassic alligator-iguana like reptiles, two legged reptiles, and great sea
monsters
Evolve before us into the Loch Ness monsters, brontosauruses, stegosauruses,
and flying reptiles of the Jurassic.
Cretaceous flowering plants rise out of the rocks here,
To feed new mammals, birds, and insects.
The great horned dinosaur, Tricerotops, the duck billed Trachodon, long
necked Brachiosaurus,
and the great Tyrannosaurus roam in the landscape of new trees,
Maple, beech, oak and magnolia.
Then, high in the dioramic layers of the gorge,
The Cenozoic ushers strange new mammals,
A reindeer horned rhinoceros, a snarling hippo, cat-like primates, tiny horses,
And a seven foot predatory bird with an eagle head, and the body of a dodo.
Primitive predators, called creodonts,
and forerunners of hoofed animals, with dog-like faces and blunt claws,
run across the gorge from the mid-high rocks.
A parade of weird, extinct mammals continues
with Oligocene oreodonts, like cougars crossed with sheep,
the eighteen foot rhinoceros with a tapir head,
and small ferocious creodonts, like a cross
between a ground hog and a hyena.
Miocene dry savannas stream out of the higher rocks,
With giant wild hyena pigs, deer-like camels, horse-like giraffes,
Small sabre toothed cats, mastodons, and the ape-like Dryopithecus.
Almost at the top, the rocks sing of the Pleistocene Ice Age,
with bison, camels, elk with eleven foot antlers,
the fearsome sabre tooth, Smilodon, and the great wooly mammoths.

We can see the Clovis point hunters stalk the woods above us for game,
Then Iroquois children, playing and splashing in the creek,
Then the memory of Dave's mom, walking among the majestic pines
on the bank, planted by Dave's grandfather, and
Dave and Hugh, as little boys running down the creek bank
to play in the waterfalls.
Right there below the tallest falls, we take our shoes off,
And bathe in the waters, that have,

with time, rinsed the ages from these rocks.
We are now part of the story washed into the stones here forever.
And the cryptic fossils of our words will tell us to the ages
like the leaves of rocks.
The rocks that tell stories of success and failure,
Of children making good, and falling by the wayside,
These books of life on the shelves here,
The winners shuffled to the top.

Days are falling out of the sky.
We watch them, beam by beam, in our own
cathedral of life, weaving in and out of time.
Here, the past is frozen, and doesn't move away from us.
The dead are singing to us in the water and in the high walls,
and in the midget dinosaur cries of birds.
From across the heavens, spreads the spangled cape of sunlight,
Around the shoulders of the gorge,
A masterpiece of God which alludes to all creation.

We emerge from the glen, just before the sun closes it to light.
We know we have navigated the Styx to the land of the longest gone.
Where the water falls furthest down,
And our lives and all our trailed memories
Come back stronger in the sun.
In each of us, the subjective is flowering myriadically from the collective,
Nevertheless, our sides of the story merge into the collective epic.
We have come back from the land of the dead together,
Like a tribe coming out of a legend,
Real and unreal, a myth shared and true,
Strengthening the outlines of our true forms,
Like figures in a storybook,
Larger than our lives.

Ruth Thompson grew up in California and received a BA from Stanford and a PhD from Indiana University. She was an English professor, librarian, college dean, and yoga teacher in Los Angeles. She was, until recently, a resident of Colden, NY, and now lives in Hilo, Hawai'i, where she teaches writing, meditation, and yoga, and runs Saddle Road Press, which has published many WNY writers. *Woman with Crows*, her second book of poetry, was published by Word Press in 2012 and was a finalist for the A Room of Her Own Foundation's *To The Lighthouse* Prize. Saddle Road Press brought out the revised edition in 2013. Her latest book, *Crazing*, has come out in 2015 from Saddle Road Press. Her chapbook, *Here Along Cazenovia Creek*, was one of *The Scrapper Poet's* "best chapbooks of 2011." Thompson's poems have won the *New Millennium Writings* Poetry Award and the *Harpur Palate* Milton Kessler Memorial Prize, and were performed by the great Japanese dancer Shizuno Nasu in 2012. Her website is: http://ruththompson.net.

Bless You, Father Walt

for lying stripped and singing
in the floes and fallows of your own body.
For granting us land-rights to your shaggy unkempt tongue
where through long syllables of scarlet leaves
we ride shanks-mare, drunk on the public road again.

Oh, bless me, Father Walt!
Lend me your large boots to caper and hoot at dusk,
make me shameless and grandiose, tender and foolish and brave.
Bless this false coin I use, stained as tinker's ware –
turn it to tigers resting in the shadows of my mouth.

Two Sections from: **Spring Along Cazenovia Creek**

vi
It's like you turn your head
for a moment or close your eyes
for a moment, like the pig-iron-
colored frost still has it all locked
for a moment longer and then

faster than you can catch in your wide
palms, in your wide eyes –

saffron-veined crocuses pushing through the ice,
then clouds of crabapples and willows and mauve
rhododendrons
and the cherry tree pouring down snow
into pools of grape hyacinths and forget-me-nots

and lilies of the valley, smelling
like that dream you had about the angel,

and purple irises and lilacs in clusters
of scented grapes, and wisteria –
and suddenly every roadside white and purple
with daisies and wild phlox

and then all along the fence,
fat mops of peonies, as big as your head,
and Renoir-fleshed roses, all
pink shoulders and gold ribbons,
and the lilies already two feet high –

and you are spinning around
to catch it inside your eyes before –

but it won't stop,
it is galloping downhill, days
like catherine wheels –

everything roistering, everything
busy being what it exactly
is, just as fatly and deliciously
as possible – like little pigs grunting
and sucking it up through their feet,
mouths open to the rain, to the held hose

and you would cry Wait!
but you're already twelve miles
down the road
and suddenly it's

vii
Fig-ripe, falling open,
heavy-breasted, deliquescing.

Melon sky, lightning-split
spitting seeds of thunder.

Caught in the grasses,
light, light, light!

Sugar shimmering in the veins.
On the skin, a slick of sweet.

Our Father's Deafness

Sometimes our father sang to himself
about dusk on the prairie and the slow murmur of cattle,
about rolling unshaven off a long-snaking train of flatbeds
with nothing but a tin can and a whistle.

There were two of us, and the mad bird
rocketing around the tall glass walls of the house
on a wheel of words. Behind his back
she snaked her neck and struck.

Then he was deaf. We thought him happy enough.
He had his work; we thought his deafness
bought him peace. But our father took to dying
as sea grass takes to salt.

Sometimes still I see his shadow
where darkness shoulders up against the glass.
He weighs the music in each hand,
turns the volume as high as it will go.

Then as the house rides out into the night
on seas and breakers of Beethoven,
he sits there hard against the speakers,
head cocked, eyes closed. Listening.

Walking Akolea Road

Two cardinals in blue ginger.
Three mynahs on a dark rock wall.

The red cocks crow, compare tailfeathers,
herd their households up the street.

Back then, the kids called it the Burma Road.
Sugar cane tall as the sky, sweetest when tasseling.

Now Mauna Kea shines above pastureland,
and down in the blue harbor, a ship has come in.

In a plowed field of bright rust-colored earth
men in broad hats are planting tamarind.

Flocks of little yellow birds consult in the wild cane.
Under the sun, the smell of molasses grass.

Three horses, two bays and a buckskin
drift down to the fence to be sweet-talked.

An old woman walks her goat on a leash,
white cockatoo and blue parrot riding on her shoulders.

Humus

Let the space
between tree and "tree"
be humus.

Let the space between us
fill with roots
that are (not) mine.

Let form come from this exact
place, be knit
to this tree's branching
as close as bark.

Because nothing is another thing
or a puppy of our thoughts
but only this
happening here between us:

let me grow a word for this

David C. Tirrell (1946-2012) had a BA and MA in English from SUNY at Buffalo. While he was in graduate school, he wrote papers on Keats and Blake, as well as dozens of poems. He also studied Anglo-Irish at Trinity College in Dublin after graduating from UB, and participated in a PhD program under Leslie Fiedler and Jack Clarke. He took graduate courses in linguistics and read and wrote extensively in that discipline. In the early 90's, he wrote a paper called "Placing Arcadia," in which he talked about the role of the poet as the "Vertical Man" who intersects with the divine, and about the role of poetry as a point of departure to divine consciousness or "ekstasis."

He wrote many books of poetry including *The Dublin Sonnets, The Lion and the Rose, Pieces of Eight, The Half-House Poems* (shuffaloff books, 1990), *Phantoms in the Mirror, Once Past Eden* and *The Darker Choruses* (all as yet unpublished), as well as several broadsides, papers on linguistics and a booklet on tantric yoga, called *Visions in the Kundalini Tantra*. He also wrote the fascicle, *Alchemy: A Curriculum of the Soul No. 19* (Institute of Further Studies, 1992). He was published in *The Buffalo News, Further Studies Magazine, Inc.&Ink, Farthar, House Organ and intent*. He started as a traditional poet and transitioned into an avant-garde writer from the 80's onward.

He loved spending time at his family's estate on Hunter's Creek in East Aurora, which is called Kenneglenn, and is now owned by the WNY Land Conservancy.

The Long Road and Perfect Visions

Lord, of the gifts you give there are but few
I can accept, for you have honored me
And I am full of wealth, and grateful, too,
That burdened of these things I still am free.
For all my trials, I have ever known
Great fields and running rivers for my ease
And even in the forests you have shown
Your voice to whisper from the towering trees.
But I am not content; I wander still,
And every crossway marks a further quest;
I cast my eyes upon the furthest hill
And wonder if I ever will find rest.
Yet if you have a hold on those that roam,
Then yoke me to the dream that brings me home.

Vision of Christ, of the Holy Tree

Now of the desert there is raised a castle,
Closed like gardens in deep Babylon.
The pavement, rust, and banner
Are all subject in the winds, nor no less
This Lord with just his pot of fish
For a last meal under heaven.

Stars are hard to understand
When whispers sharpen each one in the sky.
Fish are swimming, waiting for a transfer
To the lake; hard feet, yet; no miles to go
Across—unless they are unlike the stony hills,
The garden or the sea.
What place this is without mark
Or chance event to pass is wandering itself.
What can happen with the fish left by the staff?

Nowise is not often, but it is this once
As finely hung as a dark melody is spun,
But not so winged and fleeting—
Slower, even, than the fish
The breeze lifts branch and leaf
Exceptional, as showing earth and sky
Secreted in a palm whose thought was carried
Round the crown, until he wept to see
This laud of pain displayed
In natural order, strident prophecy
Or Word unmentionable;
Unnamed by present signatures
As well as votes from ancient times.
That made the roots and gave the wombshape
To the wood as it wept beneath its harmony
Of some six thousand future nights.

He gave words to understand, He saw,
And He saw the word hung over all the leaves
The wood grew and withered in the dark.
The handsome flowers fell off
And gave the night its heathen promises;
But the leaves turned up the faces of the race
And the Enemy lay in the flowers and
Threads of language drew the earth up
To the tree.

The Snake among the petals wove a secret spell:
　　　　Poison, become vinegar; and he spun off
Running well against the blowing dust, far back
To his own star.
Them, his sons on earth looked up, uncoiling
From around the eggs their warps encompassed
And they ate dull nails; and their sons
Sucked at splinters from the axe.

A silver girl tumbles from a hanging wisp,
The prophet's bearding of the branch,
Who split in augury of a white world
Made rippling in the likeness of this oceanic
Night which has no jewels but those
An unhinged door might hide so carelessly.
Like so, with such abandon He,
Lord and Master of the Heart beheld the starry dawn
And the seasons of the world, the final robes
That Adam flung before his bride.
King, Queen, faded like the winter rose
And the Virgin sat beneath the rushing boughs
With one small lamb while armor was prepared
Up in the castle, and spears were forged
For an almighty hand.

A scarf was tossed
And the challenge this bright morning
Mixed in the jingling of a tambourine
Spilled silver across the red blood
On His angel's sword, & then He slept.

The Tree swelled over burning mountains
To rip off the strings of the gypsy guitar,
And the song, quivering, unheralded the earth
And stopped.

Now my harvest welcome home,
The scythe is bleeding, and our work is done
The lovers lie upon the root,
And heaven cools the fish who knew no deed.

Five-twenty p.m.

When the sun sinks under
weight of gold, no more
Amber of the cloud within,
It grew large, took hold
on wounded earth
It made all men & women sing.

Birds about bright also
In that hue
The promise that tomorrow
     never knows
The feats of driving
Into, thru that night
Waiting for a moonscape
Or moving from
The window to the stars.

& where
  Is one who always
     with us
Dressed the bird,
gave wings & callings into air,
Double on Double split from
       once
As was, until it always is.

Michael Tritto, Sr. (1939-2015) was born in Buffalo, New York and taught Spanish in the Buffalo Public Schools for 37 years, including Kensington High School, Buffalo Academy for Visual and Performing Arts and Hutchinson Central Technical High School. He lived in Buffalo all his life. He loved poetry since he was very young and his work was published in journals since the early 70's throughout the US, and in England, Ireland and Australia. He had his first poem published in a journal called *Pure Light*, and had 24 of his poems published by *The Buffalo News* over the years. He won the Niagara-Erie Writers poetry competition in 1987, the Just Buffalo Writer In Residence award in 1988 and the AFL-CIO Just Buffalo Labor in Literature award in 1991. He read his work on Spoken Arts Radio, WBFO-FM 88.7, and at the Burchfield Penney Art Center and the Rooftop Poetry series, and his poems have been heard on Sirius Satellite Radio. In March, 1990, his narrative poem, "Light from a Dark Canvas," depicting a story of the Holocaust, was the basis for a dramatic ballet staged at the then Pfeiffer Theatre in Buffalo. Sadly, he died on January 30, 2015 of cancer, leaving his lovely wife, three sons and four grandchildren.

Locked in Ages

First sun edges itself into view,
elbow to elbow, scattered boots of fire,
from all the weights of night, their stillness
waits to throw shapes, catch colors,
wandering brilliance in blue.

Shadows are escapes for eyes and ears,
in the domain of woods, trees control paths,
here, now up the last hill, fields in seed,
glass boils lights from a house and barn.

The walker is upon the last hill,
celebration quickened by bone antenna,
all stops, old silences, the gasps,
a plumed tail, a mate becomes bush,
side by side they are locked in ages.

Crackles call up from the woods to the farm,
rows and plants, eyeglasses near windows,
seeds, lifts of light, paths one to another, a step.

Memory Fire

Grandma and Dad, almost all of the aunts, uncles,
radiant smiles out to the cameras, the Italian side,
thirties and forties, no sign of my Irish mother,
some tree having shadowed her, and I was ten,
watching for chickens on a Sunday of my aunt's farm,
not knowing anything of the town plan,
once, after all the family had gone away,
not a shout, nor song, not a belly laugh,
just the quiet of the yards, our hearts elsewhere,
a fire truck, a can opened to splash,
the heat backs the truck away,
while time and a world of us burn down.

A Twice a Day Wonder

Sunlight introduced penetrations
among jagged cuts of grey stone fences,
lifting stories sealed under slopes.

Seamus would join the hills
for both steady and wild shadows,
as if he could take his pick,
spread sleep with his hand, or list
the yellow blossoms by name.

Those who know the sunlit furze bush,
its power of blossoms, repeating the show,
sending off, calling back, its waves.

Auntie Faye turned quickly, walked slowly.
She had received the letter this morning,
"We're sorry" it read, . . .nothing we could do!"
And she remembered the return of the blossoms,
famous for the second times each year.

The sheep worked the fields of green
in the company of one or two lambs,
and Jimmy ran pumping his arms
around trees of a young oak grove,

quickly over stone fences, he would spin with gold.

Flights

He knew where he wanted to go,
to the night table, back towards the bed,
so I'd wheel him as close as I could,
and he'd gently put his head on the tray,
a weathered nest, coming undone.

I wanted to talk about the flight
of thirty years ago on Franklin Street,
the whitewashed, stony, basement walls,
warm in winter, dry in summer,
the yellow, blue and green stir
the birds made of the air.

The flight was huge for the birds, for me,
cages opened, they'd fly as they pleased;
he'd call them by name and they'd sing.

I'd tell him how I watch wild ones now,
as they dip to the tray, puff at the cold,
until dusk confuses wings and leaves.

But he asked to go to the closet door,
"Closer, closer, thanks. A little more!"

I wanted him to know I remembered
the Annual Regional Bird Club Outing,
where we stood at the edge of a pond,
where I first met magnificence,
a glow he called a swan.

I was as quiet as he is now,
as close to the edge as I could get,
reaching to stroke the swan's neck,
making it glide to the middle of the pond,
an aching brilliance, out of reach,
holding us in its wake.

He asks to go to the other wall,
whoever I am could get him there,
he leans and squints to point the way,
wheels to the wall, he's smaller than before,
crouching before the push.

They had him in bed when I tried again,
bits of him gone in earlier flights,
ivory white, thrashing under sheets,
opening doors, one by one.

I stood quietly at the edge of the bed,
and the room became larger for him, for me,
"Closer, closer, a little more!"
And a door opened with a rusty sigh,
then the glide, then the glide.

Live at the Philharmonic

The baton rises for all of us, orchestra and audience.
Breaths are slow in the hold of caverns within us,
then the fall to a valley, updrifts of shadows and light,
syncopations of village lights along the far roads
open into the composer's room of first marks,
each one timed for all time, the beats of hearts on wing
weaving around the conductor's arms, the woods and winds,
the composer's feed into rooms where players first found
their mastery seeds, the sounding limbs of their new flesh,
repetitions stitch their hours into freedom of melodic sweeps
out to the faces, row after row, their companions within
childhoods and today, touch sorrow, touch a new chance,
the bent figure over paper and pen across cliffs of time,
faces known in the far gray, questions with windows and doors,
all members of tonight, each in a singular flight
sit alone within each other on great blankets of sounds
that lift from rocks to rivers, hot breaths on an ear,
the harmonies, the simple tunes, raptures ablaze,
baton down, the great hall, and then the roar. . .

Buffalo Philharmonic Orchestra
JoAnn Falletta, Music Director
"The Overture to The Three Cornered Hat", Manuel de Falla
June 13, 2004 Kleinhans Music Hall, Buffalo

Verneice Turner - Poet, performing artist, "enjoys & respect the magic of words and the powers that they bring. To see things that are yet to be, feel things that are yet to be felt. The means to journey to places/feelings/thoughts/ possibilities that are, were & possibly will/can be, have been &/or hopefully may never be!"

River

i pray to always be
like a well cared for river

going where i am to go
doing what i am to do
being who i am to be
sharing what i am to share

flooding when it is time to flood
receding
when it is time to release new
soil upon the ground
from which new wonderful
things dreams can grow

never destroying

only replenishing the banks
with the love
that continuously brings
forth new wonderful
things dreams to life

continuously being
groomed, dredged,
enriched, deepened

cleansed, replenished

by all

that is
holy
divine

true

poor man's dance

how spiffy & handsome they look
in their uniforms
going to a poor man's dance

manufacturing jobs have all but disappeared
the willingness to work with one's hands
is no longer held dear
going to a poor man's dance

college education
outside of their financial reach
the rotc offer can't be beat
going to a poor man's dance

should have listened to mama when she tried to tell me
son, it's best for you to keep your grades up
so you can be all that you want to be!
going to a poor man's dance

provisions before pregnancy
genesis chapters 1 and 2 reads
but only a few take the time
to learn how to heed
to learn how to leave a life that is absent of needs
going to a poor man's dance

maybe one day we'll allow ourselves to see
the importance of dying to ego
and taking the chance and be
all that we were originally created to be
eventually destroying the selfish universal need
for a poor man's dance - WAR

me

my ancestors were warriors who happen to have lost a war
they were not some ignorant creatures standing around waiting to be
snatched up and taken to some far off distance shore
they established kingdoms, political, educational, economic, religious systems
and the arts that influence life today

Africa is not one country... it is a continent of many different countries,
different peoples, each nation having and living their own unique way

i hate and despise slavery and yet, not in the *us of a* was it birthed
the horrific price of being a loser in a war has been practiced in many
different countries throughout the millenniums/millennia here on earth

study Europe, Asia, North and South America,
then we might choose to understand
in spite of the horrific injustices inflicted upon our ancestors
as african-american, a strong, powerful, wise and responsible people
we can still in their likeness choose to stand

i choose to throw off the cloak of insecurity and the desperate
plea and need for an apology, for i now know that
God knows the whole story and in His Word it reads
i am not to depend on man to bless me

only through His powerful way of living, doing, being,
can we truly, richly, live
and be free.

crescendo (a woman's prayer)
(inspired by Mingus Fable of Faubus)

i lay.....i gaze.....
what am i seeing
stars....dancing....dancing in the sky

do be be be dao, do be be be dao
dao be be
      dao be be
         dao be di dao

my heart swells
swells, engorged with depth, pain, humor, love
it swirls in my chest rising up to be free
free of....anger, free of fear, free of
pain, hurts, disappointments
loves-past, present, future
      remember
         engage
            expecting

again it falls
back into my chest
then......a sweet chorus crescendos into a prayer
bursting thru my eyes
cloaked in tears
"may this heart bring peace"
"may this heart bring joy"
"may this heart bring divine understanding,
wisdom, power, Love
in the midst of....

chaos"

Katharine Tussing has had her poems published in *Poetpourri, Moody Street Irregulars, Honoring Women With Our Voices* and *Trees of Surprise.* She co-facilitated the Writing and Well Being classes at the Mental Health Association with Jamie May from 2004-2007. Her chapbook, *Colored Pebbles,* was published in 2010.

Katharine is also a painter, and has had her work exhibited at Artsphere and Impact Gallery, and had a two person show at Unity Gallery and, in 2010, a one woman show at El Buen Amigo.

Tree of Life
For a Tree Overhanging Ellicott Creek at Glen Park

You had to burst
Through a grey wall
Full-blown
Like Athena through Zeus' grey brain
And lean over the tumultuous water.
Your pale fans of blossom
Against the white torrent
And white ghost fungi
Contrasting with the dark limbs they haunt,
You reach out your buds
Like tiny deer hooves
Risking falling into the catastrophic river.
Craning your head up
Like a swimmer trying to keep breathing,
You struggle against your prone position.
I, too, crane my neck and reach out to you,
But I am afraid to go flat out
Over the abyss.

Winter Night

Cold snow
Scour clean my soul
With crystal winds,
Wash me with your milk dreams
Mystify me with your polygonal equations,
Your black night covering.

I am snow,
I slip past you, tiny particles wisping through your cracks.
I am the wind,
I cannot be held.
I sough through your vegetation,
Your shoulders are hills.
I keen around them,
Never settling, always drifting.

3

I come out of the grey wolf woods,
Whose branches twined around me,
Whose trees breathed wild, free
Possession and slavery
In my face,
Whose shaggy heads covered me and sheltered me.
You led me into the snowfields,
Treeless except for you,
One frail black bush.
Save me from those warm woods,
Grey as the corpse.
Surround me with your brambles,
Dark with mourning
And alive.

Cosmic Neighborhoods

You have traveled and dwelled
In so many worlds.
You have lived in a Daylight Zone
Where a benevolent sun
Glared down burning heartless and heatless
On the pale, dusty pavement.
You have been despondent with the destitute,
But you have been a seagull on a flight of ideas
In an institutional cell.
You have known a red demon
Glowing in the darkness of such horror
As most can never fathom.
You have lived aeons in one night.

But the bridge over the railroad tracks
Suspended you in a world outside of Buffalo
And outside of time.
I imagine the sky was blue
And full of dispassionate compassion
Like it was
When I walked another railroad track with you
And it seemed like it was leading to infinity
But it only led to a grey brick wall
At the end of my home.

It wasn't just your music
That made me think of you today.
It was the warm winter sun that made me think of
The lively humdrum wholesome worlds of Buffalo,
Me with Jenny and her grandma,
Telling them about the "Polish boy"
And hoping Jenny's grandma wouldn't be mad
If I warned Jenny not to be a nun.
Somewhere under the grey Buffalo sky,
You were hanging around with your brothers
Or your high school buddies
At Benny's Bar and Grill,
And just around the corner
Was a freak of nature,
A sign of God,
Some portent or epiphany,

Another Daylight Zone, this one not blinding
A subdued world
Where men who now work or once worked
For this factory or that lumberyard
Watch TV or talk about their fishing trips.
I don't know if they are poor,
But I wonder if you quote,
"Blessed are the poor in spirit"
When you think of them.
Whether you do or not,
Christ moves in this world.
Although you set yourself up naked for arrows,
You would not give up your eyes like St. Lucy,
Nor let your hair be set aflame for love.
Only inside, your soul was a tungsten wire.

I think of you this way now.
I do not like to think of the zoo
Where you said our keepers
Were our brothers and sisters;
Though you paced your cage with long strides,
Though your voice was too big
For four fake wood panel walls,
They tried to teach you to hold a pencil
and write your name legibly,
and you were a humble, sheepish lion.

I know eagle flies inside your mind.
A room black inside but glowing
With controlled creativity
Was infinity for you and your genius friend
And his entourage.
You called yourselves heroes-
Did your heads swell as you spun worlds from your words?
But you were only making the inside outside.
The bowl of your brain
Held many psychedelic mushroom dream universes.

You have traveled in so many worlds.
None of them are mine,
But I know them,
For I have traveled at Warp 3 too,
And I know brief life is long.

Sinéad Tyrone's poems have appeared in *The Buffalo News*, *The Empty Chair*, *The Still Empty Chair* and *Beyond Bones III*. In 2013 she published her first novel, *Walking Through the Mist*, a story of coming to terms with loss and moving on. "I like to paint pictures in my poems and stories," Sinéad says of her writing. Much of what she writes mirrors her passions for God, nature and Ireland, where she recently traveled. Her first book of poetry, *Fragility*, was published by No Frills Buffalo in 2014.

Memories Disturbed

He wears corduroy pants like you wore,
hair same wiry gray,
same wire-rimmed glasses,
and suddenly the literary night was lost
to memories of you,
the ache I'd buried under Ireland maps and music
and offerings of my pen
rising to the top again,
still overwhelming,
still shocking to find you are gone,
all the hope and promise of you,
your smell a mixture of wine and cigar,
your intellect challenging,
keeping me on my toes,
awaking dormant corners of my mind
others left sleeping.

I lie awake tonight,
that same old yearning so often unanswered
a constant throb in my soul,
demanding fulfillment like fists
beating against a brick wall,
voice stolen by that same gale force wind
that tore you away,
haunting my darkened room.
I wanted so much more for myself,

for you,
carried so many dreams
that now lie buried underground
like daffodil bulbs waiting for spring warmth
to draw them back to life.

Jupiter and Venus

Jupiter courts Venus
in a springtime sky,
calling to her,
drawing her near with his
magnetic gaze.
They meet,
kiss,
dance under a sliver moon.
Their love shines out,
two bright lights on a
jet blue landscape.

Moon grows fat and jealous
watching Jupiter and Venus dance,
forbids their love,
banishes them to opposite
corners of the sky.
They separate,
wink at each other
one last time,
and are gone.

Red Haired Boys

Whispering pines and red lake,
keeper of my memories,
how I wish I could return
to log forts and pine cone wars,
to balancing on wooden beams,
to mallows' pink and purple blossoms
and wild strawberries in sunny fields,
and you.

Could we play again,
wade up mountain stream
to the waterfall cascading down,
splashing over rocky path
to the manmade lake
that showed bright mineral color?
Could we walk the steep wooded trail
to the lookout tower,
feel again the spirit of Indians who formed that trail
so many decades before us,
feel triumph as we gaze across
miles of farmland below?

If I had one night to do over
it would be our late night walk,
sitting on a picnic bench,
starry skies smiling down on us,
our first real kiss and exploration.
I wish we could have found we loved each other,
the answer for what we both so desperately sought.
It hurts to think of you now,
think of you gone.

So much will have changed
under whispering pines,
it could never match my memories
so I stay away,
recall instead its wildflower fields,
the stream where cedar waxwings play,
campfires, s'mores, and stories,
and red haired boys with unsteady legs
and passion in their eyes.

Altered View

Dawn,
morning's light is new,
casting rosy glow
that hides the flaws,
shines hope and promise
on the world before me.

Noon,
full light shows cracks,
lends full illumination,
nothing hidden,
flaws spread before me
leaving me to choose
to fix or abandon.

We are tied together
with invisible bands,
so hard to break.
Life changes,
brings new twists and turns,
rivers chart new courses,
forever altering my landscape.

Dusk,
evening light colors my world
in shadow,
dark night coming on,
I adapt to moon and star light,
forge ahead with you.

Alfonso Volo attended the State University College of New York at Buffalo, where he graduated Summa Cum Laude with concentrations in philosophy, religious studies, art, art history and foreign literature. He lives on a farm in Eden, New York, where he does his art work and his writing, and earns his living as a freelance gardener. His art work has been exhibited at Hallwalls, Albright-Knox Art Gallery, Burchfield Penney Art Center, Harbourfront Centre, Maryland Art Place, Big Orbit Gallery and UB Art Gallery, among others. In 2005 and in 2007 his art was included in the Beyond/In Western New York exhibitions.

His writing has been published in *The Buffalo News, Nassau Review, Artvoice, Slipstream, Moody Street Irregulars* and numerous others, and he has given many readings throughout the years.

Constellation for Vincent

My mind is a night sky.
From darkness stars will
emerge.   I
lay upon my bed and hear
the hot, summer
wind rattling the shutters.
I dream,
open my eyes. Moon
rises upon a slow
cellular arabesque. Olive
grove's
fragrance floats the galaxies.

Stepping From a Train

Train's tight, clangorous world brakes
to silence, then
the small steps descend. For
a split second,
as eye rises from foot to
sky, the world's fresh as spring light.

    -For Jackie Felix

He never was able to
live out his heart's
desire. Life's
bitter pill downed him too soon.
Yet, his last few years
were a revival. Sweetness
seemed to have
settled to the bottom of his
cup. He said, "Though
it's a floating world, I can
build a home in it."

    -For Victor Volo

Balboa Park, San Diego

Years later, I remember the great
lath house, its cool breath
and fluttering light.
Fragrances steeped within
its damp
myriad spaces. Leaves released
green for dream's
sake. My revelry still flowers.

I'm
not
trying

to
remember

anything.

I'm
trying
to

forget-

then
I
play.

    - For Sonny Rollins at 81.

Sun Ra

Joyfully squeal all you worlds.
Gather your atoms, raise
passionate ruckus.
Dance the galactic rounds. Tickle
the void and fall till music splits
its horizons and
stardust opens its laughing eyes.

Midst my microscopic self,
who am I
less space and sparkling
particles
playing hide and seek?
Yet, here I
am, flesh, pulse, and soul gazing
at galaxies, wondering.

* * *

Beneath the ice, fish
swim and stare.
World's dim and slow, cooled
to life's verge.
Shy, iridescent
bodies
gather the diminished light.

Anna Walsh was born Anne Vera Provost on April 11, 1938 in Williamsville, NY. She attended high school and several years of college in the Buffalo area. At nineteen she married her first husband and moved to Washington, DC, where she had two children and worked in a local library. She became active in political causes and began writing poetry. After getting divorced in the early 1960's, Anne moved to San Francisco, where she met her second husband and had a daughter. She wrote and performed poetry in the San Francisco Bay area until 1985, when she returned to Buffalo, NY to care for her aging parents. She lived in Buffalo, writing and performing, as well as hosting numerous writing groups. She took her family name, Walsh, and became Anna Walsh. In 2005, she published a book with Alex Mead, called *The Poetry of Anna Walsh & Alex Mead: Invisible Fire.* During her last years Anna was active in Native American groups, and also in Women in Black, a women's peace group, and continued writing her "sacred human text."

Anna Walsh passed away on Sept. 21, 2012, leaving behind thousands of beautiful poems and many fond memories of a visionary being that will be carried with all of us who knew her.

---

how we speak
the green languages
trinity of healing
green root green mist
      green flame
how glacial winds
had torn holes
in our bodies
and we had endured
the power of ice
to receive this grace
of ethereal vernal
building to a vast music
streaming from earth
forever, for a summer
no ashes no dust
silent green intelligence

Resonance

for my daughter, Lazuli

she is singing polyphony
she is singing wind with fingers
she is singing the noon she was born
she is singing coup d'etat, nom de guerre, de plume
she is singing woman belly, woman blood
she is singing solar domes, speckled dreams, decahedrons
she is singing moon gods, salt tears, torn days
she is singing mandolins, mourning doves, silver wolves
she is singing a man who makes dandelion wine
she is singing naked
of losing her way
her lover's storms, his scent (sweat)
she is singing lightning
between her legs
a river streaming over its edges
navigating the invisible confluence
(following a braille tattoo)
leaving trails of supernatural light
she is singing to honor the goddess
she is singing while she sews
strong button-hole silk
sacred the threads: scarlet and blue
                                        scarlet and blue
she is singing at midnight
she is singing (the) (silent) power of unhealed pain
steel traps, scar tissue
years in prison
angry, hungry
hairline fractures
never spoken
she has wounds
singing a red serpent uncoiling
singing deep roots to draw from
singing heartbeat heartbeat and breath
and breath
she is singing "when Death, when Death
when Death walks in the door
what shall I do, oh Lord
what shall I do, what shall I do?"
she is singing touch my temples
touch my palms
she is singing spirit bread
she is singing to honor herself
she is singing polyrhythmic resonance

holographic ghostdance
she is singing hypnogogic retroactive opalescence
she is singing nascent neonatal green delirium
      of the weightless dreamer
wet with birth, her own
her bright skin singing
born from gnarled, dwarfed fruiting trees
she is hieroglyphic evidence
she is singing oh my dear
        grandmothers
        do not forsake me
        in this great wilderness
        of living

Wildflower

to honor
the most ancient
in each

is to behold
process
see sparks
igniting
into
fluid forms

culture:
skeletal integrity
to hold
changing gardens

to give us strength
to bear

the texture
of exquisite touch
intense heat
of this
cellular life

o thank you
for the gift
of oxygen and song
of living mandala

of heart's breath
the spilling of love
which is
pure light
in the mystery
of this
dimension

in darkness
we generate
ourselves
arise
iridescent
from deep
well of self

able are we
to walk in balance
to eat
from earth's bowl
to laugh
in tongues
to dance

to receive
the great love
of sun and moon
to dream
and find vision
to work
to find
one another
on the paths
of our lives

surrounded by miracle
of tree and bird
galaxies
created
in blessing
it is almost
too complex
a feast

too majestic
to bear
gracefully

this intelligent
sentience

this body-spirit
fusion flowering
in rock
rising, falling

light a candle
to each moment
hold unfold
each other
as we fall
into sky

Celia White is a poet and fiction writer, whose work has appeared in local and national publications, including the *San Francisco Bay Guardian* and *Exquisite Corpse*. Her collection of poems, *Letter*, was published by Ambient Press in 2007. She has taught writing to fourth graders, mental health care clients, hospice nurses and high school students. In 1995, Celia received the Just Buffalo Literary Center Writer in Residence award, and in 1998 was the recipient of University at Buffalo Academy of American Poets Prize. She has won the Best Poet award from *Buffalo Spree* in 2006, and several times from *Artvoice*. She is the cofounder of Urban Epiphany, Western New York's largest poetry event, a marathon reading where every poet in the region is invited to read.

The Poet Whose Youth Was Pursuit of Wind Waits for April

I am in trouble tonight in my timidity.
I am the trembling which makes a tulip
naked, and then kills her.

I draw these words on scrap paper as
carefully as a painter in a cave
lifts a crude brush, carrying blood
to the wall, to evoke and scrawl,
so that someone can remember, later,
what this was like, even if
it never happened to them,
never happened at all.

Can I coil myself so as to sieve through
the telephone wire, or drink
until I pour, until I can pray, evaporate away?
I long for adventure, immersion. Risk
the damp coin, the palm
a pale pond under full moon.

I write over the skeletal impressions
of the words I wrote on the page before,
where they pressed, pass through.

So the stars go out like the leg of a broken chair.

So each errand is a journey, a quick quest,
a guess. I armor myself with adornments---
beads at the belly, a hidden braid,
gold birds hung from the earlobes. A caress
of my own cheek under the guise of maintenance,
unconsciousness of gesture. I hide
the intentions of my eyes in plain sight.
I stitch language to the border of this darkness
so it will sing like light.

If I touched my finger to your finger by the candle
would you touch my finger with your finger?
Would you take me by the wrist from the room?

I will follow you by feel, and find you,
for the sake of the forbidden,
unraveling, unreeling, revealing
the knowing in you that you know me.

What I want is that stupid shake back in my legs,
the long love letter of longing, my breath rattling
like a pearl in the gutter. I want that
first kiss, one with a low, anxious moan in it.
Before that sweating palm curls around
the back of the neck. While a poem, like foam,
rises in the blood, the body, illogical,
lush. A drunken pull in the noon of the day.
I want the words which stagger out, after,
like sun struck coal miners in the light,
again, in the light, in love.

Spring in Beautiful River*

Spring, omnipotent goddess, I have seen you
break open the branches with blossoms and with ice,
certain in the sway of your sensual power,
bringing out the buds on the trees and the fuzz
out on the buds, which buzz with pre-orgasmic breakthrough
and then you blow and cold and brittle wind
like a burst of blue smoke to scatter the proud
petals of the flowers, stutter the songs of the birds,
startling and stiffening the earth who has been turning
like a well-pleased woman in her bed, her limbs
loose and akimbo and beautifully spilling.

Oh spring, you are such a tease, bristling the grass
with your fingers of breeze, pinching the flowers
awake the same way you crack open the dawn.
Like any lover who is always late you make us crazy
impatient and when you finally show up smiling, shining,
and promising some more we drop our best-dressed defenses
and say okay spring, come on, let's get it on.

Spring, you let loose a drug in the air,
a loose and floating feeling, cupped between green
warm palms, mixed-up mojo magnified, broadcast
like invisible seeds, inimitable infection, infestation.
Spring, you lush, you always want more but you're the one buying.
We wait when it doesn't seem worth it.

Faces of flowers worship you, spring. Do you
think they mistake you for the sun? We all know
that difference, we're hip to feeling gypped
when the green does not glow, when bright still
means bitter, when trees are naked, when birds
are misled and a little pissed.

Suddenly, spring, you unlock the river, another lover,
you are as usual all hands hauling in
the backstocks of birds, your dress is muddy
and you don't mind, you melt the town
into a ragged mess, a rough beauty, like rust,
and coax it into green and seen with rough love, like lust.

* "Beautiful River" is the English translation of the original name for Buffalo, New York, which French travelers called "beau fleuve." This phrase became "buffalo", though no bison were ever native to Western New York.

November, For Mom

this might be the end of leaves on trees

knowing a from b

of knowing me

a series of yellow days

dip, bounce, promenade

recollection, a pomade, a spade in the head,

in the hair, a whisper, just barely there

Here, Mom. Have a seat. A parade.

Frederick E. Whitehead is the host of the 4th Friday Poetry Series at Dog Ears bookstore in South Buffalo. He has released six collections of his work since taking up poetry as a creative outlet in 2009. That year saw the release of *songs,cradled* - partly made up of lyrics from his days in local Buffalo bands. *Protected by Paradox* followed in 2010. In 2011, *Orbs* came out, first as an e-Book and then in print form in April of 2012. This pattern was used again for *Water From A Toad*, published in June, 2012 as an eBook, and in print later that year. *All Sail No Rudder* was published by No Frills Buffalo in 2013. His latest book, *Half Speed Epiphany*, was published by Saddle Road Press in 2014. His poetry blog can be found at fewhitehead.wordpress.com.

---

sweet spaces

I knew there would be
sweet spaces in his senility
moments
filled with phrases
only the enlightened
of the world
would understand

I would shift restlessly
waiting for those times

learning the art of
code breaking
I would sit between the
machinery and bedrail
watching for the telltale
brightening of his eyes

anticipating the brief
straightening of the spine
that would signify the coming
of some great insight
he may have been
meditating on for years

one, only now

allowed to slip
through loose threads
in the faded tapestry
of his life

then this giant of a man
would again be in conversation
with any
number of people
but me
the only other
person in the room

residual heart effect

the streets we
used to run
have been
widened now
just enough to
allow for sidewalks

recent additions
not in the
photos I came across today

there was one of her
standing with arms raised
where the lawn met the street
the ground wet from
the spray of a hose
a bike on its side
a sweatshirt abandoned by
one of the trees that
used to tower above us

thinking it was dusty
I swiped my thumb
across the photo
a kid took on
some spring afternoon
when plans were big
and everything was possible

it wasn't dusty at all
just faded

under scars

in her twenties
she was cut four times
a scapel hewn
doorway for
my brothers and I
that we may leave
our first home
screaming in the
light our lungs
expanding with the cast off
breath of those who
were there before we
were there we
wiped clean
laid on her breast to
beat our hearts in syncopated
meter with hers
a few days shy of seventy
she was opened again
her insides
having rebelled
then surrendered
another scar another mark
in her travelog
under those scars
is the place I began
away in ever widening
circles I move
picking up
things she left for me
which I return to her
on my visits as if
I was the first ever
to have discovered them
she smiles
a servant now
to her solitude
silent mostly but
seemingly assured
that she was as good
a guide as there could
have been her hair now
grown back enough so that I
have to brush it from
her forehead a kiss there

her eyes letting me know
it is not complete
I have got
so much more to do

the river waits

the suggestion,
small as it was
came in a still moment
a spirits fingerprint
on your forehead

go not
into the river
if
stones of regret
are what
you carry

and there
beside you rests
the jackal of hearts
reclined
mouth moist
from where you
kissed away deception
yet again
the field you occupied
an impressionist
palette holding up
a sky Picasso blue
you in crimson
as if pearl would
be too much of a stretch

you wonder what
thoughts are in the
minds of lilies
lowering their
heads as light subsides

they bow from
shore as
the river waits

Max Wickert was born in Augsburg, Germany. After receiving his doctorate from Yale, he taught English at UB until his retirement in 2006. He has published three collections of poems, *All the Weight of the Still Midnight* (1972, second, expanded edition, 2013), *Pat Sonnets* (2000) and *No Cartoons* (2011). Over the years, his poems and translations have been featured in journals, including *American Poetry Review, Chicago Review, Poetry, Sewanee Review* and *Shenandoah*. His short story, "The Scythe of Saturn," was among the winning entries in the first annual *Stand* Magazine International Fiction Competition in Newcastle-on-Tyne (England). He has also been a winner or runner-up for the New Poets Prize, the Mason Sonnet Award, the Albright-Knox Poems-on-Paintings Award and the Burchfield Center Poetry Prize. Long active as a translator of German poetry, he has in recent years shifted to Italian literature. His verse translation of Torquato Tasso's *The Liberation of Jerusalem* was issued in 2009 by Oxford University Press, and his version of Tasso's *Love Poems to Lucrezia Bendidio* in 2011 by Italica Press. He has published translations from German into English (including poems by Georg Trakl) and from English into German (Tuli Kupferberg's *1001 Ways to Live Without Working*). He is the founder-director of Buffalo's Outriders Poetry Project, and the editor of *An Outriders Anthology: Poetry in Buffalo 1969-1979 and After*.

From: **Departures**

> *--for Esther*

I love your fingers, the little bones
in them, your shoulder blades when the light
is on your back.
> And why aren't we
frightened by the blaze in the west
behind the buttonwoods? Sudden gold
on our lips, and a queer voice somewhere,
a wail of music from the rivers
of Babylon.
> Stars.
> There will be fog--
brook and flat valley milling with white
dancers. Oh, the small bones. The sweetness.

*

A beast crashes through the dry thicket.
Apples drop with a thud. Blades of grass
snap, frost-brittle.
     Your lips at my mouth.

I'm transparent, a giant of glass
brooding on the edge of the dark world.
Slowly the weight of the still midnight
shifts onto my shoulders.
      The sweetness!

*

And Herod murdered all the children.
Two toys lie broken on a white sheet.
Two lovers awake.
     Thick smoke of blood
rises to the sky. The animals
are coming to the river to drink.

*

Love, you are all the morning I have.

Serenade 3

Night stretches all her wires tight to lure the sightless
Heirs of wretchedness here or there or another place
Strings of silver or steel singing pass from stars
To tipped grasses tie frost to tree-bark transfix the apples
With worms or steadily pull at the ring in the nostrils of
A patient white bull the moon: night organizes courts
Of desire where all things squirm or thrill at appointed centers
The bat secure at the place of the moth the moth rejoicing
In a mansion of little flames the flame ringing a last faint
Vibration of venom and honeycomb: night has tuned her wires
Precisely has strung them through the ears of her blinded
inheritors is making them yearning for justice try to guess
At the one the final direction by piercing melodies crossing
Recrossing turning their heads this way or that: they know
Their eyes no longer avail in the magical night they listen
For the seat of the harpist themselves musical with regret
That it beckons from no place that two ears are not enough

Pat Sonnet 25

There is a darkness darker than each night
in which our solace suffers an eclipse,
a silence far more silent than each slight
silence of love on our unkissing lips.
There is a word behind each word we say
That qualifies our love, a thunderous noise
quite overwhelming noises on our way
which mark the pathlessness our path destroys.

The greater darkness makes the less be seen.
The final silence lets our lips declare
what word behind our words it is we mean
in each endearment we obscurely dare.
There lies our path, which both our loves must mark,
toward the dark behind the darker dark.

Pat Sonnet 31

A common story: Once upon a time
the hero and the heroine awoke
In fading starlight to a distant chime.
"You are apart!" it sang, and with each stroke
the distance grew from him to her and from
the bell to both. He rose, and she, before
the sun rose, while the bell tolled "Find the door!"
Bravely they ran. Faintly the bell chimed "Come!"

And was the door where he heard her voice, or
was it where she heard his? Or was it more
a matter of the chime's dark source? They ran
in zigzags as their afternoon began.
The bell tolled "Soon!" and yet more distance yawned.
Night fell. The bell tolled "Now!" The next day dawned.

Heroic woman and heroic man
were lost forever in a night beyond
all distance. You and I did not respond
when the next teasing bell began
its common story: "Once upon a time
there was no ever after and you two
were fated by my melancholy chime
to reach the door but not to make it through."

The Figures Beneath

(Jackson Pollock's "Convergence II")

Here is where we started out. Here is
where we return. You will not gauge our force
until you learn that we are not the source,
nor guess our number till you see that this
is not the background and is not the goal.
We're here to help you, but we come uncalled—
splayed, charred, uncertain, spurned, benighted, scrawled
myths of the body, axioms of the soul.

In our effects you know us. In the plane
where your own gesture makes its marks to chart
the lightnings of our absence, in the pain
you feel when you begin, we live. Our part
is merely to confirm the urge. The urge
is yours. Open your eyes, and we converge.

The You Who Homages 32

After we marry, I hope to be seduced by you.
Already I'm trying to feel less stupidly stunned.
Don't leave me now, and don't lead me by the nose,
just look a bit longer at my bovine incomprehension,
my innocence, my celibacy, my grand climacteric.
Really, I begin to understand. (I'm left-handed

when it comes to emotion. Having to feel with my right
cramps my style, makes me clumsy. When all is lost,
what *is* my right? What's left? I feel for you and I
insist you feel for me whatever side you're on.
I join you when I know I'm there.) I begin

to understand the look in your eyes when you see
how much I take for granted, the smile on your mouth
when you let me please you, the seduction in your every
other response to me, the tone in your voice
when you seem to say "I will never marry" as naturally
as a cow in the evening mist might say "*Moo!*"

Blows

Nothing I like makes sense,
all mere preference.
Make me happy. Rate me.

This sense of merited
discomfort seems to
make me comfortable.

I'll be honest with you:
I'm really just as
chickenshit as I sound.

Give me a break! You've been
at me from the day
you tried to be in me.

You'd have to eat my flesh
to find out how not
to be fascinated.

You hit me because I
was hurting you. I
hit you because I hurt.

Not the threat of your blows,
not your blows falling,
but my sores make me smart.

No matter how slowly
you add my fuel,
I spin out of control.

Do not let me punish
myself too harshly
once I learn what I've done.

Torquato Tasso, from: *The Liberation of Jerusalem* (Canto XVI:14-15)

"Ah, see," he sang, "the modest virgin rose
first bursting her green bud all timidly,
half hidden and half bare: the less she shows
herself, the lovelier she seems to be.
Now see her bosom, budding still, unclose;
but look! she droops and seems no longer she--
not she who in her morning set afire
a thousand lads and maidens with desire.

"So passes in the passing of a day
the leaf and flower from our mortal scene,
nor will, though April come again, display
its bloom again, nor evermore grow green.
Ah, let us pluck the rosebud while we may.
It all too soon fades from its morning sheen.
Let us pluck the rose today, to love and burn
while we can love and be loved in return."

Lisa Wiley is an English professor at Erie Community College in Buffalo, NY, where she lives with her husband and three children. Her poetry has appeared in *Beyond Bones III*, *Earth's Daughters*, *Epiphany Magazine*, *Red Booth Review*, *Seven CirclePress*, *Teaching English in the Two-Year College*, *Word Worth* and *Yale Journal for Humanities in Medicine*. Her chapbook of villanelles, *Chamber Music*, was published by Finishing Line Press in 2013, and her collection, *My Daughter Wears Her Evil Eye to School*, was published by The Writer's Den in 2015. She seeks poetry in everyday objects and conversations, searching for the grace notes which surround our daily lives.

Return to Goldfish Point

A bold marine layer spars with the sun,
I'd forgotten about this morning battle.

The sun will win—he always does even
in this tucked away spot on a one-way street.

I've never been to the South of France.
But it must look like this, sandy bluffs

I used to run. I can't linger long enough
by water's edge to glimpse Garibaldi,

fleeting threads of light. Their orange flicker
eludes me, yet thousands of fireflies

dance below. My firstborn catches them
in the nets of his Peter Pan eyes.

When I peer down, King Palms sigh;
I only hear my lost daughter's cry.

Alice

You used to call me *Alice*, in the rain,
and I wished the sun would never come out.
A sort of sadness in that sweet refrain.

Like a daydream sparkling with pink champagne,
we always had something to talk about.
You used to call me *Alice in the Rain*.

No need for a jewel to hang from a chain.
Alice wasn't the type of girl to pout.
A touch of sadness in that sweet refrain.

Any creature at all, you would have slain.
Protection from an evil queen—no doubt.
You used to kiss me, *Alice,* in the rain.

Time, on the young, is always spent in vain;
I had no idea I'd want to shout:
Dance me away in your haunting refrain.

Our old umbrella couldn't entertain
that teeming downpour. It had too much clout.
You used to sing me "Alice, in the Rain,"
a bitter sweetness as our last refrain.

Somewhere Between Locks 34 and 35

For Max and Wiley

Between Locks Thirty-four and Thirty-five
and the engine's hum, I saw you reveal
the boy you'd be when you learn how to drive.

One who understands respect and to arrive
on time. All because of a simple meal
shared between Locks Thirty-four and Thirty-five.

Standing tall with your blue eyes so alive,
you noticed cotton snowing—I could feel
the boy you'd be when you learn how to drive.

Canal songs chimed; history seemed to revive
cool shade under the low bridge where kids kneel
between Locks Thirty-four and Thirty-five.

Waiting for the lock to fill—not like a hive,
but very slow—you were patient, no big deal,
like the man I hope you'll be when you know how to drive.

The canal tunes you whistled will survive,
just as my glimpse of you behind the wheel.
Between Locks Thirty-four and Thirty-five,
I saw the man you'll be, when you learn how to drive.

Under a Bipolar Sky

For Vanessa's fortieth birthday

I met you under a bipolar sky,
an ephemeral flash, consuming dark.
I couldn't help, just heard your pretty sigh.

So many times, I observed your cry.
After, you'd want to go out on a lark.
I met you under a bipolar sky.

So many nights, I thought you might die.
Your stories always traced the same sad arc.
I couldn't help, just heard your Southern sigh.

Together we dreamt we'd meet the right guy:
loyal, handsome, one who'd make his mark.
I found you under a bipolar sky.

All the ridiculous things you'd say, *Why
don't we dance with the gators at the park?*
I wouldn't jump, just felt your pretty sigh.

Your storm tore us apart; we can't deny.
You left Collegetown in a flaming spark.
I met you under a bipolar sky,
I wanted to help—not just hear you sigh.

Janna Willoughby-Lohr has been writing poetry since she was 5, and performing since age 12. She graduated from Warren Wilson College in 2004 with a BA in Integrative Studies: Entrepreneurial Creative Business Arts. Since graduation, she has been performing poetry and music steadily as her alter-ego, MC Vendetta, and as her singer-songwriter self, Janna-Ruth. She was a Grand Slam finalist in 2005-2008 for the Nickel City Poetry Slam, and a member of the 2006 Nickel City Slam team at the National Poetry Slam. She is also an editor and layout artist for *Earth's Daughters* literary magazine, the longest running women's publication in the country. Since 2008 she has been performing with her band, The BloodThirsty Vegans, a lively mix of energetic hiphop, rock, funk, ska and blues, topped off with socially conscious, positive lyrics. She currently runs her own business, Papercraft Miracles, and works as a teaching artist in Erie County and as a graphic designer for Bodycandy.com.

Death is Not Pastel

Sympathy is a strange animal.
Your acquaintances feel they need to volunteer
like you're a soup kitchen

No, I don't need meals, I'm still breathing.

But they don't actually want
to be called to active duty
just feel like they should—
buy the card
pen a message
peel the stamp
and toss it in the blue metal mailbox
with the groan and squeak.

There, I've done my part.

Sympathy cards always have
large swirly letters
rimmed with silver glitter
over pastel pansies

with an overly meaningless message.

And it doesn't matter
what the person writes inside, none of it
sinks in, floating on the surface
like dead skin on old bathwater.
I'm just waiting for that plug to be pulled,
for some of it to get sucked down the drain.

The only real card I've ever read in grief
was one from the other end of the aisle,
Celebration.
It was a solid vibrant red and black design,
no pre-printed script, she simply wrote:

Your mother is smiling and yeah, it still sucks.

Finally, someone who really knows about loss.

The Scornful Look

I hate the scornful look you give me when
I reach up to play another TV show on NetFlix,
another hour of blissful relaxation, watching
old episodes of Law & Order, lounging on the couch.

You get up and leave the room,
do the crossword from the Artvoice,
check your e-mail, go to sleep,
while I delve a little deeper
into this drama
because for me it's not just TV,
I'm hanging out with my mother,
this was her favorite show.
I'm reliving the many
Thursday nights
or Sunday nights
that we watched these episodes together,
hearing her proclaim her not-so-secret
crush on Chris Noth
and her scorn for Jerry Orbach,
the way she always prayed for justice
for the person who was wronged
and how she cried whenever
a child lost a parent
or a parent lost a child.

But you don't get it,
having never lost a parent—
my need to reminisce here with this show,
and so I also love that scornful look
you give me when I press play again,
your innocence calling me to bed,
saying, *stop wasting your life*.

Soap

There's a certain way that certain sounds
can pull your heart aside
sit her down and tell her again about memories.

My grandma's kitchen drawers have a tell-tale
smooth gliding, rattle-click that I have never heard elsewhere,
and it immediately brings to mind
big silverware with smooth rounded handles,
blue enameled fry pans, scrambled eggs hand-beaten with cream
cooking slowly on the stove.
Toast with soft butter (stored in the cupboard, never the fridge)
cut in triangles, like a restaurant,
laid out perfectly on a large oval plate with napkins and placemats
cotton soft from fresh wash and the smell of her perfume
mingling with cleanser.

I step to the sink to wash my hands before eating and am surprised
that I no longer need tiptoes to reach the soap.

Ah, the soap, a large oval bar,
yellowish blue, splitting around the edges, sitting in the oval soap dish,
even the soap makes my memory surge.

The cracks like grandma's fingers, curled with arthritis and 80 years of
holding everyone else's hands,
the cracks like my tiny child hands pruned from the bath,
big copper pitcher filled with hot hot water,
rinsing my hair, twisting a pristine white washcloth to clean out my ears,
skin scrubbed red, flushed from the hot hot water
wrapped in a fluffy white towel, being buffed dry by grandma's strong hands
surrounded by the scent of Dial soap and caring.

My hands may someday cradle babies but they will most certainly
twist with arthritis, crack along the edges like that big oval bar of soap
and there, split open, they will hold my memories.

Robin Kay Willoughby was a poet, translator, artist, singer and so much more. She learned to read by age 4 and began writing immediately. A constant devourer of books, she read (and remembered) everything she could get her hands on. After graduating high school and college early, she continued to work on her master's degree thesis, *The Effect of Jesus Christ on the Work of Stephen King*. She was one of the first editors of *Earth's Daughters* literary magazine, as well as their layout artist for many years, and she was omnipresent in the WNY poetry scene. Robin was also a teacher at Erie Community College City Campus, as well as the longtime director of the Women's Center there. She eventually obtained her masters in Divinity and was very active in the church until her untimely death in 2002. In 2004, a special issue of *Earth's Daughters* (No. 65) was issued to showcase Robin's achievements. Her personality and talent is widely known in the community of Buffalo; she was truly--one of a kind.

The Field Behind the Row of Pine Trees III

In the winter, the waterfall becomes a cave of ice
We crawl inside and sing our highest notes
Hans Christian and the Grimms can't get us here
the icicles are like pipes on some frigid organ
we blow into them; they whistle, our lips stick.
We dream of waiting for spring like an Iroquois ordeal of
human-being-ness, until we're free.
On the contrary, our singing brings us loose at once
melts us
free water trickles sweet down our chins, inside our anoraks

From: **Electric Buffalo**

II.
Mark Twain found love here and went nuts. Electricity
had got him. He had his first typesetter
fantasies here.
Buffalo (you know) as the first city
with electric in the streets?
The electric power kills things.
Some of them a lot stronger than volition.
Plenty of rare marble was brought over by
real Italians to make the big church
and monuments in Forest Lawn. The
power in the air began to chew before
they even finished carving. The angels
around the graves, the lions downtown,
now look fluffy—fuzzy—from afar.
Only the fellow in his glass dome near
the gate is safe.
The craziness that made that dome helps you survive.
Buffalo breeds it. Burchfield painted the
electricity of here zinging out of the butterflies
and trees, glowing in the Lackawanna hovels.
Gold and grey should be the Buffalo blazon.
Conducting wires—gold sparks.
The man who made the electric chair
came from here; it's true: He was a
dentist, which seems *apropos.*
'He-keeps-them-awake' knew the white
men who came here would be named
"We'll-put-you-to-sleep," before the fact
came home to any of the
guys with gold lace on their coats.
The first one to die in it was a female.
They used the electric chair to kill Czolgosz, too.
He didn't mind a bit. He admitted that he was
happy to die for his ideals. This man didn't really
come from Buffalo, though, and brought his Power
and craziness from the north lake.
This power comes home to us now.

An Invitation to the Dance
Gretchen admires the jewel-box

A complex cheesy mystery &
not too nice
this being of a woman
this being me
Something put too cryptically
w/smacks of vice
the way the ballet-dancer
with the rag of skirt
twitches
her random arabesque
poco à poco più lento
that mirror
and she don't care if she's dancing for the wall
or away (towards us)
or --inelegant!—no, say it:
with the klutziness that looks like
playing around, but is really mortal—
Goyaesque//
to flop straight back as the lid goes down
It's not real dancing
Doesn't go with the music, ever...but,
She always beats the lid coming down//
It must be a trick of the spring.

Swimming

"It's ages since I've swum...." I say, fudging with the truth for the
tantalizing man, shortly before he disappears.
I'd prepared myself to swim, bought an appropriately
matronly suit, flowered like the sleazy dress of some Flannery
character. I had muttered, "Daddy, don't die," in the fitting room.

I remember the feel of my first suit (this is when the man disappears...)--
If I had had my daughter's words,
I would've told everybody: "Mommy, it itches my bootie!"
with her freedom, I'd've gone in nude. ---
Wool, with button and straps, and a dangerous navy-blue with a cream-crust
white panel, Schiffli navy-&-red sailboat in the center:
It was tight when I struggled into it and sagged nearly to falling off when wet.
I became heavy with water, heavy with fear.

I would watch my father swim and float
as my water-burden ran down my legs on shore.
He would swim out to the middle of the pond without lifting his face,
slithering along like a water-creature
like those I saw on TV in "THE JUNG-le"
(a show that always started out with a fight to the death
between some constrictor-snake and a black black black panther)
When he got to the center where no one else went, he would flip to his back
and float forever with no motion at all.
He would say, each time we walked the hidden path to the pond,
"This time, I 'll teach you to do the dead man's float,"
but I couldn't.
I said my suit made me sink, which was not a lie,
but my itchy, wet fear was heavy, too.
I thought you had to let yourself be dead to float this way,
and I didn't want to be, not even a little bit.
I thought it helped to be a man, as well,
and I knew I couldn't be.
I'd grow to something else.

I know how my father looked after he died. He was floating.

Blue Wojciechowski is a fiction writer, humorist and mediocre poet who avidly collects rejection letters which she plans to wallpaper her bathroom with. Her only published piece prior to this anthology is a short story, "A Wizard's Hands," which is in *Nickel City Nights, Erotic Writing in Western New York*. She is best known for her rambles which are based on her warped view of the world around her. On the weekends Blue is the roadie for her boyfriend Tom Young (guitarist for the band, Mid Life Crisis), a job that has become a source of much inspiration for her writing. The other source of inspiration is the 38 voices in her head that she always makes a point to listen to. Technically she's not a writer, she just takes dictation.

Ode to That Guy

He seems to know everyone in the bar, yet no one knows exactly who he is or cares for that matter.

No one ever sees him arrive or leave so no one can tell if he's there with anyone or came alone.

He knows the words to his version of every song that exists which he sings very badly and very loud.

He stands right in front of the guitarist alternating between playing air guitar and shouting "You rock!"

He drinks his beer out of a pitcher with a straw.

He wears a cowboy hat with shorts and sneakers.

When he dances he looks like a cross between someone having a seizure and Wile E. Coyote with his ass on fire after an Acme equipment malfunction.

He insists on holding onto his beer while dancing. As a result, most of it gets spilled on him, the floor and other dancers.

In his drunken state he will probably knock over some piece of the band's equipment, usually a mic stand with a full glass of beer in the cup holder.

He will get up on stage and play air guitar or pretend he's the singer even while the band takes a break.

He stands in the middle of the dance floor and rips off his t-shirt while the band plays "War Pigs".

Without him the band will never have a reason to look totally confused.

He's the one who shouts "Freebird" repeatedly throughout the night. Even after the band plays it.

He's over 40 and still wears his baseball cap backwards.

He shouts into his cell phone in the middle of a crowded bar just so everyone can see he has a cell phone and that he has people to talk to on it.

He'll play death metal music on the internet jukebox.

He's usually buzzed by the end of the first set, totally drunk by the end of the second set and completely passed out by the end of the evening.

He'll ask the band to play a song that no one ever heard of.

He will show up in the background of every photo you take, usually doing something to take away from the focus of the photo.

He uses "freakin" as an adjective in front of every noun in every sentence he utters.

He wears shorts all winter long with a heavy winter coat.

He will babble for hours in drunken-eze about absolutely nothing to anyone who is unfortunate enough to have made eye contact with him.

He always manages to say something stupid, annoying or pointless.

The ATM machine completely confuses him.

He sings "Crazy Bitch" to every woman in the bar, confident that will get him laid.

He will wear a concert t-shirt for a band that broke up 20 years ago insisting they'll make a comeback even though no one else cares if they do.

He can offend anyone without saying a word.

He usually ends up leaving the bar with fewer pieces of clothing than he came in wearing.

He'll pick up your beer and drink it before you realize it's gone.

He doesn't drink Dos Equis like that other guy, nor does he drink beer that even tastes good. It only has to be cheap and get him drunk.

He's not "The Most Interesting Man in the World", he's That Guy.

Mom's Table

Standing in the empty dining room
I close my eyes and can feel the past
The chandelier's warm bright glow
The sounds of forks on china
Clinking glasses, scraping bowls
The music of loud laughter
Amid words wafting over the table
Uncle Chuck's latest story
Most likely more fiction than fact
Mom's sing-song voice offering more
Turkey, stuffing, potatoes, squash,
Jellied cranberries, stuffed celery,
Olives, make sure Snowy gets a green one
And the crunchy part of the stuffing
Uncle Chuck always gets that
I remember the time I almost forgot
Until his fork rescued it from my plate
The wine, always Blue Nun, mom's favorite
Dad never asked what tribe that was

A smile spreads over my face
Two families were joined over dinner
Catholic and Jewish, it didn't matter
At Mom's table we were all family
Blood relation wasn't important
Her home was everyone's home
She always said first time you're a guest
The next time you're family, get it yourself
And they always did
Everyone felt at home in Mom's house

Dinner and conversation uninterrupted
As dishes and leftovers are slipped away
Mom putting things in containers
Women scraping plates, filling a dish pan
While men retire to the living room
For talk and football games
We talk in the kitchen while drying dishes
Mom never lets anyone wash
She always does it better
When we finish we find our places
Among the men in the living room
Or quiet talk at the dining room table
With snacks, cookies and candy
On every table big or small

Six o'clock Mom slips away to the kitchen
I follow her knowing what she's up to
We carry plates of turkey, cold cuts, cheese,
Rye bread, rolls and of course placek
Cold stuffing in case anyone wants it
It's even good cold
Celery, olives, Snowy wants another
Don't give him one, it's worse than catnip
Mom gives the command to return to the table
Andy turns to me looking amazed
"We just ate a couple hours ago"
I quietly tell him to shut up, sit down and eat
Mom won't let you leave until you're stuffed
My brother-in-law will soon learn the Polish tradition
Eat until you have to roll away from the table

Mom's dining room table is now mine
With all its many memories of holiday meals
A piece of Mom and her traditions
But in this empty house, the ghosts still linger
If I close my eyes and really listen
I can hear her say those words
That truly made this house a home
SIT DOWN AND EAT!!!!!

Theresa Wyatt was born and raised in Buffalo, NY. She credits study in the Siena Program through Buffalo State College and later teaching in the NYS Department of Corrections among her major life experiences. Now retired, Theresa enjoys exploring creative writing. Initially attracted to poetry for its therapeutic benefits, she enjoys exploring many subjects. Her work has been published in the *Yale Journal for Humanities in Medicine, Magnapoets, Raving Dove, The Healing Muse* and *Earth Speak Magazine,* among others. She received a Pushcart Prize Nomination for her poem, "To Chromosome 22," which appeared in *Beyond Bones II.* Her first collection, *Arrowheads Everywhere,* was published in Spring of 2014. Theresa and her husband live near the beautiful shores of Lake Erie in Derby.

Trostle Farm at Plum Run
(July 2, 1863, Gettysburg)

The breastworks seemed
to whisper

go lie in this open field
and feel the earth
speak to you

allow the ground
to tell you its story

how stampedes and strife
were often daily

and how,
the in between times
accommodated lovers
at the beginning of their thirst

allow yourself
the curiosity of tall tales
and sad but true testimony

of how this battle
or that battle
changed the course
of history

and how,
as you see it,
lying there in an open field,

how drops of ruby blood,
invisible to sight or touch,

have mingled into blooms

Niagara Falls

Sometimes love floats like cork on liquid
sauntering an indolent river
toward a shallow end

and sometimes love rushes hell bent,
frenzied currents birthing waterfalls
with stupendous drops

but sometimes love in its own migration,
stops completely in midair, decides its
own course with neither speed
nor indolence in view

takes its own time to cipher
form and shape, to separate
the quiet from the roar

becomes instead
the magnificent
mist

and lingers

After the Flamenco Lecture, I Can Not Sleep

Insomnia spirits, so misguided, why do you persist
in haunting me so, cursing me like a gypsy
for raising rosewood coffins?

Why stand me accused? I have taken nothing
from you, did not dig up your grave to poach
the treasured cypress wood

You are a thousand fold mistaken, I play
no guitar, wear no jewels, your evil eye and
secret whispers land meaningless on me

A solitude untouched is what I wish for,
after your stomping heels of frenzied
dance subside can I truly hope
to rest

I pray, do send instead the good *palmistas*
to me in peaceful dream only, singing
soft and slow beside my pillow's
wrinkled spine

There is sometimes truth in rumor,
you, insomnia spirits, you are
the real thieves in the night,
not the gypsies

Tomorrow, dark circles under
my eyes will prove your
brazen guilt!

Restoration on Church Street
  The Guaranty Building

Baked earth hieroglyphs my city's helter skelter,
brings me up and down idyllic space that soars
and weaves the leafy terracotta, how my heart
climbs free within this easy undulation!

Circles plenty crown this infant prince
with vaulting forehead, eyes shaping
the modern gods of place

You, Sullivan, gifted father of skyscrapers,
utterly broke in your last days, this jewel
is what you left us in your final book
of generosity

Remember the seed germ

Now look down upon the street, see all
the students sketch and stare as if in
trance, a trance like lasting bounty,
brilliant for the everyman
in Buffalo, backbone
of steel

Ruddy skin of genius clads
thirteen floors of bone
and sinew, blood flow
restores

and foliated
seed pods
incubate
anew

Ryki Zuckerman is the author of the chapbooks: *body of the work* (Textile Bridge Press), *the nothing that is* (Benevolent Bird Press, 2015) and *a bright nowhere* (FootHills Publishing, 2015); and the poetry collection, *Looking for Bora Bora* (Saddle Road Press, 2013). Her poems have appeared in *Black Mountain College II Review, Pure Light, Slipstream,* Swift Kick, *Monthly Planet, Lips, Paunch, Escarpments, The Other Herald, The Buffalo News* and *Artvoice.* She has had poems published as broadsides by Serendipity Press, Textile Bridge Press and the Tea Leaves Collection. She is anthologized in the Buffalo collection, *Brigid's Fire.* She has been a coeditor for decades of *Earth's Daughters* magazine, the longest continuously published feminist literary periodical in the U.S. She has created *The Gray Hair Reading Series* and the *Wordflight Series,* and curates both of them.

---

on the ponte milvio

on the oldest bridge in rome,
arched across the water below
for more than two millennia,
the young italian writes the name
of his beloved on a padlock,
closes its metal arch
tightly over the links of chain,
fitting it in amidst hundreds of other locks.

the chains, stretched out like welcoming arms,
weigh down the ancient lampposts
pooling light onto the walkway,
until the lamps crash down.
the weight of love is heavy.

the keys are always tossed into
the dark, dried-blood hued tiber,
sinking to the bottom of the old river,
where the bones of ladies of the night,
also tossed over the side,
are dancing on slippery wedges
of rusted metal,
remembering flesh.

the absence of joy
for joy walsh (1935-2011) -- poet, editor, publisher, kerouac scholar

grey sky pressing down,
dripping angst,
a soft rain, a whimper.

her warrior heart
silent now.
no more motorcycle-roar
no more mary magdalene journeys

suburban grandmother, yes.
oh, child.
don't email me cyber-roses.
don't you have something to say?

here, protect my treasure,
my words, my poems.
i was a keeper of jack's legacy.
i have done my work.

she floats off to join him
somewhere
on the road.

patina: copper entry roof

go me green
soft ox
oxy daze
oxy oxy ollingfree
drowsing the weight of years
lift up arms to
a goose-down gray sky:
clouds, rain, snow, air
make me what i am.

blue me green,
kin of portico,
protector of heads,
i give my sheen
that they might be spared
clouds, rain, snow, air.
i know what i am.

the tower

my friend alicia's uncle
brought her mother
a candy tower at christmas:
smaller boxes stacked
on top of increasingly larger boxes,
each filled with a different
variety of chocolate,
wrapped in lustrous paper, drenched in ribbons--
gourmet grandeur.

her mom both smiled and wept,
puzzling my already awed
8-year-old brain.

never had i seen anyone
blessed by such generosity;
my family had few rituals,
except turkey for thanksgiving,
and nary an occasion for gifts;

every year,
watching scrooge's transformation
in black and white and envy,
i, too, vowed to always keep christmas;
each holiday season, i learned again
how to know when an angel earns wings;
each christmas
i wanted a snow-kissed victorian day
of plum pudding, family,
and presents stacked under a tree --
yearning for love wrapped up
as a tower of sweets;

instead, here, in the light,
waning now, as my days wind down,
a gift from h.h. richardson,
his soaring architectural wonder,
twin romanesque towers on the grounds
of the nearby state asylum for the insane.

standing on the outside looking in;
sane, but haunted
by ghosts of christmas never,

a prisoner of a past
that lives only in fiction, in film,
not once letting my hair cascade down
out the window of my storied tower.

gentleman caller

the man in the moon
followed me home,
bobbing up and down
behind the boxy tops of
concrete condos,
peek-a-booing from behind
the pointed eaves of houses.

it's hard to keep my eyes
on the road when
his buttery-yellow
ochre-creased face keeps
smiling down,
radiating night kindness.

a perfect man,
who lights the way,
never burns or scorches,
but will move the tides for you.

he's waivering in his ascent,
hanging half-way down
between stars and the edge of earth
in a maxfield parrish sky
still backlit by sinking sun—

cobalt blue dripping down
to water-thinned blur
then a stack of juicy colors —
orange, peach, lemon,
and pink, at the bottom,
holding it all up.

the clouds, a giant's fistfuls
of denim fluff,
are squeezed lower and lower
to the horizon—
so dense a blue,

the man in the moon
is having trouble standing up,

the man in the moon
follows me home,
his face lit with that
contagious gentle grin.

i sing him a night aria —
  fair moon, to thee i sing!
  bright regent of the heavens!
he glows brighter;
i promise him an opera.

i think he winked

Made in the USA
Charleston, SC
07 May 2016